Can the World Be Wrong?

Where Global Public Opinion Says We're Headed

CAN THE WORLD BE WRONG?

WHERE GLOBAL
PUBLIC OPINION
SAYS WE'RE HEADED

DOUG MILLER

Routledge
Taylor & Francis Group

LONDON AND NEW YORK

First published 2016 by Greenleaf Publishing Limited

Published 2017 by Routledge
2 Park Square, Milton Park, Abingdon, Oxon OX14 4RN
711 Third Avenue, New York, NY 10017, USA

Routledge is an imprint of the Taylor & Francis Group, an informa business

Copyright © 2016 Taylor & Francis

Cover by Arianna Osti (ariannaosti.com)

British Library Cataloguing in Publication Data:
    A catalogue record for this book is available from the British Library.

    ISBN-13: 978-1-78353-422-7 [hbk]
    ISBN-13: 978-1-78353-421-0 [pbk]

Contents

Figures and Tables

Figures

Table

Foreword

by John Elkington

You can prove almost anything you want about public opinion if you resort to the modern vox pop method of thrusting a microphone into the face of people you have reason to believe will say what you want them to say – and then asking them a leading question.

Thankfully, that's not the way Doug Miller and GlobeScan operate – which is why they have become such a lifeline for leaders and decision-makers wanting to feel the pulse of the greatest power in the land.

Unsurprisingly, Miller quotes the General Secretary of the US National Council of Churches to exactly that effect. "There are two superpowers in the world," concluded the Rev. Bob Edgar, way back in 2002, "the United States and world opinion."

Well and good, but leaders through the ages have struggled to get a sense of what they should do to align with – or subvert – public opinion.

Some consulted augurs, some gurus, basing their decisions on the behavior of birds, the shape of entrails or the pattern of thrown yarrow stalks. No doubt, some great choices resulted, with advisors such as the priestesses of Delphi tapping into a wider world of intelligence and rumor.

But then came the Age of Science – and very different routes to analyzing public attitudes, opinion, and values.

A public opinion master from whom both Doug Miller and I have learned much over the years is (as he is now styled) Professor Sir Bob Worcester, founder of MORI (Market & Opinion Research International, now part of Ipsos MORI).

And here is how Worcester explained the difference between opinions, attitudes and values over 20 years ago:

- **Opinion.** The ripples on the surface of the public's consciousness – shallow, and easily changed

- **Attitudes.** The currents below the surface, deeper and stronger

- **Values.** The deep tides of public mood slow to change, but powerful

Among pioneering multi-country polling efforts they would both reference – and Miller does later – are those conducted by the University of Michigan, the University of Chicago, Gallup International, the Pew Research Center, and WorldPublicOpinion.org.

But each of these would no doubt insist that theirs is the secret sauce to end all secret sauces. So why have I so assiduously tracked GlobeScan's work for over a quarter of a century?

The reasons include these: GlobeScan asks the world the sorts of question I would ask if I could. They do so in a scientific way. And they present the findings in easily accessible formats – with the result that I have used their diagrams in most of the presentations I have done this century.

Why? Because I believe in democracy, despite all its faults, and I also believe that leaders in the private, public, and citizen sectors should take our opinions, attitudes, and values into account.

I don't believe in the power of yarrow stalks and entrails. Nor do I have much confidence in most computer simulations, for all they have improved in recent years.

Instead, and maybe this is simply the *zeitgeist*, the spirit of the times, I believe in what is now called the wisdom of the right sorts of crowd. As Miller puts it:

> Masses of people can sometimes become mobs ruled by lesser passions. But public opinion pollsters mainly find wisdom in crowds. As James Surowiecki said in his landmark book on the subject, "Under the right circumstances, groups are remarkably intelligent, and are often smarter than the smartest people in them."

So how best to capture this wisdom? GlobeScan's answer is described later. We learn that:

> Well-constructed surveys conducted with proper scientific samples provide these "right circumstances" for delivering the collective wisdom of the general public (and sometimes more specialized publics) on topics ranging from globalization, nuclear proliferation, and

climate change through to assessing the performance of countries, companies, and leaders.

A challenging question at the core of the evolving sustainability agenda is: How do we give voice to the world's population, to other species, and to the future? How can leaders access tomorrow's intelligence about business, markets, and society?

You could argue, and Doug Miller does, that:

> multi-country polls provide an early form of global democracy by giving voice to a large and increasing percentage of the Earth's people. More scientific than street protests, global polling does challenge us pollsters to give appropriate "political space" to the views of people in developing countries as well as in the industrialized ones.

But he also warns that, "Some of our best global polls are scientifically representative of only 2.5 billion people worldwide – well short of the current 7 billion global citizens."

So, to this book's question, "Can the World Be Wrong?," the answer has to be yes, on occasion. But, to date, GlobeScan's surveys have polled over 750,000 citizens across 20 countries. In a world where ripples can herald tsunamis, leaders ignore other people's values, attitudes, and opinions at their peril.

John Elkington is co-founder of ENDS (Environmental Data Services), SustainAbility and Volans Ventures. His 19th book, co-authored with former PUMA Chairman and CEO Jochen Zeitz, is *The Breakthrough Challenge: 10 Ways To Connect Today's Profits With Tomorrow's Bottom Line.*

Acknowledgments

Many people must be acknowledged for their critical roles in creating the unique body of global polling data on which this book is based. In fact, there are almost a million people worldwide to thank.

First, my mentor and first Chairman of GlobeScan, Lord Holme of Cheltenham ("call me Richard"), for his enormous and continuing contributions, including suggesting the title of this book.

Next, my major business and research partners over the years – Michael Adams, Steven Kull, and now, Chris Coulter and the next generation of leaders who are taking this work forward at GlobeScan. And Sir Robert Worcester, founder of the UK polling firm MORI (now Ipsos MORI), for his kindness and help in the early years of building our international network of researchers.

I especially want to showcase and thank a special group of committed social researchers forming the nucleus of GlobeScan's 50-nation network of Research Partners, many of whom have fielded our research at their own expense as part of their contribution to society. I particularly want to acknowledge Anna Andreenkova, Paolo Anselmi, Marita Carballo, Jo Ebhomenye, Yashwant Deshmukh, Fabian Echegaray, Gines Garrido, Ijaz Gilani, Bulent Gundogmus, Huixin Ke, Marta Lagos, Dan Lund, Irma Malibari, Bernhard Reider, and Urpi Torrado.

As for my wife of 35 years, Margot, she is beyond words.

Last but not least, I want to acknowledge the over 750,000 citizens across 20 countries who have generously shared their time and views with us in responding to our surveys over the last decade. It is our debt to them that has most driven this project.

So in addition to my talented colleagues at GlobeScan and the clients who have supported our work, this book is dedicated to our research colleagues around the world and to all who have given us their views. Without them, this book would simply not have been possible.

If I can speak for all of them, we offer this book as a contribution toward the world we intend for ourselves, our children, and future generations. I do so in the belief that when humans are involved, everything is possible, including achieving our highest aspirations and best intentions.

Doug Miller
Toronto, Canada
June 2015

1
Where on Earth are we going?[1]

A futurist is someone who deeply understands the present.
Michael Adams, President, Environics
Research Group, Canada, 1991

There are two superpowers in the world: the United States and world opinion.
Rev. Bob Edgar, General Secretary of the
US National Council of Churches, 2002

In early 2009 we all got somewhere we'd never been before. Almost everything about our world flew off whatever maps we'd been using to navigate our economic, political, and geopolitical lives. We felt on the brink of an abyss. We didn't know where we *were*, let alone where we were all headed. And, if we're honest, we're just as lost today.

In describing today's world, the US Army War College coined the term a "VUCA World" – for volatile, uncertain, complex, and ambiguous.

It is not only the global financial meltdown and continuing Great Recession. There are many other factors. The historic decline of the USA as the world's superpower. The rise of China. The climate crisis. The inadequacy of the global governance system. The rise of new kinds of leader and new kinds of power. The decline of trust and the rise of both hope and hopelessness. All of these phenomena have the thoughtful among us casting about for our bearings and scrambling for some way of predicting the future.

---

1   With acknowledgment and thanks to Maurice Strong, Secretary-General of the UN's 1992 Rio Earth Summit, who chose this as the title of his book (Texere, 2001).

Even today, with nothing really changed, our worst fear is that economist Raj Patel was right about the Great Recession when he said in 2009, "Our faith in a gentle return to earth is misplaced, for there is not, and never has been, any solid ground beneath our feet."[2] A number of other economists are expecting a long period of "secular stagnation." Some social commentators are even beginning to fear that the biblical "seven bad years" that we think we've just been through (2008–15) might actually be "seven good years" compared with even worse conditions that could shape the next seven years.

In this period of history that might be dubbed "The Rising Dread," it seems important to ask ourselves "Where are we headed?" To answer this question we can do far worse than to look where the majority of us humans aspire for us to go, and explore the values and attitude trends that are already shaping the world.

As this book hopefully demonstrates, not only is exploring global public opinion a valid, fascinating, and surprising exercise, but the value shifts and attitude trends it uncovers help us understand the present and predict the future. This is because public opinion can be shown to powerfully and materially affect the course of history.

A review of history shows that the "street" has always been a political force in the world. Even before the emergence of public opinion research, street crowds in ancient Rome, revolutionary France, and Reformation England demonstrated that the ultimate mandate for leaders and ideas comes from the public.

More recently, the civil rights movement and anti-Vietnam War demonstrations in the USA, the Orange Revolution in the Ukraine, the anti-US sentiments generated by President George W. Bush's Administration, Tunisia's 2011 Jasmine Revolution and the subsequent Arab Spring across the Middle East, and the Occupy Wall Street movement in the USA have underlined the power of public opinion.

Masses of people can sometimes become mobs ruled by lesser passions. But public opinion pollsters mainly find wisdom in crowds. As James Surowiecki said in his landmark book on the subject,[3] "Under the right circumstances, groups are remarkably intelligent, and are often smarter than the smartest people in them."

---

2   From his brilliant and thought-provoking book, *The Value of Nothing* (Harper-Collins, 2009).

3   James Surowiecki, *The Wisdom of Crowds* (Doubleday, 2004).

Well-constructed surveys conducted with proper scientific samples provide these "right circumstances" for delivering the collective wisdom of the general public (and sometimes more specialized publics) on topics ranging from globalization, nuclear proliferation, and climate change through to assessing the performance of countries, companies, and leaders. At very least, our research findings document the evolution of collective thinking on these topics.

While opinion polls have been an authoritative part of national life in many countries for some time, global outrage at the foreign policy of the Bush Administration in the USA galvanized and demonstrated the potency of "global opinion." The emergence of global-scale concerns including climate change and extreme poverty has also contributed to this rise of what has been called "the other superpower."

This globalization of issues, together with pioneering multi-country polling efforts by the University of Michigan, University of Chicago, Gallup International, the Pew Research Center, WorldPublicOpinion.org, and GlobeScan Incorporated, has resulted in global opinion surveys becoming established sources of comparative insight that are now widely used by major media organizations, UN (United Nations) agencies, global companies, national governments, and NGOs (non-governmental organizations).

At its best, global polling taps the collective wisdom of average citizens the world over. Pollsters have the privilege and responsibility of "letting the people speak" and bringing global opinion to the decision tables where leaders grapple with issues affecting everyone. Be it G7 (Group of Seven) or G20 (Group of Twenty) summits, the UN Security Council, the World Economic Forum in Davos, or boardrooms of major companies – these are where decisions on issues such as trade, climate change, and human rights are taken. Even when it doesn't affect decisions, good polling can help us more deeply understand current history.

It could also be said that multi-country polls provide an early form of global democracy by giving voice to a large and increasing percentage of the Earth's people. More scientific than street protests, global polling does challenge us pollsters to give appropriate "political space" to the views of people in developing countries as well as in the industrialized ones. Currently, in spite of our best efforts to include more populations in our polls, social researchers often give greater political weight to those in industrialized countries. Some of our best global polls are scientifically representative of only 2.5 billion people worldwide – well short of the current 7 billion global citizens.

Truthfully, we are in the early days of global polling. So-called global polls can be trotted out with only eight or ten countries represented. Others are conducted online so only represent the views of "Netizens" – still a minority of citizens in many countries. Relatively few social research organizations are even engaged in giving voice to the global public on important issues.

It is also vital that pollsters ask the right questions – well-crafted, culturally neutral, and balanced questions that give people a true choice and an appropriate context within which to register their views.

This book draws mainly from a decade-and-a-half of global public opinion research that my colleagues and I at GlobeScan have conducted, to map some of the key trends that are shaping the world. It then goes on to suggest where these trends are likely to lead – with the implications for nations, companies, NGOs, world leaders, and individuals.

In this time of great concern and uncertainty over the state of the world, we believe long-term polling trends offer an important source of insight into where things are headed.

Together with its national research partners, GlobeScan has conducted regular 20-nation public opinion surveys since 1997 to track views on a wide range of issues shaping the world. Clients have included the BBC World Service, the World Economic Forum, the World Social Forum, the UN, national governments, the National Geographic Society, Oxfam, and scores of global companies. We believe the resulting trend lines are powerful, unique, and indicative of what the future will hold.

While single polls can provide a good snapshot of views, tracking surveys that ask the same questions in the same way over time generate the equivalent of a motion picture of trends – much more compelling findings and reliable predictors of likely scenarios shaping the future.

The current world situation is unprecedented in its uncertainties but also in its possibilities. The trends revealed in this book speak to both the risks and the opportunities; and we hope will help you and your organization navigate the medium-term future.

Summary

- Many factors put the future of human civilization in doubt. Long-term trends in global public opinion help us understand the present and predict the future.

- History shows us that the "power of the street" is the ultimate mandate for leaders and ideas. More scientific than street protests, studying public opinion is valid, fascinating, and surprising – as this book hopefully demonstrates.

- At its best, global public opinion taps the collective wisdom of average citizens the world over, and is an early form of global democracy.

- International polls have become established sources of comparative insights, widely used by major media organizations, UN agencies, global companies, national governments, and NGOs.

- This book draws from a decade and a half of global public opinion research to map some of the key trends that are shaping the world. It then goes on to suggest where these trends are likely to lead.

2
Can the world be wrong?

> Public sentiment is everything. With public sentiment, nothing can fail. Without it, nothing can succeed.
>
> Abraham Lincoln

> There are lies, damned lies, and statistics.
>
> Mark Twain

Welcome to my world: the world of public opinion polling.

It's a world of questions and answers, of samples and surprises. The better the questions and the samples, the better the insight into the world. The more often over time the same good questions are asked of fresh scientific samples, the better the insight into the trends shaping the future.

The central thesis of this book is that global public opinion polling, tracked over time across key countries, can help predict the future – or at least yield clear insights into the likely scenarios within which the future will unfold.

Pollsters and other social scientists are fascinated not only by the views held by majorities of citizens on a wide range of topics but on the processes and influences that change these views over time.

I'm very grateful that I found my way into public opinion research because it satisfies two of the big themes in my life. First, numbers have always spoken to me. I get as much from reading a set of number tables as I do from reading a good book. And second, equality has always been important to me – something that I didn't really understand until I visited my family's early 1800s sharecropper homestead in Scotland. We Scots do seem to rail on against inequality and arbitrary authority!

So stumbling into polling (after taking mathematics/physics in university and beginning an issues communication consultancy) has been like coming home for me, because statistical research involves numerical measurement of opinion and one of its basic principles is that everyone's opinion is equally important.

I remember when GlobeScan fielded its first global poll in 1997 – to measure environmental concerns across 30 countries to present at a UN environment conference. For a number of weeks I would wake up every morning imagining the thousands of interviews that were taking place with all those people around the world on perhaps the first global issue that was touching all of our lives. I felt honored to be part of giving voice to their collective views. I still feel the same today.

International polling has also introduced me to a world of interesting and committed colleagues in countries around the globe. In addition to GlobeScan's hand-picked research partners in each of 30 countries, I'm grateful to all my fellow members of WAPOR (World Association for Public Opinion Research) for the opportunity to work with and learn from them over the years, both at our annual professional conferences and when I have been able to visit with them in their countries.

One of my earliest memories of my many "country visits" over the years was drinking Turkish coffee till dawn in Istanbul with one of that country's finest pollsters, who regaled me with wonderfully insightful tales of opinion and trends in his fascinating country where Europe meets Asia. You can't learn about a country more deeply than this.

But what about at the global level; can this level of accuracy and insight be achieved? And what about the bigger question that this book tackles: can the world be wrong? In other words, can comparative polling across multiple countries result in wrong conclusions about where the world is heading? My answer is, "Yes it can be wrong, but rarely from my experience."

Using polling to predict the future can be wrong in at least five possible ways. Polling can variously be deliberately misleading, technically wrong, conceptually flawed, or factually incorrect. Polling can also be accurate yet not predictive of actual events. Let's take these each in turn.

In today's distrustful world, everyone is treated with skepticism and pollsters are obviously not immune (nor should we be). Some people assume that pollsters practice the dark arts and regularly ask questions in ways designed to get the results desired by their clients or their own political leanings. Unfortunately, this is sometimes the case, and it drags down our profession as surely as a self-interested politician drags down political life.

Some less-than-honorable polling agencies have publicly released survey results designed to be supportive of their (often unnamed) clients. I've seen

examples of such polls on nuclear power, climate change, and a raft of political platforms. Extreme examples come from the use of "push polling" techniques, where faulty facts and biased question wording are used to skew the
results. But this is not the truth about the vast majority of polls or pollsters.

Polling can also be technically flawed and therefore misleading. It may
use a weak sample that is not representative of the total population, an
inappropriate methodology, or make other technical errors such as faulty
translation of the questions into local languages and dialects. Online polls
in countries with very low internet penetration that purport to represent
broad public opinion are another example, which can be as misleading as
polls sponsored by self-interested organizations. The established research
industry has long argued that media organizations should have strict policies of not reporting "junk polls" such as these. Reporting of any poll results
that do not include enough information to enable the reader to judge its
accuracy and neutrality, deserve to be treated with skepticism.

Third, in spite of our best intentions we pollsters can sometimes get it
wrong even with a good sample. A flawed question wording on a complicated topic can produce findings that misrepresent the public view. This
can particularly be a problem when we ask too few questions on a topic or
form conclusions based on superficial questions that don't get to the substance of the issue.

A simple question that forces respondents to choose between spending
cuts or tax increases to reduce overall government deficits is a good example. Detailed research shows that opinion changes by spending area and
most want a combination of the two. A pollster can also confuse respondents with question wording that muddles concepts that are already unclear
in the public mind, such as deficit and debt, or climate change and ozone
depletion. In other cases, local, cultural, or religious factors can make global
questions irrelevant in certain countries. For example, a question about
belief in God is not salient in the (humanistic) Buddhist and (multi-deity)
Hindu worlds. Polling is like other fields of activity: garbage in, garbage out.

Fourth, polling can accurately measure perceptions of the public that
are factually incorrect. Polls showing that most Europeans see immigra-
tion as bad for the economy accurately reveal perceptions that don't have
the added advantage of being true. Economic studies show migration to be
strongly positive for economies.

Finally, polling may result in a totally accurate picture of public sentiment
that will never be reflected in public policy or eventual societal outcomes
because of strong opposition from powerful forces with vested interests.

FIGURE 1   Seriousness of global warming
"Very serious," BRIC vs. G7 (without Japan and Italy), 1992–February 2014

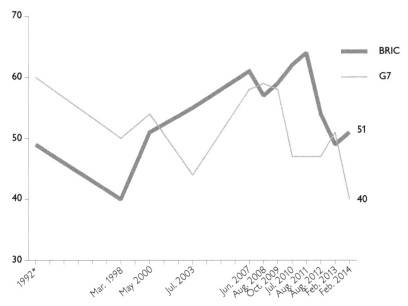

BRIC includes Brazil, China, India, and Russia. G7 includes Canada, France, Germany, UK, and USA.
Brazil not asked in 2013. Canada not asked in 2011. China not asked in 1992. France not asked in
1992. Russia not asked in 2012.
*Source: Gallup International Institute's Health of the Planet survey

From my 25 years of experience, while power elites can choose to ignore
public opinion for a while, strong opinion trends revealed through our
tracking research have almost always prevailed in the end, be it in China or
in Western democracies.

There are inevitable lags in any governance system, but generally we have
found that strong polling trends eventually get manifested in changed government policies and citizen behavior. This is the reason we are emphasiz-
ing tracking research in this book – where the same questions are asked in
the same way over a number of years.

Figure 1 shows the power of long-term trend research in telling a story. It
shows the evolution of concern about climate change between citizens of
the G7 industrialized countries and citizens of the so-called BRIC countries
(Brazil, Russia, India, China). Back in 1992, G7 citizens were on average 10%
more likely than citizens of BRIC countries to rate climate change as a "very
serious" problem. By 2014 the reverse was true, mainly due to a decline in
perceived seriousness among G7 citizens.

FIGURE 2   Participating countries

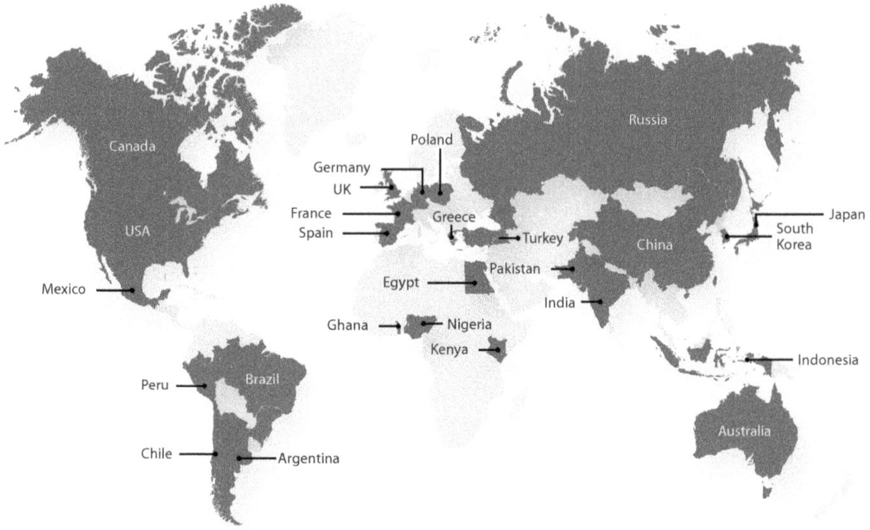

Polling is both an art and a science. We social researchers definitely get it wrong at times just like anyone else, but generally our industry standards are good and our methods and results are sound.

Most social researchers really want to understand how society is evolving. We follow rigorous sampling and survey methods to ensure the laws of statistics apply. Most reputable polling firms are members and follow the standards laid down by our global professional bodies, WAPOR and ESOMAR (the European Society for Opinion and Marketing Research). Most of us also regularly present our methods and results at professional conferences, opening ourselves to peer review.

Much of the polling that underpins this book was conducted by GlobeScan Incorporated, a company founded (as Environics International) in 1987. We have been fortunate to have built a network of respected local research partners across 30 countries, many of them willing to field global polls as part of their societal contribution. A list of the fine research institutes contributing data to this book is included in Appendix 3.

The research findings presented here usually involve over 20,000 interviews across 20 or more countries from six continents, and are statistically representative of a universe of 2.5 billion of the world's people. Most of the 20 largest economies in the world (the so-called G20 countries) are included in each poll. In each country, the surveys use the same methodologies as those used to predict national elections, being accurate within 3.5%

nationally, 19 times out of 20. Figure 2 shows the countries usually included in GlobeScan's polls.

GlobeScan and its national research partners use in-home or telephone interviewing. This ensures the key scientific underpinning and therefore legitimacy of polling is respected – that the sample is constructed in a manner that gives everyone in the population being surveyed an equal chance of being selected for the survey. Random digit dialing for telephone research is a good example of this. Fresh samples are drawn each time.

All this methodological rigor, plus the fact that tracking polls ask the same questions in the same way over time, mean that the resulting trends in key opinions are reliable metrics for both understanding the world today and developing likely scenarios for the future. Hence, they form a good basis for making well-informed decisions at both the personal and organizational level.

As mentioned earlier, the crafting of questions is key to the art and science of polling. This is especially true when doing multi-country research in 20–30 languages across many cultures. Simple language, free of cultural bias, is key. The neutrality of questions is another key factor – neutrality in both tone and content. In my experience, most social researchers are passionately neutral and really want to understand where society is heading.

Given the importance of the research questions, exact question wording for all the findings presented in this book is provided in Appendix 1; please judge for yourself. Many of the tracking charts in the book use multi-country averages to keep complexity to reasonable levels; but in the interest of transparency detailed country-by-country results for these questions are given in Appendix 2.

At the end of the day, my 25 years in the polling business suggest that many people's definition of good polling is research that agrees with their prior views on a given subject. You might watch for this yourself so that you're open to some of the surprising findings in this book.

There is also real opposition among power elites almost everywhere against increasing the influence of the will of the people on the affairs of state. A senior official in one country's foreign service reacted to one of my research presentations with the admonition, "Surely you're not suggesting that we shape our foreign policy on public opinion!" I told him they could do far worse. And they have.

But strong trend lines such as those presented in this book will very likely become manifest in the world eventually, through market and policy changes. There are delays in every system, and major events such as 9/11 and the Great Recession can definitely change the course of certain things. But most of the trends presented in this book have been affected very little by even these mega-events (as can be seen from the tracking charts).

Over the years, GlobeScan has generated a number of research results that some people couldn't quite believe at the time but which ended up being very predictive of subsequent events:

- The huge expectations of companies to act on broader societal issues, revealed in our 30-country Millennium Poll in 1999, led to a decade in which companies have had to out-compete each other in demonstrating their CSR (corporate social responsibility).

- Our 1998 poll for a global consumer product company showing American and Chinese citizens similarly wired on environmental topics has been followed by a decade in which the environmental concerns of the Chinese population have actually overtaken those in the West and transformed Chinese government policy into a leading position on renewable energy and sustainability.

- Our 1999 research and analysis for the UN Environment Pro-gramme identifying a surprisingly large ethical consumer segment of the global population has been followed by the recession-defying growth in ethical consumerism generally and the Fairtrade brand specifically.

So can the world be wrong? Yes it can, but I would argue polling trends are going to be less wrong than almost every other way of predicting the future. I would strongly advise organizations and individuals that are significantly vulnerable to the trends outlined in this book to at the very least develop a planning scenario for the kind of future suggested here.

The future of global polling

The rise of global polling is one of the things that has significantly shaped the first decade-and-a-half of the 21st century; and it promises to grow in importance and influence.

Pioneering efforts in the 1980s and 1990s by the University of Chicago and University of Michigan have been greatly broadened since the late 1990s by the Pew Research Center, Gallup International, WorldPublicOpinion.org, and by GlobeScan.

At its best, global polling taps the collective wisdom of average citizens the world over. It can be seen as an early form of global democracy, giving voice to a large and increasing percentage of the Earth's people, using scientific methods.

At its worst, polling can live down to the serious skepticism that some hold for this "devil science." Mark Twain's quotation at the beginning of this chapter was far from the last to cast dispersion on statistical research. However, the pervasiveness of statistics these days from many sources, and the hunger for a factual basis for understanding our world and for making decisions, has brought survey research into much wider favor. Whether it's the consumer confidence index, voting intentions, product usage, or views on specific policy options expressed through referenda or polls, scientific survey research based on rigorous samples has become an important source of understanding and an authoritative input to decision-making.

But to live up to this role, global polling must evolve quickly. And it is.

I predicted five years ago that truly globally representative polls will be a reality within a decade. Sure enough, the Gallup Organization in the USA has recently launched its World Poll claiming annual polling in 140 countries around the world, using telephone or in-person interviews.

I believe we can't rest until we have established a number of annual surveys of truly representative global samples that accurately reflect the weight of opinion in proportion to their percentage of the global population. We also need to develop better ways of presenting global opinion. Currently almost all pollsters use the UN model for weighting global opinion of "one nation one vote," even though this weights the importance of Chinese and Indian opinion equally with smaller countries such as the Netherlands and Colombia. The polling profession needs to develop and agree a more suitable weighting system and then all major polling organizations should follow it.

While more scientific than street protests, polling is equally reliant on the "Fourth Estate," media, for its power and impact. Both the polling profession and media organizations have much to do to live up to our responsibilities as the influence of these polls grows and takes on almost a global governance role.

Researchers must do a better job of addressing skepticism toward polling by better educating people on the scientific validity of representative random samples, and finding better ways of portraying and interpreting multicountry results. For its part, the media must develop its internal expertise and policies that can differentiate good polling methodology from bad polls; then do a better job reporting the former and never reporting the latter.

The role of survey research is not limited to public opinion but can also involve stakeholders who are paying close attention to or have knowledge of particular topics, organizations, or sets of issues. For example, surveys of climate experts and decision-makers, chief executives of companies, or Nobel Prize-winning scientists can tap the views of people that are particularly knowledgeable or engaged in specific issues and are therefore able to go beyond their personal opinion to give a considered judgment on topics based on their professional or life experience. Similarly, the views of citizens living near industrial facilities, or those most affected by a particular government policy, have sometimes more relevant and important perspectives than the general public.

GlobeScan has found that our best contribution to important policy debates is to combine the contextual insight from public opinion polls with more detailed findings from surveys of experts and stakeholders. In this book, I draw on findings from GlobeScan's surveys of an authoritative panel of sustainable development experts[1] across more than 60 countries to illustrate this added value.

I suggest that transparent, quantitative and iterative surveys of particular stakeholders will become increasingly established as part of global governance processes in the internet age. Transparency International's "Bribe Payers Index" is a good example, where business executives across the world rate how likely companies from 28 different countries are likely to pay bribes in order to win business.

Another increasingly surveyed sub-audience is the "Netizen," an online citizen reached using online samples and survey techniques. In many countries these surveys cannot be credibly presented as representative of public opinion in the country due to low penetration of the internet in households. However, online polls are relatively inexpensive to carry out and, if done rigorously, can be representative of the online community, or "Netizens," in a given country. This can be seen as a surrogate for surveying the more wealthy, educated and informed citizens who often tend to be influential in

---

1   This hand-picked panel of 5,000 experts and stakeholders across the world includes sustainable development leaders from business, government, academia, NGOs, think-tanks, consultancies, and the media. About 1,000 of them answer each of our quarterly surveys, now co-managed by GlobeScan and SustainAbility.

TABLE 1   Home internet access by country (G20 countries)

Does your home have access to the internet?	Yes
Australia	89%
Canada	87%
South Korea	87%
France	85%
UK	84%
USA	80%
Germany	77%
Saudi Arabia	74%
Japan	73%
Italy	63%
Russia	51%
Argentina	41%
Brazil	40%
Turkey	40%
China	34%
Mexico	25%
Indonesia	21%
South Africa	16%
India*	3%

* Most internet connection in India is through mobile telephones.

Source: The World Poll 2011, by Gallup Organization. Results are based on telephone or face-to-face interviews with at least 1,000 adults in each country, aged 15 and older.

shaping social norms and political trends. However, in most countries this is not the same as true public opinion.

To demonstrate how far this is from being representative of the general population and therefore public opinion in most countries, we need only look at the percentage penetration of household internet use in countries across the world (Table 1). Even among the so-called G20 largest economies, there are countries where the percentage of the national population that have internet in their home is too low for online surveys to be representative of public opinion.

We must always remember that the key scientific underpinning and therefore legitimacy of polling is to have balanced questions and a sample constructed in a manner that gives everyone in the population being surveyed an equal chance of being selected for the survey.

Having said this, conducting public opinion surveys in countries with high internet penetration (such as the USA, Canada, UK, Netherlands, Germany, France, Japan, South Korea, etc.) yields reliable results, especially using internet panels that have been built in a rigorous manner – for example, by giving computers and internet connectivity to citizens unable to afford it, so their opinions can be included in proper measure.

With all its blemishes, it can be successfully argued that using strong trends in public opinion across even the G20 countries will still be better than other methods for predicting the future, because the sampled populations constitute the most influential portion of what could be called the global "body politic."[2]

For a more definitive proof of this, please reread this book in 20 years' time! What seems challenging and unrealistic at a certain point in time can appear prescient a decade or so in the future.

Summary

- The central thesis of this book is that global public opinion polling, tracked over time across key countries, can help predict the future.

- Multi-country public opinion polls give a good approximation of what can be called a global "body politic" with real influence.

- However, using polling to help predict the future can be wrong in five possible ways:
    - Some polls are deliberately misleading, with biased questions designed to support (often unnamed) clients.
    - Polls can be technically wrong due to weak sampling methods or faulty translations of questions or responses.
    - Some questions are conceptually flawed due to overly simplifying possible responses or muddling concepts (such as deficit and debt).

2   See "Global public opinion: a valid proxy for the global body politic," chapter by Doug Miller in the book *Voice of the People 2015* (Gallup International Association), available at http://www.globescan.com/images/GlobeScan_Foundation/Doug-Miller-Can-the-World-Be-Wrong-GIA-chapter.pdf.

- Polls can accurately reveal perceptions that are factually incorrect and hence unlikely to make it through the policy development process.
- Even the highest-quality polling can result in findings that do not get reflected in public policy or societal outcomes because of strong opposition from powerful elites, at least for a while.

- Polling is both an art and a science. We social researchers definitely get it wrong at times just like anyone else, but generally our industry standards are good and our methods and results are sound.

- This book, based as it is on decade-long trends from scientific surveys across scores of countries, provides reliable metrics for both understanding the world today and developing likely scenarios for the future.

- To help readers come to their own judgment, the exact question wording, methodological details and country-by-country results are given for all questions in the appendices.

- So can the world be wrong? Yes it can, but this book argues that polling trends are going to be less wrong than almost every other way of anticipating the future.

3
A post-superpower world

The strongest is never strong enough to be always the master, unless he transforms strength into right, and obedience into duty.

Jean-Jacques Rousseau, philosopher

One of the big lessons of the Iraq War has been that, even for the United States, legitimacy in the court of global opinion ultimately counts for as much as military might.

Philip Stephens, columnist, *Financial Times*, January 2009

How long can the world's biggest borrower remain the world's biggest power?

Lawrence H. Summers, Economic Advisor in the Obama Administration, 2009

In the first decade of the 21st century we have seen the globalization of long-time American values such as excellence, free markets, and the rule of law. At the same time, we've seen the USA heavily criticized for offending these very values.

In a way, the first decade of the new millennium (the "noughties") was defined by the George W. Bush Administration's defiance of global public opinion. As a result, world opinion savaged Brand USA, with material effects on America's stature, influence, and economic success. The Obama Administration on its own has not been enough to fully regain America's leadership, and his continuation of an invasive electronic surveillance program and his escalation of drone warfare continue to tarnish views of America around the world.

I expect history will show that the global outrage over Americans allowing the Bush and Obama administrations to conduct such foreign policy, not the 9/11 terrorist attacks, will most shape the future of the world. In other words, it wasn't the terrible act of hatred perpetrated on the Twin Towers, it was what America did next. As the British would say, it was an own goal of historic proportions.

I was a mile from the Pentagon at 9 a.m. on September 11, 2001 when the plane went in. I was just off a flight at Reagan National Airport. I felt the impact, saw the after-explosions, walked through the plume of smoke on my way to a scheduled presentation in downtown Washington. Due to the ensuing travel disruptions I ended up spending the next week there, huddled around television sets in the hotel lobby with everyone else. I experienced America's shock, grief, and fear at first hand.

I can say from this experience that it was a totally self-absorbed week in America with the crowds around the televisions watching CNN coverage of the latest FBI raids on houses in Miami. The fact that much of the world stood by America at that moment simply wasn't reflected in American media coverage, and was therefore not received by Americans. They totally missed the vast outflowing of sympathy around the world. "Why do they hate us?" was the phrase on the lips of many Americans, but at that point most people across the world supported Americans in their hour of national mourning.

In a poll conducted in November 2001, two months following the collapse of the Twin Towers, GlobeScan found majority support in 19 of 23 countries for what would become America's invasion of Afghanistan (expressed as "using military force against countries harboring terrorists," Fig. 3). This near-consensus support of America has not been seen since.

I was also in London on the morning of July 7, 2005, just entering the London Underground when terrorist bombs went off on three trains and a bus. I experienced the British reaction: a quiet stoic resolve, the proverbial stiff upper lip. Things quickly got back to normal, including transit ridership.

Fear breeds bad decisions, as a wise man said, and Americans in my judgment got overly spooked by 9/11. They circled the wagons too tightly, smothering dissent for a while through a climate of self-censorship, enabling wrongs to be done in their name.

By November 2006, four years after 9/11, more than twice as many people (57% across 11 countries) saw the world's only superpower as a mainly negative force in the world than those who saw it as a positive force (25%, Fig. 5).

In analyzing the results from a series of questions on American foreign policy asked across 20 countries in 2005, GlobeScan was surprised by what most drove negative views of the USA. The second Iraq war was the most

FIGURE 3   Use military force against countries harboring terrorists
"Agree" vs. "Disagree," November 2001

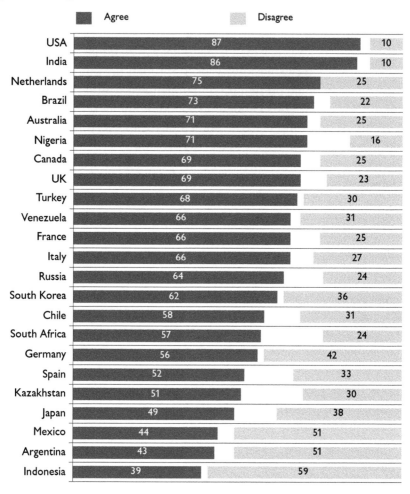

The white space in this chart represents "DK/NA."

powerful factor, as expected, but not much stronger than two other factors. The Bush Administration's retreat from multilateralism on climate change was tied for second place with the Guantánamo Bay detentions. This suggests a much more complicated set of reasons for the faltering of American leadership in the world than simply Iraq.

Some months before, GlobeScan's first Chairman, the Right Honourable Lord Holme of Cheltenham and I wrote the following unpublished op-ed piece:

Regaining trust in America

By Lord Holme and Doug Miller
May 4, 2004

In the words of a prescient print ad created a few years ago for the global consultancy Accenture, "Trust is the oxygen of the new economy." Trust is also the oxygen of the new world order.

As revealed by GlobeScan's latest 20-nation public opinion tracking research, just released by the World Economic Forum, trust in global companies has bounced back to pre-Enron levels in over half of the 20 largest economies in the world.

While global companies continue to be the least trusted of the seven institutions tested, the results do suggest that citizens see recent regulatory and legal actions as helping moderate and punish the corporate abuses that have so undermined corporate trust in recent years.

As for the new world order, the same poll shows that non-governmental organizations and the United Nations continue to enjoy the highest public trust. As many are learning the hard way, this is an upside-down world where those with least power are most trusted and those with most power are least so.

The fact that trust in the United Nations is at the same relatively high levels it enjoyed in August 2002 is nothing short of remarkable. The early 2003 diplomatic breakdown over the invasion of Iraq was clearly not as damaging to the UN as many commentators believed at the time. In fact, all roads may well lead to the United Nations for American and British policy-makers on more than just Iraq.

The same poll shows that the war on terror, as currently executed, is losing popular support across the world. The proportion of citizens agreeing that "military force is the most effective way of reducing international terrorism" has dropped significantly since 2002 in over half the countries surveyed, including the US. Today, majorities of citizens in only five of the 20 countries agree that hard power is most effective.

European Union President Romano Prodi's view that the military approach is "insufficient," and that "soft" approaches are also needed, appears to have clear popular support, especially in Europe.

Effective military force, at least on a global stage, is in the hands of one actor, the United States. The poll shows that, over the period since December 2002, agreement that "the United States is having a mainly positive influence in the world" has dropped significantly in half the tracking countries, to the point where only five countries have a majority positive view. In today's world, with numbers like that, US policy-makers cannot hope to wield the influence they wish to in world affairs.

Nor should Europeans congratulate themselves. The perception that Europe is having a mainly positive influence in the world has also eroded. However,

Europe is seen as playing a much more positive role than the US in all but three countries.

At a time when trust in both the USA and Europe is dropping, it is striking that trust in the United Nations has remained at a high level and, in a number of countries, has actually increased. This may suggest that people believe that the UN stood on the correct side of history in not granting its legitimacy to the American invasion of Iraq.

Countries that seek to influence world events need to be adept at wielding both soft and hard power, just as global companies that seek to maximize long-term shareholder value have to excel at both business acumen and corporate social responsibility.

The world needs a strong and influential America, just as it needs a strong and influential Europe and a strong and influential Arab world. The US will not succeed as we need it to, by treating the rest of us like failed Americans.

Clearly, the US needs to become much better at "the trust thing." Unless it does, in this asymmetric world, America will be unable to convert its unparalleled hard power into global influence, and it will be caught in a world shaped by others.

It has been said that, if we compare today's world with medieval Europe, and argue that the US President is the Emperor, then [UN Secretary-General] Kofi Annan is the Pope. What the world is looking for now is the legitimacy which only the Pope can give in blessing the arms of the Emperor.

Even under the much-less-popular "Pope" (current Secretary-General Ban Ki-moon), the UN continues to be one of the most trusted institutions in the world (Fig. 10), and is seen as having a more positive influence in the world than the USA even with the much more popular "Emperor" (President Obama).

But the American government wasn't alone in being impacted by falling trust through the Bush years. American business also paid a price for a faltering Brand USA. A demographic analysis of 2007 international polling data showed that those most upset with America included the world's educated and the world's wealthy – important markets indeed.

As GlobeScan presented to the US Chamber of Commerce in early 2008, fewer citizens across 17 countries agreed that "American companies are having a mainly positive influence in the world" in 2007 than was the case in 2004 (Fig. 4). The biggest declines occurred in Europe and Latin America, where only 28% and 39% respectively agreed with the statement. Europe is a major market for American goods and services, and this declining view of American companies had a negative impact on sales.

FIGURE 4   American companies are having a mainly positive influence in
the world
"Strongly" and "Somewhat agree," average of 17 tracking countries,* by region,
December 2004–June 2007

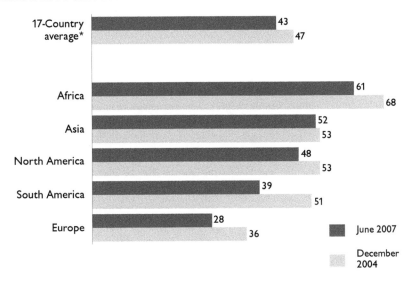

17-Country average*: 43, 47

Africa: 61, 68

Asia: 52, 53

North America: 48, 53

South America: 39, 51

Europe: 28, 36

■ June 2007

▫ December 2004

*Tracking countries include Brazil, Canada, Chile, China, France, Germany, India,
Indonesia, Italy, Mexico, Nigeria, Philippines, Russia, S. Korea, Turkey, UK and the USA.

Data analysis shows that by far the biggest driver of these views of US business was the respondent's view of the overall US role in the world. No wonder
a number of major US businesses formed Business for Diplomatic Action to
urge the US government to apply what US business had learned about reputation management in order to turn around a faltering Brand USA.

As damaged as it has been in the court of public opinion, America is still
very much in the game. But even under the leadership of President Barack
Obama, its influence continues to be viewed negatively by significant numbers of people.

One of the benefits of tracking views annually is that it is easier to attribute changes in opinion to specific events or policies. This is particularly
the case with the annual tracking of views of countries done by the BBC
World Service (Fig. 5).

BBC findings from November 2006 showed that anti-Americanism had
reached a fever pitch. By December 2008 it showed an "Obama bounce"
with views of the USA back up to 2005 levels – still quite negative. By the
end of Obama's first year in office in December 2009, positive views of the

FIGURE 5   Views of US influence
"Positive" vs. "Negative," average of 11 tracking countries,* December 2004–
February 2014

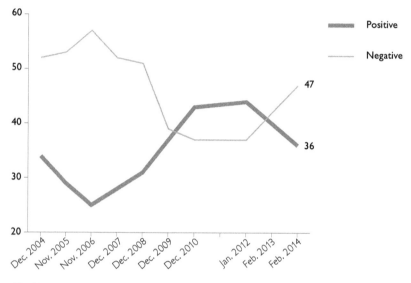

*Tracking countries include Australia, Canada, Chile, China, France, Germany,
India, Indonesia, Mexico, Russia, and the UK.

USA equaled negative views. But, as GlobeScan and others predicted, the
turnaround has been much slower than many Americans thought it would
be. It's hard work, regaining trust. And then came the escalation of drone
warfare and Edward Snowden's revelations about the extent of the US government's electronic surveillance in 2013 to turn opinion of the US net-
negative again.

Other global brands that have suffered similar losses of trust (e.g., Nike
over sweatshops, Shell over human rights in Nigeria) have shown that it
takes 5–10 years of hard work to rebuild trust. While easy to lose, trust is
hard to win back. It requires humility, apology, and walking the walk more
than talking the talk – attributes that have rarely been manifested in many
nations' foreign policy.

I think many people would agree with former President Bill Clinton when
he said, "There is nothing wrong with America that can't be fixed by what
is great with America." In a way, many of us want our favorite superpower
back, providing positive moral leadership in the world. But it is not at all
clear that enough Washington insiders yet understand the depth and nature
of their challenge.

American policy-makers from both parties will need to recognize how badly trust in the USA and in Americans has been affected by events of the past decade. GlobeScan noticed from its tracking data how the reelection of President Bush in 2004 spread the global outrage from only being focused on the president to include the American government and individual Americans. (Just talk to Americans who had to travel internationally during those years.)

The Obama Administration has struggled to find more than fine words as it has worked to regain American influence. The US government will need to ensure a consistency between its foreign policy and the values for which America has always been admired. Only in this way will trust be rewon.

Almost immediately, the Obama Administration ran into difficulty. Its failure to stop Israel building more illegal settlements on Palestinian land, its failure to close its much-maligned Guantánamo Bay detention center, and its increasing use of racial profiling to protect its borders all weighed against an early recovery of trust and hence moral authority in the world. More recently, the Snowden revelations of the NSA's online surveillance has put the USA back in net-negative territory on the BBC's tracking survey of country influence.

A poignant example of this lack of moral authority came in February 2010 when Secretary of State Hillary Clinton accused Iran of "moving toward a military dictatorship." Her statement seemed to fall on deaf ears in many parts of the world after Iran's Foreign Minister Mottaki snapped back, accusing the USA of being "the very symbol of military dictatorship." Clearly, Iran's progress toward developing a nuclear weapons program is part of the price the world is paying for America's loss of soft power.

With Europe's reluctance or inability to become the world's first soft superpower, the USA may yet recover before the rise of China and India threatens to eclipse the West. This is certainly one of the scenarios for the geopolitical future that our research suggests. But it is not the most likely scenario.

In today's world, "soft power" of opinion trumps "hard" military power,[1] so it will be whoever is best at winning hearts and minds that will come out on top.

---

[1] With apologies to Joseph Nye of Harvard University, who first coined the phrases hard and soft power in 1990 to refer to military strength and diplomacy. I submit, a decade-and-a-half later, that the growing potency of global opinion is making this the new soft power, especially given the relative decline of effective diplomacy.

It is clear that America, through the Obama years, will accomplish some laudable things on the world stage. But the USA is unlikely to get much credit for them.

America's key challenge in earning back the global leadership mantle is that its two-party system so polarizes political debate and splits the US electorate that a US-led world will always be just an election away from the kind of mean-spirited leadership the world doesn't want. The Republican sweep of the November 2014 US midterm elections made even America's friends lament. GlobeScan's global polling for the last two US presidential elections shows that the world consistently wants a Democrat.

Of course the USA isn't the only big power that isn't doing so well on the soft-power front. The BBC World Service country-rating poll suggests that China's Tibet and South China Sea policies and India's treatment of women have both held back their national reputations and therefore legitimacy. People just expect and demand far more from the US hegemon, which holds itself up as a nation with high vision and standards.

Another challenge for the USA is that the world is moving rapidly onward in the meantime. America's decline as a moral force has set many other things in motion.

The ongoing BBC World Service Poll suggests we have a post-superpower world (or a "non-polar world")[2] featuring the rise of regional "champions." Initially, these regional players included "bad boys" – such as presidents Putin in Russia, Chavez in Venezuela, and Ahmadinejad in Iran – who defined themselves by opposing American hegemony. This was a natural stage. The world will get more interesting as the emerging great powers of China and India find their voices.

Aiding and abetting the rise of these regional players as well as the emerging great powers is a growing cynicism about many things American, exacerbated by what a significant minority see as a failure of the American model.

In late 2009, a year following the collapse of Lehman Brothers, GlobeScan asked 21,000 people across 21 countries to name "who or what would you say is most to blame for the current global financial crisis?" (Fig. 6). Without prompting, most respondents (31%) named their national government as being most responsible. However, the USA was named by 18% and a further 9% named either "capitalism" or "globalization," both associated with the

---

2   Coined by Richard N. Haass, President of the US Council on Foreign Relations, in May 2008.

FIGURE 6   Who is to blame for the global financial crisis?
Unprompted, combined mentions, average of 22 tracking countries,* July 2009

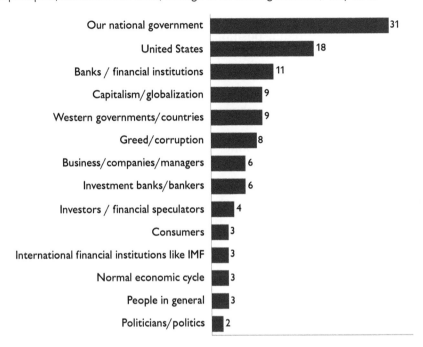

Our national government	31
United States	18
Banks / financial institutions	11
Capitalism/globalization	9
Western governments/countries	9
Greed/corruption	8
Business/companies/managers	6
Investment banks/bankers	6
Investors / financial speculators	4
Consumers	3
International financial institutions like IMF	3
Normal economic cycle	3
People in general	3
Politicians/politics	2

*Tracking countries include Australia, Canada, Chile, China, Costa Rica, France, Germany, India, Indonesia, Italy, Japan, Kenya, Mexico, Nigeria, Pakistan, Panama, Philippines, Russia, Spain, Turkey, UK and the USA.

American model. Another one in five named financial institutions (11%), bankers (6%) or speculators (4%) as being most to blame.

As covered in other chapters, even before the 2008 US banking collapse, our research showed declining regard for a number of key values previously associated with the American way. This included declining trust in the free enterprise system (covered in Chapter 8, especially Figure 28) and increased cynicism about the application of democratic principles even in long-established democracies (see Fig. 56). Government by the will of the people just doesn't ring true to many people anymore, probably because of the perceived role of private and moneyed interests.

A key challenge is that, at least temporarily, we seem to have created a world without a moral compass, in which individuals and nations are encouraged to bring their narrowest interests and worst behaviors to the world instead of their broadest and best. President Obama provided a refreshingly different role model for the world for a brief while, but the Republican-controlled US Congress certainly has not.

This rise of self-interest rather than common interest has been reflected in everything from negotiating positions at international climate change conferences through to the strategies of some nations (e.g., the clear regional strategic plays of Venezuela and Iran, and the clawing back of power and terrain by President Putin of Russia). Even universal threats such as the global economy and climate change seem unable to galvanize collective action in the common interest.

Short of a dramatic turnaround, all of this suggests we have entered a multipolar world that will be more dangerous, for a while at least, than the "Pax Americana" world we inhabited after the fall of the Berlin Wall and before the world's sheriff (the USA) fell off his horse. The US Army War College's "VUCA World" seems to describe the present nicely – volatile, uncertain, complex, and ambiguous. The "A" could also stand for asymmetric to reflect the ease with which underfunded, upstart players can disrupt established state or corporate powers. ISIS (Islamic State of Iraq and Syria) and the online hacker group Anonymous are two such asymmetric powers that come to mind.

With America's global image declining, the only other entity able to fill the leadership gap in the near term is the EU (European Union). In spite of the European elite's seeming inability to rise to this challenge, and the current economic challenges in the eurozone, this is a second geopolitical scenario suggested by our research.

For years Europe consistently scored near the top of the BBC World Service poll in terms of people's positive views of its role in the world, until 2012 when it began to decline due to the economic troubles in the eurozone. In a December 2004 poll, the University of Maryland and GlobeScan found citizens in 20 of 23 countries polled found the prospect of Europe being more influential than the USA in world affairs as positive. Americans, Filipinos, and Indians were the only ones opposed (Fig. 7).

Europe already has attained greater influence in some ways. There was a time when developing countries needing new laws went to Washington looking for model legislation on everything from environmental protection to financial market oversight. Now they travel to Brussels and use European legislation as a basis for their own laws. European leadership also caused the Kyoto Protocol on climate change to be brought into force in spite of US opposition, and the EU continues to benefit from its continuing leadership

FIGURE 7   European vs. US influence in world
December 2004

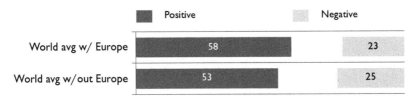

The white space in this chart represents "Depends/Neither," and "DKNA."

on the climate file in spite of its failure to influence a positive outcome at the December 2009 Copenhagen Climate Conference.

In detailed 2006 research used to brief EU President José Manuel Barroso, GlobeScan explored aspects of Europe that most drove favorable views of the EU among Brazilian opinion leaders. It found that Europe's support of multilateralism, its commitment to human rights, and its protection of the environment were most admired and valued. We also discovered two things that would most drive views of the EU to be even more positive: improving respect for immigrants and further strengthening Europe's leadership on climate change.

But having a popular global mandate to lead is different than being willing and able to step forward to provide this leadership. A senior European official once candidly confided to me, "There is no more reluctant a leader than Europe." Perhaps so, I answered. But in today's arrogance-weary world, this is part of Europe's charm, and possibly an essential attribute of effective global leadership in the 21st century.

It is true that the EU has done almost every possible thing it could to sideline itself from playing a more active global leadership role, including almost crashing its economy and currency, and naming unknown compromise candidates to the key roles of European president and foreign policy director. However, this is not due to Europeans being reluctant to project more to the rest of the world. The lack of success in passing a grand, new, European constitution, and the many years it has taken to formally ratify the watered-down Lisbon Agreement, appear mainly due to the political elite being too aloof to renew the European project in the hearts and minds of Europeans.

Figure 8 tracks the declining perceptions of the EU's role in the world since 2010, when the European economy began to falter in the aftermath of the 2009 global financial crunch. The resulting severe economic troubles in

FIGURE 8   Views of European Union's influence
"Positive" vs. "Negative," average of 15 tracking countries,* November 2005–
February 2013

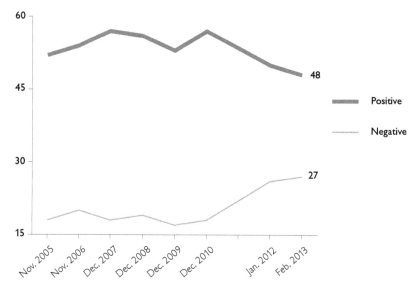

*Tracking countries include Australia, Canada, Chile, China, Egypt, France,
Germany, India, Indonesia, Kenya, Mexico, Nigeria, Russia, the UK, and the USA.

Greece and Spain in particular have taken a heavy toll on views of the EU's
role in the world. Across 16 countries tracked by the BBC World Service Poll,
the percentage seeing Europe's role as positive has declined and the percentage saying negative has grown steadily since 2010. However, Europe is
still viewed much more positively than the USA on this measure.

While the EU has not been able to take advantage of the historic opportunity offered by the past decade to become the world's first soft superpower
(and indeed "soft superpower" may be an oxymoron), Europe would bring
real strengths to a renewed transatlantic partnership with the USA, even
to the point of warranting a partnership of equals. The global legitimacy of
Europe's soft power, together with a humbled America's hard power, would
be hard to beat, and is the most likely geopolitical scenario in our judgment.

Neither the USA or Europe are likely to regain superpower status on their
own quickly enough to firmly reestablish Western dominance in the world.
The USA under President Obama has been trying to do it solo, but I predict
that America will come to see that power-sharing with Europe is the most
desirable, achievable, and sustainable way forward. NATO's role could be

FIGURE 9   Views of China's influence
"Positive" vs. "Negative," average of 11 tracking countries,* December 2004–
February 2013

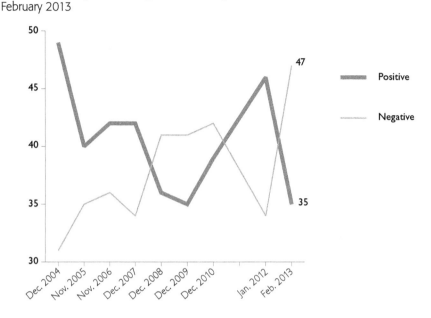

*Tracking countries include Australia, Canada, Chile, France,
Germany, India, Indonesia, Mexico, Russia, the UK, and USA.

key in building such a partnership, perhaps initially in response to Russian
territorial ambitions.

This transatlantic partnership is "the other superpower" that could capture hearts and minds worldwide and be sufficiently responsive to evolving
global opinion to provide inspired leadership for the next chapter of human
history, until China's chapter begins. An expansive US–Indian partnership,
as envisaged in President Obama's 2015 state visit to India, would be the
only other possibility.

As for China, BBC tracking in Figure 9 plots what the Chinese call their
"Peaceful Rise." It has been a wild ride that was negatively affected by media
coverage of their harsh treatment of Tibet in advance of the 2008 Beijing
Olympics, resulting in falling ratings even with their successful hosting of
the Olympic Games. More recently in 2013, views of China have sharply
eroded after a period of steady improvement. A slowing Chinese economy,
their aggressive stance in the South China Sea, and alleged China-based
hacking of Western websites may all have influenced this decline.

Clearly, Chinese leaders are still learning how to win hearts and minds globally, but they appear to be learning rather quickly. And few argue that China's time will not eventually come to exercise global leadership.

Summary

- The first decade of the new millennium was defined by the George W. Bush Administration's defiance of global public opinion. As a result, world opinion savaged Brand USA, with material effects on America's stature, influence, and economic success.

- By November 2006, four years after 9/11, more than twice as many people (57% across 11 countries) saw the world's only superpower as a mainly negative force in the world compared with those who saw it as a positive force (25%).

- As damaged as it has been in the court of public opinion, America is still very much in the game. But even under the leadership of President Barack Obama, it is viewed more negatively than positively.

- A key challenge is that, at least temporarily, we seem to have created a world without a moral compass, in which individuals and nations are encouraged to bring their narrowest interests and worst behaviors to the world instead of their broadest and best.

- We are not alone in suggesting that we have entered a multipolar world that will be more dangerous, for a while at least, than the "Pax Americana" that followed the fall of the Berlin Wall until the world's sheriff (the USA) fell off his horse. The US Army War College's "VUCA World" seems to describe the present nicely – volatile, uncertain, complex, and ambiguous.

- In today's world, the "soft power" of opinion trumps "hard" military power, so it will be whoever is best at winning hearts and minds that will come out on top. And the USA isn't the only big power that isn't doing so well on the soft-power front.

- With America's global image declining, the only other entity able to fill the leadership gap in the near term is the EU. But having a popular global mandate to lead is different than being willing and able to step forward to provide this leadership.

- Europe would bring real strengths to a renewed transatlantic partnership with the USA, even to the point of warranting a partnership of equals. The global legitimacy of Europe's soft power, together with a humbled America's hard power, is the most likely geopolitical scenario in our judgment.

- This transatlantic partnership is "the other superpower" that could capture hearts and minds worldwide and be sufficiently responsive to evolving global opinion to provide inspired leadership for the next chapter of human history, until China's chapter begins.

4
How the mighty are falling

One thing I learned during my years as CEO is that perception matters. And in these times when public confidence and trust have been shaken, I've learned the hard way that perception matters more than ever.

Jack Welch, former Chairman and CEO of General Electric, 2006

Over the last few years the trust between the public and the elites has completely collapsed.

David Gergen, Center for Public Leadership,
Kennedy School of Government, Harvard University, 2008

The sharp decline in trust in institutions and the rise in internet and social media use across the world are not just historic trends. They have real consequences in the world.

The 2011 Jasmine (or Facebook) Revolution in Tunisia followed by the subsequent Arab Spring insurrections across the Middle East, including the ousting of long-time Egyptian strongman Hosni Mubarak, are some of the latest examples of the power of the street. Occupy Wall Street's success in raising economic fairness as a political issue is yet another.

But it is not only the prospects of nation-states that rise and fall with public opinion. Global companies, multilateral agencies, the media, faith-based organizations, and even NGOs are all being negatively affected by declining public trust.

BP's oil platform disaster in the Gulf of Mexico, Siemens' bribery and corruption scandal in Germany, and illegal trading practices by a number of global banks have all exacted huge reputational costs to these companies, as has the entire banking industry's excesses and role in the 2008 financial crisis. We have seen similar reputational hits on the Catholic Church due to widely reported sexual abuse. Furthermore, we've seen declining trust in the traditional broadcast and print media in a number of countries.

One could argue that the growing pervasiveness of the internet and social media, together with the growth of global media outlets and public opinion polling, is causing a "great leveling" to occur. An increasingly outraged and empowered citizenry is bringing down strongholds of self-interest, privilege, and greed. These are important dimensions of the "flat world" concept first described by Tom Friedman of the *New York Times*.[1]

In this world, everyone's motives are questioned and only the worthiest goals supported. Combined with growing public alarm at the extent of our global challenges (poverty, the economy, climate), this is creating unstable political climates in many countries, where volatility and change will be the norm.

This has been called the "Age of Transparency"[2] and the "Age of Accountability." It's where secrecy meets virtual strip search. And where legitimate privacy can also be violated.

This is not an environment in which global companies like to navigate. As a result, risk management and reputation management are ascendant disciplines within global companies as they work to find a way through their issues much as a forester might move through a tinder-dry forest, where the slightest spark can cause an immolation.

What do we know for sure? Public trust in institutions has been mainly declining throughout the first decade-and-a-half of the new millennium, with only a few exceptions.

GlobeScan's "Trust in Institutions" tracking research shows that global companies, the media, and national governments are least trusted to operate in society's interest, while NGOs and the UN are most trusted (Fig. 10). In other words it is an upside-down world where those institutions with vested power are least trusted and those institutions with no formal power are most trusted. These are not conditions that foster efficient action on global problems, as we've seen.

After wondering how low these levels of trust could possibly go, the 2013 polling revealed a sharp recovery in trust for all institutions tracked. Alas, it was not to last, and the 2014 trust levels are continuing the downward trend, with NGOs and global companies at decade-long low points.

---

1   Thomas L. Friedman, *The World is Flat* (Farrar, Straus & Giroux, 2005).

2   Don Tapscott and David Ticoll, *The Naked Corporation: How the Age of Transparency Will Revolutionize Business* (Free Press, 2003).

FIGURE 10   Trust in institutions

Net trust,* average of 13 tracking countries,** December 2000–February 2014

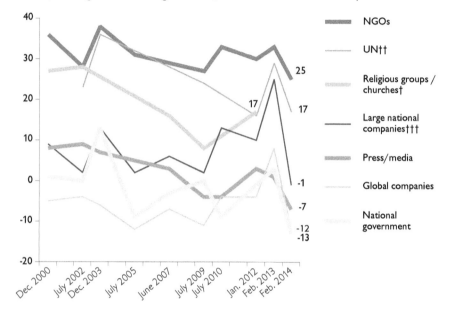

*"A lot" and "some trust" minus "not much" and "no trust at all"

**Tracking countries include Brazil, Canada, France, Germany, India, Indonesia, Mexico, Nigeria, Russia, Spain, Turkey, the UK, and the USA.

Note: There is no data for France in July 2002, for Spain in June 2007, nor for Brazil in February 2013.

†Not asked in Brazil and Spain, not asked in 2014

††Not asked in Russia

†††Not asked in Nigeria in December 2003

The decline in trust through much of the last decade parallels a similar fall in the number of people holding the view that the world is headed in the right direction (Fig. 11). Majorities today, in countries around the world, disagree with the world's direction, a significant reversal from the quite positive views expressed at the dawn of the new millennium.

These findings suggest that, while our 20-nation Millennium Poll in 1999 showed that citizens worldwide had a hopeful and aspirational agenda for the 21st century, they now feel that world leaders have delivered the 19th century instead – more war, more injustice, more fear and insecurity.

People will not trust leaders taking them in a direction they don't like. Research suggests this distrust of leadership is mainly related to people seeing leaders not doing what they say they will, or not operating in the interests of overall society but in their own narrow self-interests. The 2003 World

FIGURE 11   The world is going in the right direction
"Agree,"* average of ten tracking countries,** December 2000–February 2014

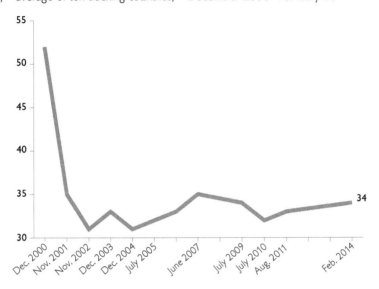

*"Strongly" and "somewhat agree"

**Tracking countries include France, Germany, India, Indonesia,
Mexico, Nigeria, Russia, Turkey, the UK, and the USA

Economic Forum Poll (conducted in November 2002) explored the issue of
leadership and concluded that leaders were less trusted than their institutions. When this same poll asked people across 21 countries to identify the
factor that most leads them to distrust a given political or business leader,
four in ten (44%) chose "not doing what they say they will" and three in ten
(27%) said "self-interest" (Fig. 12).

While this question has not been asked since 2003, it is likely that the 2008
financial collapse, together with the subsequent media coverage of extrava-
gant bonuses and other perks to executives, has only deepened this perception of self-interest among leaders. Extensive media coverage of the 2013
collapse of the Rana Plaza clothing factory in Bangladesh likely contributed
to the sharp drop in trust of global companies seen in 2014 (Fig. 10).

Where do people see institutions serving the public interest rather than
narrow self-interests? Scientific bodies, NGOs, and, to a lesser degree, the
UN are seen to be closest of any that we have tested. Hence the rise of soft
power in these realms as well, where a trusted UN agency or collection of
NGOs combined with supportive public opinion (and an effective use of the

FIGURE 12   Factors causing distrust in leaders
Average of 21 countries,* November 2002

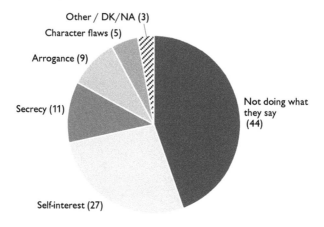

Other / DK/NA (3)
Character flaws (5)
Arrogance (9)
Secrecy (11)
Not doing what
they say
(44)
Self-interest (27)

*Includes Argentina, Australia, Canada, Chile, France, Germany, India,
Indonesia, Italy, Japan, Mexico, Netherlands, Nigeria, Qatar, Russia, South
Africa, South Korea, Spain, Turkey, UK and USA.

internet and media) can lead to major beneficial changes. Examples include
the banning of landmines and getting millions of people around the world
to turn off their lights at the same time to press for action on climate change.

All this is corroborated by the Edelman Trust Barometer survey.[3] For the
first time in 2006, and annually since, the Edelman survey showed that
NGOs such as Amnesty and Greenpeace are now among the most trusted
brands in the world, along with top corporate brands such as Microsoft and
Coca-Cola.

Where will this overall decline in trust lead? It is worrying indeed. It
reminds one of a stressed ecosystem in the natural world that becomes
more susceptible to weeds, disease, and collapse. A distrustful society is
susceptible to instability, radicalism, and populism – just as we're seeing in
the world in general, let alone in countries such as Nigeria and Turkey where
levels of trust are generally lowest.

Take the global financial meltdown that began in the USA with the collapse
of Lehman Brothers in September 2008. When Congress initially refused
to pass the administration's US$700 billion bailout package due to broad

---

3   Produced annually by Edelman Public Relations, the Trust Barometer is based
on an online survey of citizens across 27 countries. See http://www.edelman.
com/insights/intellectual-property/2015-edelman-trust-barometer/.

public opposition, David Gergen at the Kennedy School of Government pointed out (in a *Financial Times* interview) that public opposition was understandable because four of the five least-trusted institutions in the USA were involved – Congress, the President, business, and the media.[4]

In other words, trust matters a great deal, especially in crunch times. The lack of trust in the equities markets following the 2008 banking collapse contributed to the spread of the crisis into the "real economy" in record time. While the stock market has since recovered, the "real economy" is still languishing.

Continuing low trust in the economy, due in part to high levels of unemployment and widespread perceptions of economic unfairness, means that the consumer confidence index – that key economic indicator based entirely on polling data – continues at low levels in many countries.

The fall-off in trust is perhaps the most important trend covered in this book. While there are some signs of recovery, low levels of trust will need to be fully reversed in order to get to any world we're going to want to live in. Distrust and cynicism are future-killers.

Summary

- It is not only the prospects of nation-states that rise and fall with public opinion. Global companies, multilateral agencies, the media, faith-based organizations, and even NGOs are all being negatively affected by declining public trust.

- One could argue that the growing pervasiveness of the internet and social media, together with the growth of global media outlets and public opinion polling, is causing a "great leveling" to occur.

- Research shows an upside-down world where powerful institutions (including global companies, the media, and national governments) are least trusted to operate in society's interest, while relatively powerless institutions (such as NGOs and the UN) are most trusted.

---

4   K. Guha and E. Luce, "Failure to lead fuels Main Street backlash," *Financial Times*, September 30, 2008.

- This is not an environment in which global companies like to navigate. As a result, risk mitigation and reputation management are ascendant disciplines within global companies.

- The decline in trust through much of the last decade parallels a similar fall in the number of people holding the view that the world is headed in the right direction. People will not trust leaders taking them in a direction they don't like.

- The fall-off in trust over the last decade is perhaps the most important trend covered in this book, because distrust and cynicism are future-killers.

5
Retreat from economic globalization

> Globalization is a reality, but one with the ability to mutate into a monster.
> Horst Köhler, former President, International Monetary Fund, 2005

> Another world is possible.
> Motto of the World Social Forum, Porto Alegre, Brazil, 2001

GlobeScan first began polling on the topic of globalization in late 2000 when pitched street battles were being waged between anti-globalization protesters and police outside every major meeting of world leaders. "The Battle of Seattle" in streets outside the WTO (World Trade Organization) ministerial meeting in November 1999 had launched a progression of escalating protests not seen since the Vietnam War era.

GlobeScan had the opportunity to do pre- and post-surveys around the Summit of the Americas in Quebec City in April 2001. There were 34 heads of state barricaded inside a ten-kilometer perimeter fence, with hundreds of protesters outside threatening to pull the fence down.

Our polling showed the associated street battles – covered live on television – made a significant impact in lowering overall support for globalization among Canadians. However, the impact on young people aged 18–24 was especially pronounced. As we can see in Figure 13, youth were the very people in December 2000 who were among the most positively inclined toward globalization. It seems that seeing other young people getting their heads cracked by police batons on television turned them off. What this research suggests is that the anti-globalization protesters were beginning

FIGURE 13 Canadian support for economic globalization
"Very" or "Somewhat" positive, by age, December 2000–May 2001

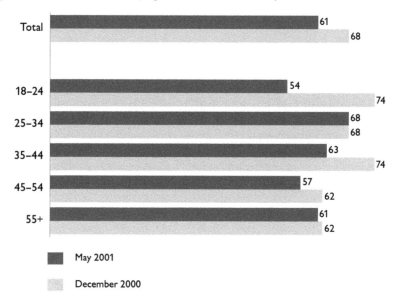

to win the battle for hearts and minds – yet another example of the power of the street.

Conspiracy theorists could have a field day with GlobeScan's tracking research. Just prior to September 11, 2001, not only did the above research suggest support for globalization was beginning to fall,[1] but GlobeScan's 20-nation research revealed increases in the perceived seriousness of many environmental concerns from 1998 to the year 2000 (Fig. 14). This suggested the possibility of a next "green wave" of public environmental concerns which would further undermine support for globalization.[2]

All in all, conspiracy theorists would say it was a perfect time to start a war if you wanted to protect vested economic interests.

An alternative view saw al Qaeda and their terrible attack of 9/11 as simply the most radical of the attempts to stop the Americanization of the world – another word protesters used for globalization at the time. Certainly one of the most immediate impacts of the 9/11 attack was the end

---

[1] While the May 2001 research was conducted only in one country, Canadian opinion is often at or near the average of views across the G20 countries, suggesting broader representation.

[2] Please see Figure 16, which shows the public believed globalization was having a negative impact on environmental quality.

FIGURE 14   Seriousness of environmental issues

"Very serious," G20 countries,* March 1998–May 2000

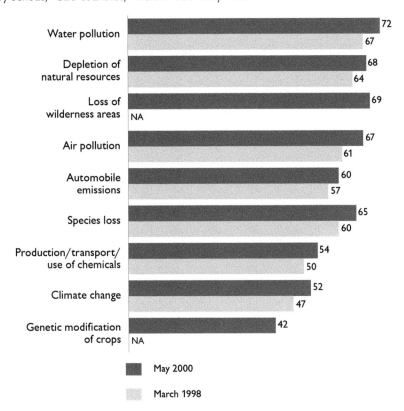

Water pollution — 72 / 67

Depletion of natural resources — 68 / 64

Loss of wilderness areas — 69 / NA

Air pollution — 67 / 61

Automobile emissions — 60 / 57

Species loss — 65 / 60

Production/transport/ use of chemicals — 54 / 50

Climate change — 52 / 47

Genetic modification of crops — 42 / NA

■ May 2000

▨ March 1998

*Includes Argentina, Australia, Canada, China, France, Germany, India, Indonesia, Italy, Mexico, Russia, South Africa, Turkey, UK and USA.

of anti-globalization street protests. It wasn't OK anymore to express such outrage over something like trade.

Tracking research (Fig. 15) shows that in fact the 9/11 attacks briefly unified the world and temporarily increased support for globalization (in December 2001 polling). The wagons were circled and the world had a brief moment of solidarity.

I remember how relieved my audience was at the World Economic Forum's "Davos in New York" meeting in early February 2002 in New York City when I presented GlobeScan's December 2001 tracking results on globalization.

It was a brilliant move by World Economic Forum President Klaus Schwab to take his annual meeting to New York (from Davos, Switzerland) in the immediate aftermath of the 9/11 terrorist attacks, but it was definitely a

FIGURE 15   Support for globalization vs. trade barriers
December 2000–February 2015

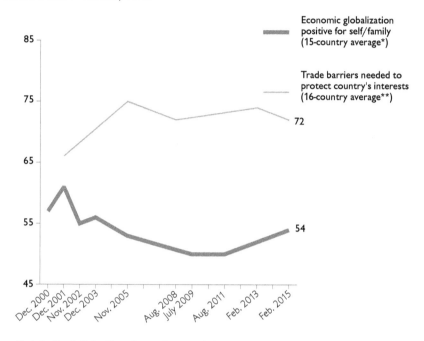

*Includes Brazil, Chile, China, France, Germany, India, Indonesia, Italy, Mexico, Nigeria, Russia, Spain, Turkey, UK, and USA.

**Includes Australia, Brazil, Canada, Chile, China, France, Germany, Kenya, Nigeria, Pakistan, Russia, South Korea, Spain, Turkey, UK, and USA.

Not all countries were asked in all years.

bunker mentality there. Five thousand of New York's finest guarded only 2,000 of us meeting at the Waldorf Astoria Hotel in midtown Manhattan.

This time hiding from a possible terrorist attack rather than from the anti-globalization protesters of the year before, some rather worried corporate executives assembled for my morning briefing session on our poll results. I remember one chief executive of a global food company, sitting in the front row looking particularly intent until he saw my slide showing that global support for globalization had increased from December 2000 to December 2001. The relief in the room was palpable.

Alas, it was not to last. The lower line on Figure 15 shows that support for globalization dropped significantly the following year (2002) and continued a slow decline until 2011. The latest tracking indicates a modest improvement in views of economic globalization, but they remain more negative

FIGURE 16   Effects of globalization on ...
Percentage saying "Better" vs. "Worse," average of 25 countries,* November 2001

■ Better   Worse

	Better	Worse
Access to foreign markets	66	22
Availability of inexpensive products	63	25
Your family's quality of life	60	23
National culture	60	28
Human rights / freedom / democracy	57	28
National economy	56	33
Your income and buying power	54	27
Economic development in poor countries	51	36
Quality of jobs	48	39
Peace and stability	47	38
Workers' rights / working conditions / wages	47	40
Economic equality	45	40
Number of jobs available	42	46
Poverty/homelessness	41	45
Environmental quality	41	47

*Includes Argentina, Australia, Brazil, Canada, Chile, China, France, Germany, India, Indonesia, Italy, Japan, Kazakhstan, Mexico, Netherlands, Nigeria, Qatar, Russia, South Africa, South Korea, Spain, Turkey, UK, USA, and Venezuela

than they were during the anti-globalization street protests in the first few years of the new millennium.

The upper line on the same chart shows the real problem for those working on trade liberalization – continuing strong popular support for the use of trade barriers "to protect national industries and jobs." With protectionism at these levels – over 70% throughout the last decade – new trade deals are almost impossible to pass through the court of public opinion.

An equally important part of my World Economic Forum presentation back in February 2002 was that, while globalization was seen as positive overall, the research showed that it was widely seen as bad for the environment, jobs, and economic equality (Fig. 16). These drivers of negative views were not sufficiently addressed by those championing globalization, and the subsequent rise of public concern about all three of these issues caused support for globalization to decline through the first decade of the new millennium.

Many thought economic hardship would reverse this downward trend. However, the economic recession that began in 2009 continued the decline in support for economic globalization. July 2009 polling results (Fig. 15) showed that, for the first time since tracking began, support for economic globalization had lost its majority support across the world. Support fell from 62% in 2001 to 50% by mid-2009, across the same tracking countries.

It has been the sustained majority support for "using tariffs and other trade barriers to protect national companies and jobs" that has most shaped the last decade, however. Across 16 tracking countries (see the top line in Figure 15), support for trade barriers peaked at a lofty 75% average in 2005, up significantly from 66% in December 2000. This foreshadowed pro-tectionist actions by a number of national governments during the Great Recession and also resulted in no real progress on multilateral trade nego-tiations. Support for protectionism remained high at 72% in February 2015 across the same 16 countries.

Trends among the BRIC countries make particularly grim reading for those working to expand global trade. Over the period from 2001 to November 2005, there was a sharp drop among urban Chinese and Brazilians in the view that globalization is in the interest of them and their families, with lesser but significant declines in India and Russia over the same period.

To underscore the political impact of such findings, a decline of only 11% in American public support for economic globalization between 2002 and 2005 was enough to pave the way for the election of the new batch of anti-free-trade legislators in the midterm elections there in November 2006.

Looking more deeply at the numbers, it is clear that this worldwide growth of protectionism is not limited to those whom the French call "Altermon-dialistes" – those likely to subscribe to the World Social Forum's motto of "Another world is possible."

In a 2007 segmentation analysis of international data, GlobeScan found an anti-globalist segment representing an average of 19% of the population. While this segment existed in all 19 countries studied, it was not of suffi-cient size to define the politics of globalization, except in Turkey and France where it was a larger percentage of the population.

The analysis showed that the defining political weight comes from a segment called the "Protect-Me Globalist." Members of this much larger segment of the population (28%) express both theoretical support for globalization *and* strong support for measures to protect their jobs and national champion companies.

On the face of it, the views of this new segment could be seen as fundamentally inconsistent. However, Steven Kull at PIPA (Program on International Policy Attitudes) at the University of Maryland contends it is not necessarily inconsistent for the same individuals to support both globalization and increased protectionism. In an early 2007 poll of Americans for the Chicago Council on Foreign Relations, PIPA found strong majority support for including minimum labor and environmental standards as part of trade agreements – "protectionist" measures that can in part mitigate public concerns for the way globalization has been implemented. PIPA's earlier polling of Americans had also shown that retraining programs for displaced workers was key to achieving majority support for free trade agreements among Democrats.

India's demanding stance during negotiations on the Doha Trade Round can in part be explained by the fact that India has the largest percentage (49%) of Protect-Me Globalists among the 19 countries covered in GlobeScan's segmentation analysis, with Indonesia and Nigeria following closely.

Increasingly authoritative studies by economists suggest that average workers in a number of key economies have seen their share of economic benefits from globalization diminish over the last decade – in part due to unequal distribution of economic benefits,[3] as well as the impact of technology. It is likely, therefore, that the Protect-Me Globalists will increasingly influence the international trade agenda, with even bilateral trade agreements affected.

Given this analysis, achieving *fairer* trade, rather than *freer* trade, will likely become a more central point of trade debate and negotiations. Fully seven in ten citizens of wealthy countries did not think their governments were negotiating fairly with less developed countries during the early Doha trade talks. Nor do they think economic globalization currently delivers fairness to workers or protection to the environment.

In 2003, GlobeScan presented Figure 17 at the World Social Forum in Puerto Alegre Brazil, showing that majorities in ten out of 15 countries surveyed believed that globalization was having the effect of concentrating wealth more than providing opportunities for all.

---

3   See especially *Capital in the Twenty-First Century*, by the French economist Thomas Piketty (Harvard University Press, 2013).

Figure 17   Effect of globalization
"Concentrates wealth" vs. "Brings opportunities to all," November 2002

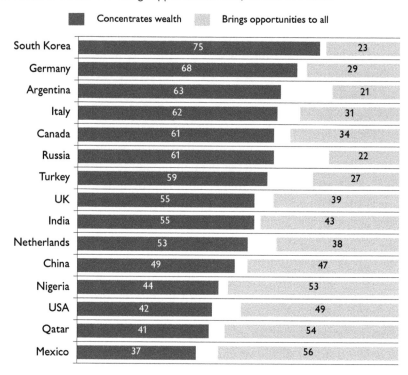

The white space in this chart represents "DK/NA."

In light of this research, it is understandable that attempts to push ahead with the WTO's Doha Trade Round have largely failed over the last decade. We predicted as early as May 2007 that "All the king's horses and all the king's men won't put Doha together again."

In fact, a small portion of the Doha Round's agenda (i.e., paperwork reduction at borders) formed part of the much-touted "Bali Package" signed at the WTO Ministerial Meeting there in December 2013. However, short of another significant financial downturn, continuing protectionist public opinion and unmotivated national governments will mean that the Doha Trade Round's initial ambition of being the "Development Round" and greatly helping developing countries' economies is unlikely to be realized.

Those wishing to further economic globalization would be well advised not to spend their limited political capital on negotiating a watered-down Doha trade agreement that will only be seen as contributing further to inequities. Rather, they should act with equal resolve to put in place corrective measures at both the national and international levels aimed at mitigating widely recognized problems that undermine political support in both rich and poor countries.

The rise of the Protect-Me Globalist suggests that, without serious government interventions to protect the environment, reduce rich/poor gaps within and between countries, and provide job security at least through retraining and other social safety nets for displaced workers, economic globalization as we know it will be more and more constrained by national self-interest. We have already seen this during the global food pricing crisis of 2008 and the protectionist provisions of economic stimulus programs adopted by major G20 countries during 2009–13.

Only a concerted approach to addressing the unfairness and negative impacts caused by globalization will convince an increasingly skeptical public that the economic power being unleashed through globalization will deliver real benefits to them and the planet. Only this will put Humpty Dumpty (i.e., Doha) together again.

As Christine Lagarde, Managing Director of the IMF (International Monetary Fund), put it in January 2014, "In far too many countries, the benefits of growth are being enjoyed by far too few people. This is not a recipe for stability and sustainability."

Let's not underestimate the magnitude of this challenge. A BBC World Service Poll in August 2008 found that most people worldwide see inequality in the economic sphere (Fig. 21). Asked if the "benefits and burdens of the economic developments of the last few years" have been shared fairly or not, majorities in 27 of 34 countries polled said "unfairly" – on average 64% (59% across the 16 tracking countries included in Figure 21).

So, well before Occupy Wall Street's popularizing of the concept of the 99% and the 1%, fully 64% of people across 34 countries believed the economic system in their country was unfair. And the income distribution statistics of governments year after year confirm an ever-widening gap between the richest and everyone else. This trend has become so powerful that even the World Economic Forum and the IMF in early 2014 called inequality the biggest threat to stability in the world.

On top of this, we have seen that the financial meltdown in late 2008 and the ensuing economic recession, far from strengthening support for globalization, simply slowed a continuing decline in support for globalization (Fig. 15). All this suggests there is little trust left that globalization is doing anything other than making a few people and companies richer at the expense of the poor and the planet.

FIGURE 18   Frequency of consuming locally grown food
"Daily" and "Several times a week," percentage of consumers in each country, trends: 2008–2014

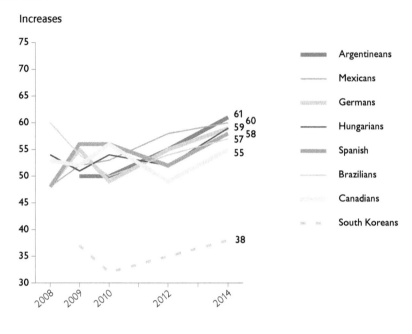

Increases

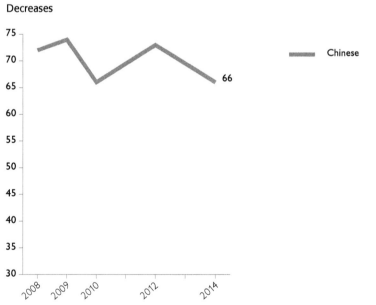

Decreases

The pervasiveness of these beliefs and the momentum of views will require an unprecedented effort to turn around declining support for globalization. However, the evidence suggests this will not happen. The protectionist actions of national governments during the Great Recession suggest that the pendulum of history will continue to swing away from economic globalization. The major focus at the global level will be on better protecting and sharing the so-called "global commons" – our common water, food, and atmospheric resources on which all life depends.

As a result of these and other trends, our prediction is that *local* rather than global will be at the center of culture and commerce in the coming decades. One of the early drivers for this has been the local food movement. Figure 18 shows the growth of this phenomenon across a wide diversity of countries.[4]

However, this new localized world will be the *new* local – brought to life over the internet. The word "glocal" has been coined to describe this new focus (or "global local"); where excellence and connectedness are valued, and where innovation and transformation happens. This is the new frontier.[5]

Summary

- Evidence suggests that street battles between anti-globalization protesters and the police, in the early days of the 21st century, undermined support for economic globalization, especially among youth.

- The terrorist attacks on the USA in 2001 caused global support for globalization to briefly rise then begin a long slow decline in the decade from 2002 to 2011. Majority support for globalization across 16 tracking countries was lost in 2011 when an average of only one in two saw it being "in the interest of their family." Support has since edged upwards slightly.

---

4   From the National Geographic Society's Greendex survey of self-reported sustainable behaviors across 18 countries, conducted by GlobeScan.

5   For more on the rise of local and the reemergence of the city-state, please see Chapter 13.

- Polling conducted for the World Economic Forum in 2001 showed that globalization was widely seen as bad for the environment, jobs, and economic equality. These drivers of negative views were not sufficiently addressed by those championing globalization, causing support for globalization to remain lower than it was during the anti-globalization street protests in the first few years of the new millennium.

- The real challenge for those working on trade liberalization is continuing strong popular support for the use of trade barriers "to protect national industries and jobs." With protectionism at these high levels, new trade deals are almost impossible to pass through the court of public opinion.

- The research and analysis presented in this chapter suggests that achieving *fairer* trade, rather than *freer* trade, will likely become a more central point of trade debate and negotiations.

- Those wishing to further economic globalization are advised to put in place corrective measures at both the national and international levels aimed at mitigating widely recognized problems that undermine political support for economic globalization in both rich and poor countries.

- As a result of these and other trends, our prediction is that *local* rather than global will be at the center of culture and commerce in the coming decades. But it will be the *new* local – brought to life over the internet.

6
Toward a sustainable economy

The global economy looks and acts more and more like a global casino.

Hazel Henderson, 1998

In far too many countries, the benefits of growth are being enjoyed by far too few people. This is not a recipe for stability and sustainability.

Christine Lagarde, Managing Director,
International Monetary Fund, 2014

An economic crisis is a period when you should step back and think: is this a moment to make some fundamental changes?

Gerard Kleisterlee, CEO of Philips, 2009

I considered calling this chapter "The Great Recession" but I thought that would be overly simplistic given the times we are in. I think the Australian Paul Guilding has said it best by calling it "The Great Disruption" – when Mother Nature teams up with Father Greed to give us kids some tough love. It's what happens when so few of us humans have been acting like adults lately. Too much "gimme, gimme;" not enough focusing on the real needs of everyone.

As the economist Raj Patel states after writing of the unsustainability of our present consumer economy, "But the reverse of consumerism isn't thrift, it's generosity."[1]

Could the global financial crisis of 2008 and the ensuing long recession turn out to be the start of an historic tipping point that enables humans to achieve a more secure and human economy? The jury is still out, but some believe the transition may have begun from an unsustainable economic

1   Raj Patel, *The Value of Nothing* (Portobello, 2009).

FIGURE 19   Changes needed in economic system as a result of financial crisis
Average of 24 countries,* January 2009

The white space in this chart represents "DK/NA."

*Includes Australia, Brazil, Canada Central America, Chile, China, Egypt, France, Germany, Ghana, India, Indonesia, Italy, Japan, Kenya, Mexico, Nigeria, Philippines, Portugal, Russia, Spain, Turkey, UK, and the USA.

model based on never-ending growth, to a dynamic equilibrium economy that respects the limits of both human nature and Mother Nature.

In September 2013, I had the pleasure of speaking at the annual Stern Stewart Institute at Schloss Elmau in the German Alps. This Davos-like retreat for mainly German and other European industrialists was preoccupied with the bleak economic prospects, especially for Europe.

One of the other speakers was the brilliant Czech economist Tomáš Sedláček who shocked the business leaders present by likening the current global economy to a manic-depressive patient – teetering between highs of growth and lows of debt. He stated that an economic policy or system that only pursues growth will always lead to debt. In his view, the current unbridled free enterprise system is geared totally to growth, not stability. And he argued we need stability first and growth perhaps fourth.

After Tomáš's talk a group of us were standing outside on the Schloss's elegant terrace in the pristine mountain air, having a glass of wine. A German CEO was vigorously challenging him on his assertion that growth wasn't the primary goal we should be pursuing, using the argument that his shareholders insisted on getting a good return on their investment in the company he led. Tomáš just waved his hands at the gorgeous mountain setting and suggested that the CEO and his shareholders were not having it too rough. Later, in a *Der Spiegel* interview, he said, "Greed is an engine of progress, but it's also the cause of our collapse. Enough is always just beyond the horizon."

When GlobeScan asked people across G20 countries in 2009 who or what caused the global financial crisis, they mainly pointed to governments, presumably for not protecting the public interest; but 8% spontaneously

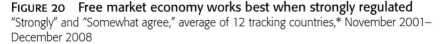

FIGURE 20   Free market economy works best when strongly regulated
"Strongly" and "Somewhat agree," average of 12 tracking countries,* November 2001–
December 2008

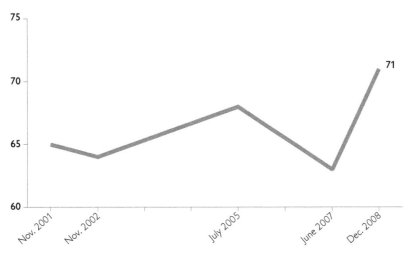

*Tracking countries include Canada, China, France, Germany, Indonesia, Italy,
Mexico, Nigeria, Russia, Turkey, UK, and the USA.

named greed or corruption (Fig. 6). For an unprompted question this is a significant result.

Even more interesting, the research suggests that people around the world viewed the global economic crisis of 2008 as a systemic problem needing fundamental changes rather than simply a cyclical downturn needing only stimulus.

A January 2009 24-nation poll for the BBC World Service showed that fully seven in ten citizens around the world believed major changes were needed in the global economic system, and indeed their own country's economy, in order to achieve a durable economic recovery (Fig. 19). Only 4% thought no significant changes were needed to the global economic system – yet, that is pretty much all we've gotten so far.

The same survey showed that seven in ten held the view that the free enterprise system works best when accompanied by strong government regulations – its highest level in our eight years of tracking across these countries (Fig. 20). Clearly, the pressure on governments to strengthen over-sight of the free market is enormous.

In this context it is unfortunate that G20 leaders at their summits through-out the recession, including the key 2009 London and Pittsburgh summits, made relatively few systemic changes in the global economic architecture. The bulk of most countries' economic stimulus packages were also aimed mainly at bolstering the existing system and institutions that got us into the mess in the first place.

No wonder the current recession is the longest lasting of any in modern times, approaching near-biblical proportions of "seven bad years." As Einstein famously remarked, "We cannot solve our problems with the same thinking we used when we created them."

If greedy bankers, declining support for economic globalization, and a collapsing belief in the unfettered free market system were all we were dealing with, the current crisis would be daunting enough to fix. But we are in much more challenging times than this.

US President Barack Obama put it this way in his January 2009 inaugural address: "Our economy is badly weakened, a consequence of greed and irresponsibility on the part of some but also our collective failure to make hard choices and prepare the nation for a new age."

Many argue that we have so neglected some of the fundamental underpinnings of continued prosperity, and so externalized some of the real costs to people and the planet, that we are faced with solving many problems at the same time. For example, we have been pricing one of Earth's most precious of resources, a benign climate, at zero.[2] But it goes far deeper than simply adding the climate challenge to the mix of problems to solve.

One of the deeper economic problems we have is distrust, not just in economic actors such as banks and their regulators, but in the economic system itself. The popular support for Occupy Wall Street, Spain's Indignados and other demonstrators calling for more fairness for "the 99%" suggests that regaining trust will be one of the principal challenges that will need to be met in order to restore economic confidence and emerge from what at best will be the Great Recession. Trust is also a key underpinning of a healthy social contract between economic actors.

It's interesting how little we talk about the social contract today, given it has been one of the most influential moral and political theories in all of human history, since Jean-Jacques Rousseau's 1762 book on the subject.[3] A tangible sense of social contract, or social cohesion, was a key element in the building of the economic miracle that led us out of the Second World

---

2   A point made far more eloquently in a commentary by the economists Joseph Stiglitz and Sir Nick Stern in the *Financial Times*, March 2, 2009.

3   Jean-Jacques Rousseau, *Of The Social Contract, Or Principles of Political Right* [*Du Contrat Social, ou Principes du droit politique*] (1762).

FIGURE 21 How fairly benefits and burdens of economic developments have been shared
Average of 16 tracking countries,* December 2007–February 2015

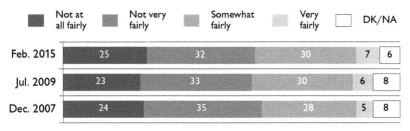

*Tracking countries include Australia, Brazil, Canada, Chile, China, France, Germany, India, Indonesia, Kenya, Mexico, Nigeria, Spain, Turkey, UK, and USA.

War and created much of the wealth that exists today. There was a shared belief that there was something in it for everyone.

Some of the elements of a social contract – the perceived bond between rich and poor; between the powerful and the governed; indeed, our trust in the very economic system under which we labor – have eroded quite badly over the past decade, according to public opinion research.

However, the major element of the social contract that has more than compensated for the decline in other elements has been the continuing ability of the free market economy to deliver benefits that people value – principally more "stuff."

One doesn't need public opinion research to accept that many people in industrialized countries haven't seen more stuff for an unprecedented period of time. With this fundamental pillar of our social contract weakened for the foreseeable future, and the need for social cohesion in this time of challenge, it stands to reason that we will have to focus on rebuilding other underpinnings. Hence, I predict that the social contract, or social cohesion, or simply trust, will be a continuing theme of debate and reconciliation.

A key economic underpinning of trust or social cement, especially in hard times, is the extent to which people believe there is a level playing field in the current economic system; that there is a fair sharing of economic benefits and burdens.

The BBC World Service Poll explored the economic views of people across 34 countries in December 2007, a year before the global financial crisis. In

FIGURE 22   Most rich people in my country deserve their wealth
"Agree" vs. "Disagree," by region, August 2008–January 2012

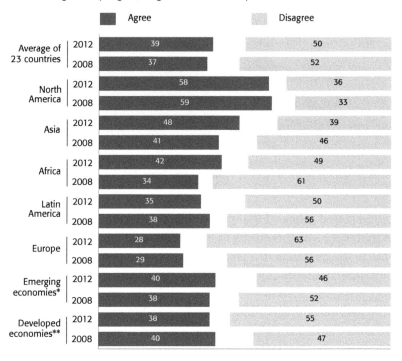

*Emerging economies include: Argentina, Brazil, Chile, China, Ghana, India, Indonesia, Kenya, Mexico, Nigeria, Pakistan, Peru, and Turkey.

**Developed economies include: Australia, Canada, France, Germany, Greece, Russia, South Korea, Spain, UK, and the USA.

The white space in this chart represents "Depends," "Neither agree nor disagree," and "DK/NA."

the BBC's media release[4] I was quoted as saying: "There is real public unease about the direction of the economy, but it's not only about a downturn. It also has to do with how fairly benefits and burdens are shared, and the pace of globalisation."

Majorities in 27 out of the 34 countries in the BBC poll held the view that the benefits and burdens of "the economic developments of the last few years" have not been shared fairly in their country. On average 64% felt this way. As Figure 21 shows, across 16 tracking countries, majorities continue to see economic unfairness today; this average percentage has remained

4   "Widespread Unease about Economy and Globalization," BBC World Service, dated February 7, 2008.

close to this level and far from where it needs to be in order to help build the social contract.

A second fundamental element of a social contract relates to whether people see the rich in their country as deserving of their wealth. In a spring 2008 poll in collaboration with the New Economics Foundation in London, majorities in 11 out of 23 countries disagreed that "most rich people in our country deserve their wealth" (Fig. 22). This was particularly the case in Europe and Latin America, where 56% disagreed. When GlobeScan asked the same question again in 2012, the results did not change significantly.

In other words, fully one in two citizens do not believe that wealth is necessarily associated with hard work or cleverness – surely one of the beliefs needed to underpin the current economic system. This suggests that views on inherited wealth, including the taxation of same, will be an interesting area to explore further in coming years.

True to the American dream, US citizens remain among the most convinced that the wealthy do in fact deserve their wealth (57% in 2008). Canada was the only country surveyed where an even bigger proportion of the population believe this element of the social contract.

Other research underscores how fragile the conventional economic paradigm has become. Citizens do not believe that the way we measure our economic progress, namely GDP (gross domestic product), adequately reflects the underpinnings of true progress.

In a 2007 ten-nation poll conducted by GlobeScan for presentation at an EU-hosted economic conference, fully three-quarters supported going beyond GDP to include environmental and social indicators along with economic ones. To ensure we were asking a balanced and accurate question, the wording was approved by the chief economist at the OECD (Organisation for Economic Co-operation and Development) at the time.[5]

As Figure 23 reveals, the 11-country average in both 2010 and 2013 represents a majority rejection of the adequacy of GDP in measuring true progress. It also suggests that the three pillars of sustainable development – economic, social, and environmental – are all seen as important by most citizens across these countries.

5   This 11-country research was funded by Hazel Henderson and Alan Kay of Ethical Markets Media LLC. See http://www.ethicalmarkets.com.

FIGURE 23 Trends in support for "Going Beyond GDP"
July 2010–February 2013

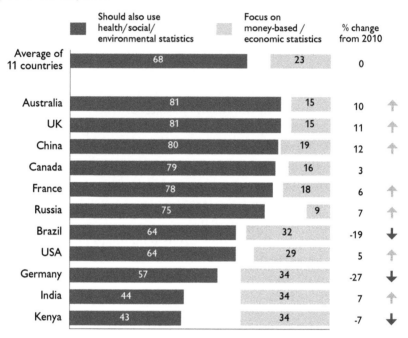

The white space in this chart represents "DK/NA."

Column of figures and arrows on outside right refers to % change in support for using health/social/environmental statistics since 2010.

A final piece of evidence related to achieving a sustainable economy concerns the perceived economic impact of action on climate change. For 15 years GlobeScan has tracked whether respondents agree or disagree with the statement "Our national economy will be significantly damaged if we try to cut our emissions of climate-changing gases" (Fig. 24). Over this time, majorities of citizens across wealthier (OECD) countries have consistently disagreed, suggesting citizens of OECD countries see climate action as not only necessary but also not a drag on their economy. It is only citizens of emerging economies (non-OECD) that are increasingly worried about this possible impact.

Given all the above evidence, it is clear that policy-makers need to better address the loss of trust in the economy. Trust can only be rebuilt by responding directly and substantively to the perceptions that have worked to undermine it.

FIGURE 24   Economy will be damaged if climate-changing emissions reduced

"Agree," OECD vs. non-OECD countries,* December 2000–February 2015

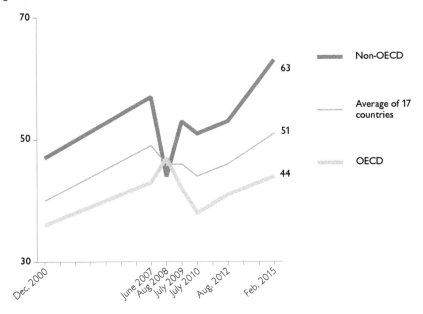

*OECD countries include Australia, Canada, Chile, France, Germany, Mexico, Spain, Turkey, UK, and USA; non-OECD countries include Brazil, China, India, Indonesia, Kenya, Nigeria, and Pakistan. Not asked in all countries in all years.

Regaining Trust in the Economy

Economic perceptions needing to be addressed in order to get people believing in the economy again:

1. **Fairness.** Even before the current economic crisis and controversy over excessive executive compensation, majorities in most G20 countries held the view that economic risks and rewards were not being shared fairly in their country. History tells us that perceived injustice is one of the most powerful drivers of social unrest.

2. **Rich/poor gap.** The growing gap between rich and poor both within countries and across the world has been widely reported for years. With the actual gap widening even more through the recession,[6] this trend is not taking us anywhere we want to go.

6   According to the Capgemini/Merrill Lynch World Wealth Report 2011.

3. **Oversight.** People want more regulation of their national economy and of the global economy. While valuing the benefits of companies and the free market, citizens are clearer than ever before that strong oversight is needed. With the "invisible hand" of the market showing itself to be a flawed concept, citizens want government's hand back on the steering wheel.

4. **Sustainability.** Strong majorities of citizens think that GDP is an inadequate measure of progress and that it should be expanded to include also measures of environmental and social progress.

5. **Climate stability.** Majorities or pluralities of citizens in most countries across the world see action on climate change as urgent, and citizens of OECD countries believe investments in climate protection will be good for the economy.

Leaders of the G20 (the 20 largest economies) certainly have had the worldwide constituency necessary to support bold actions to strengthen global financial governance. Unfortunately, they have not acted with nearly enough boldness. And if they haven't done so seven years into the longest recession in modern history, they are unlikely to do so without another economic shock to spur them on.

Widespread perceptions of inequality will need to be addressed more fundamentally than a few isolated and superficial limits on bankers' bonuses and executive compensation. As the Executive Director of Oxfam International, Winnie Byanyima, said in early 2014, "It is staggering that in the 21st century, half the world's population – that's 3½ billion people – own no more than a tiny elite whose numbers could all fit comfortably on a double-decker bus (i.e., the 85 richest individuals on the planet)."[7]

And last but not least, the so-called externalities of climate protection and social cohesion will need to start to be valued in the economic and business equations.

In a way, the worst thing that could happen is for the Great Recession to be over before we make the systemic changes required to secure the stability and moderation most people seek and the planet needs.

---

7   "Oxfam – 85 richest people as wealthy as poorest half of the world," *The Guardian*, January 20, 2014.

Unfortunately, this is indeed the most likely scenario – that the biblical "seven bad years" will end not by chance or good government, but because wealthy people get tired of low returns on their investments and collectively decide to throw a vast stream of money at the New York Stock Exchange, taking the Dow Jones Index to historically high levels. While this has already happened to some extent, without enough benefit trickling down to average people the economy will continue to be a political problem in many industrialized countries.

Even with some success, a refloated status quo economy will not be able to defy gravity for long. The elements of public trust outlined in this chapter will need to be rebuilt, especially the tattered social contract between rich and poor. At best, it will be a tenuous, short-lived recovery.

Without real economic reform, it is hard to imagine reaching the year 2020 without another serious economic downturn. The key question is, will the basis be laid by then for real reforms to be made to an economic system that will have failed us again?

Certainly, opinion research trends suggest that by the next crisis public opinion will have solidified further to create a real opportunity for reform-minded politicians to build the basis for a New Economy (rather than a refloat of the old economy) – a New Economy with fundamental improvements in oversight, fairness, and sustainability.

Only this will gain the public trust and confidence needed to truly emerge from the Great Recession into a sustained period of economic stability.

Summary

- There is evidence to suggest that the Great Recession may be the start of an historic tipping point that enables humans to achieve a more secure, inclusive, and green economy.

- The global public saw the global economic crisis of 2008 as a systemic problem needing fundamental changes rather than simply a cyclical downturn needing only stimulus.

- Over the past seven years, some key elements of the social contract have eroded. The most important underpinning of social cement, especially in hard times, is the extent to which people believe there is a fair sharing of economic benefits and burdens. Majorities in countries around the world see unfairness.

- A second fundamental element of a social contract relates to whether people see the rich in their country as deserving of their wealth. Fully one in two citizens do not believe that wealth is necessarily associated with hard work or cleverness.

- Strong majorities even disagree with the way in which we measure progress, with almost seven in ten across ten key countries saying we should go beyond GDP to include social and environmental indicators of progress.

- A final piece of evidence relates to the perceived economic impact of action on climate change. Majorities across OECD countries see climate action as not only necessary but also not a drag on the economy.

- Given this evidence, it is clear that policy-makers need to better address the loss of public trust in economic fairness and economic oversight, and implement substantive measures to reduce the rich/poor gap, move beyond GDP to measure true progress, and ensure climate stability.

- In a way, the worst thing that could happen is for the Great Recession to be over before we make the systemic changes required to secure the stability and moderation most people seek and the planet needs.

- Without real economic reform, it is hard to imagine reaching the year 2020 without another serious economic downturn.

- Only a New Economy with fundamental improvements in oversight, fairness, and sustainability will gain the public trust and confidence needed to truly emerge from the Great Recession into a sustained period of economic health.

7
The evolution of business 1975–2015

> What's good for GM is good for the country.[1]
> Charles Wilson, CEO of General Motors, 1953

> I cannot think of a time when business over all has been held in less repute.
> Henry M. Paulson, Jr., Chairman of Goldman Sachs, June 2002 (prior to becoming President Bush's Treasury Secretary)

Watching business evolve over the last 40 years has been fascinating; and evolve it has. As Plato said, "Necessity is the mother of invention," and this was no exception to that rule.

There is no more dramatic a representation of public skepticism about business than Figure 25, provided by Sir Robert Worcester and his colleagues at Ipsos MORI in the UK. They have tracked responses over 35 years to a poll question that asks whether corporate profits "make things better for everyone." Results show a steady decline in the percentage of Britons agreeing with this statement, with the more recent results showing a total reversal of views observed in the 1970s.

All of this is somewhat ironic given attempts by business, in the last decade especially, to address broader societal challenges.

In 1969, the head of human resources at 3M Canada introduced the role of business to some new employees by saying, "Business makes money,

---

1   While this quotation has entered popular culture, Mr. Wilson's actual statement made during his confirmation hearing as President Truman's choice for Secretary of Defense was, "For years I thought what was good for the country was good for General Motors and vice versa."

Figure 25　Faith in benefits of profits

UK, general public,* 1976–2012

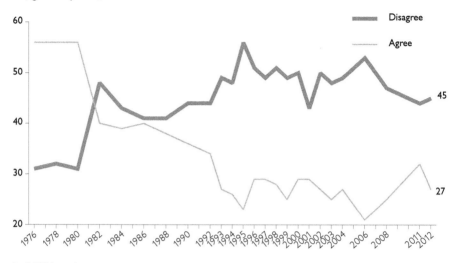

*n=1,000 for each year

government spends it." This view – of business as the generator of wealth and government as the protector and developer of societal "goods" – largely shaped the 1970s and 1980s and, some would argue, was the basis for a period of unparalleled economic growth. Unfortunately, it was accompanied by business doing its utmost, through lobbying and other means, to blunt government's effectiveness at protecting anything other than the ability of business to make money.

An example of this kind of thinking, but also of its undoing, comes from a client situation we had in the late 1980s. A North American railway company was under attack by nearby property owners over the chemical spraying of its track beds. The company insisted that chemical spraying was essential to prevent weeds undermining track stability and hence passenger safety. The citizen activists insisted that the chemical agents were carcinogens that were getting into their water supply and harming their children and animals.

After being hired to help the company effectively manage this situation, we were invited to corporate headquarters for an initial client meeting. Near the end of this first meeting I came to appreciate the professional challenge facing us when the senior vice president (who only a few years earlier had stopped wearing a fedora hat on the job) said, "It's my damn railway, and I'll do whatever I want with it." It was classic "old-think" at its finest – prioritizing the role of business above everything else.

In the course of our interviews with company officials we chanced on one of their young scientists who was conducting field trials with various alternative ways to maintain safe tracks. We suggested the company involve the activists in observing these field trials, which quickly changed the tenor of the public debate. And the field trials quickly bore the most delicious fruit.

It turned out that old-fashioned steam, which diesel locomotives have in abundant supply, when directed down into the track bed under a slow-moving train, worked extremely well in killing weeds, and was far cheaper for the company to use than chemicals. Needless to say, it was also far more acceptable to the neighbors.

The crowning touch to this story? The company patented the system of steam nozzles they developed for the front of their trains and turned it all into a profit center by selling scores of these systems to other rail companies around North America.

One thing that business does very well is learn quickly. Learning how to turn lose–lose situations into win–win situations like that of the railway was obviously good for business. As a result, business thinking began to change through the early part of the 1990s in North America and Europe – spurred on by some spectacular examples of how business "old-think" would regularly lose out to popular NGO campaigns, and cost companies dearly.

A good example of this was the North American forest industry. In the early 1990s they were facing growing public outrage over their forest practices and mill pollution. The hottest issues were their logging of old-growth trees in the temperate rain forests along the West Coast as well as their pulp mill effluent containing dioxin that research showed was linked to cancer.

We were asked to conduct some public opinion research to feed into the industry's communication strategy, which up to then was to stonewall on both issues, claiming current practices were necessary to ensure the jobs and economic activity of this major industry. I was asked to present our research findings directly to 48 forest industry CEOs meeting in Vancouver in 1993.

Given the strongly negative public views that our research uncovered, I must say I was nervous walking into that room. I was expecting one of those "shoot-the-messenger" grillings, and I wasn't disappointed. While initially lulled by the months-from-retirement faces staring back at me out of the gloom, as soon as I had finished presenting our findings, an outspoken chief executive of one of the largest companies in the room said the last thing the industry should do is base any of its decisions on public opinion, which he characterized as ignorant and blind.

Forgive me for having blotted from memory much of the next half-hour's discussion, but I do remember finishing off the session in exasperation:

> Regardless of what you think of public opinion, you're treating this situation like a minor brush fire, and trying to stamp it out with your boots. But it's a major forest fire raging down the valley toward you. You need to get well out ahead of it and cut a fire-road of fresh policies and practices in order to quench the flames. If you don't, you're looking at a couple of hundred million dollars off your industry's bottom line.

It was one of a number of times when my predictions were not accurate. Actually, in this case I was off by an order of magnitude. Within two years of my presentation, the industry's continued stonewalling had cost all their companies a couple of hundred million dollars off *each* of their bottom lines, mainly due to the cost of complying with new federal legislation in both the USA and Canada that forced them to end all emissions of dioxin into public waterways and the atmosphere. The public outrage revealed in our research forced these laws through in record time.

The chemical industry is another sector that ran into trouble in the late 1980s and early 1990s, but they made out much better than the forest industry by being more proactive in addressing concerns. In their case, it was the perceived human health risks associated with the production, use, and disposal of chemicals that created public controversy. It got so bad that chemical industry executives' own children were coming home from school asking how they could possibly work for a company that was killing people.

We were working with the Canadian Chemical Producers Association at the time, advising on a new initiative they were developing called "Responsible Care." Developed and applied in Canada in 1985, this voluntary initiative was intended to address public concerns by demonstrating the industry's commitment to responsible stewardship.

"Responsible Care" required signatory chemical companies to commit themselves to improve their performance in the fields of environmental protection, occupational safety, health protection, plant safety, product stewardship, and transportation.

Given the focus on improving industry behavior and accountability, "Responsible Care" worked well to assure the public, and moved the chemical industry off the political agenda in Canada. It has since been adopted by the chemical industry in over 50 countries, and is seen as one of the most successful voluntary industry initiatives ever.

What was missing through this period in the evolution of business thinking and action on broader societal responsibilities was a compelling framework within which to balance the competing interests. This was being developed in parallel with some of these real-world battles through the unlikely instrument of a UN commission – the World Commission on Environment and Development, under the able leadership of Norway's former Prime Minister, Gro Harlem Brundtland.

The 1987 Brundtland World Commission report, "Our Common Future," both coined the term "sustainable development" and outlined ways in which its three pillars of economy, society, and environment might be balanced. It provided the framework that business and others needed in order to become proactive rather than just reactive. And it enabled the business case for such actions to be built inside organizations.

It can actually be argued that the term "sustainable development" is one of the most successful and lasting concepts ever coined – and the Brundtland Commission one of the most influential UN initiatives ever.

Almost 20 years later, in a 2004 global survey[2] of civil society leaders around the world that GlobeScan conducted for the King Baudouin Foundation together with the Rockefeller and Mott Foundations, we were struck by the extent to which sustainable development had established itself as the common framework for thinking and action by civil society leaders in both the industrialized and developing world, regardless of their issue orientation. Activists working on human rights and community development were every bit as likely to value sustainability as a framework for their efforts as were activists working on nature conservation or energy issues.

More recently, GlobeScan's February 2008 survey of its authoritative global panel of sustainable development leaders showed that such development was more influential in organizational decision-making than it was a decade before (Fig. 26). At the same time, three-quarters of those leaders say progress in achieving sustainable solutions is not happening fast enough to avoid dire planetary consequences. Most believe that business will have a key role to play in achieving such progress.

---

2   "What Global Leaders Want: Report of the Third Survey of the 2020 Global Stakeholder Panel" for the 2020 Fund, New York City.

FIGURE 26   Potency of term "sustainable development" in decision-making
1996–March 2008

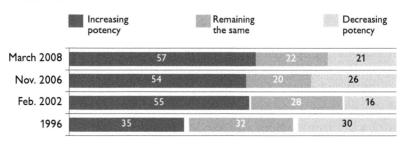

The white space in this chart represents "DK/NA."

While business was initially slow to engage, it has arguably become one of sustainable development's major standard-bearers.

Through the 1990s, there were only a few pioneering companies and executives interested in sustainable development – Swiss industrialist Stephan Schmidheiny's 1991 launch of the BCSD (Business Council for Sustainable Development), Interface Inc.'s CEO Ray Anderson, and Dow Chemical's CEO David Buzzelli come most to mind. In 1995, the BCSD fused with the WICE (World Industry Council for the Environment) to form the WBCSD (World Business Council for Sustainable Development), which has been a major driving force behind corporate engagement and action ever since.

But it wasn't until the dawn of CSR at the turn of the century and new millennium that broader business engagement really took hold and straddled all three pillars of sustainable development – the social, environmental, and economic.

During the first decade of the new millennium, CSR was all the rage among business on both sides of the Atlantic. In August of 2001, I was invited down to an innovative US firm that had grown quickly to become the 85th-largest company in the world and was taking the energy business by storm. They were setting out to grow a CSR initiative just like they did all other aspects of their business – as a market-leading activity that was so innovative that it could become its own profit center.

They liked what we had to offer and within a month had us under contract to survey their stakeholders around the world to help identify CSR initiative areas that would most differentiate them. Just as we were starting fieldwork, we read in the newspaper that we didn't have a client anymore.

The company was Enron and the rest, as they say, is history.

FIGURE 27   Most important factors in forming impressions of companies
Unprompted, USA, April 1999–July 2005

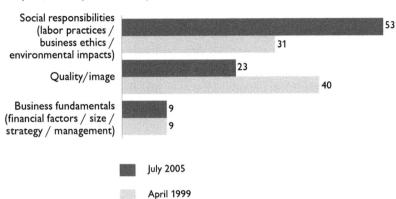

The fact that a company that became emblematic of capitalist greed and corporate irresponsibility was in the process of embracing CSR is enough to validate the worst views of NGO leaders – that CSR is nothing more than corporate public relations.

But this would miss the larger significance and impact of the Enron/ Arthur Andersen/WorldCom/Parmalat phenomena in undermining trust in business as well as fundamentally changing the exercise of entrepreneurship and corporate governance from then onward.

Clearly greed is not dead. We didn't need a bunch of greedy bankers taking down the global financial system a decade later in 2008 to know that human greed will ever be with us. However, following these and other shameful examples of corporate malfeasance, capitalist greed is definitely out of favor, even reviled (as Figure 25 documents). And governments are being called on to toughen the regulation of corporate behavior.

A parallel trend that also demonstrates how some businesses are evolving is the rise in corporate philanthropy. The exemplary philanthropic initiatives of Bill Gates and Warren Buffett (and Ted Turner before them) are good examples of how some business leaders are working to right the balance and give back to the societies in which they make their profits.

However, voluntary efforts by a few leaders will not be sufficient to regain the levels of trust and legitimacy that business enjoyed a few decades ago. For capitalism's sake, a more systemic realignment is no doubt called for; something that would bring along the laggards as well as the leaders. I explore what this might look like in Chapter 8.

In the meantime, GlobeScan's tracking research reveals just how significantly the business environment changed over the first half-decade of the 21st century. Asked to name the factor most influencing their impression of companies, representative national samples of 1,000 Americans were much more likely to volunteer CSR-related factors in 2005 compared with six years earlier, putting these factors well ahead of brand image (Fig. 27). This remarkable triumph of substance over image, also seen in Canada and western European countries, has changed almost everything about running companies today.

So ends our story of the very long and bumpy road business has traveled in getting to the present day, where it is faced with such a magnitude of challenges that it will need to continue evolving at an even greater pace. For this, it will need a new paradigm of itself in order to build a renewed and durable contract with society.

Summary

- Forty years ago, business was seen as the generator of wealth, and government as the protector and developer of societal "goods." But business hubris and government inaction soon led to change.

- Business thinking began to change through the early part of the 1990s in North America and Europe – spurred on by some spectacular examples of how business "old-think" would regularly lose out to popular NGO campaigns, and cost companies dearly.

- What was missing through this period was a compelling framework within which to balance competing interests. Sustainable development (and, to a lesser extent, CSR) has answered this need.

- While business was initially slow to engage, it has arguably become one of sustainable development's major standard-bearers. Nevertheless, public pressure for greater government regulation of business continues to grow.

- The deep public distrust of business today is somewhat ironic given some credible attempts by leadership companies, in the last decade especially, to address broader societal challenges.

- However, voluntary efforts by a few leaders will not be sufficient to regain the levels of trust and legitimacy that business enjoyed a few decades ago. For capitalism's sake, a more systemic realignment is no doubt called for; something that would bring along the laggards as well as the leaders.

8
A new social contract for business

Shareholder value is the dumbest idea in the world.
Jack Welch, former Chairman of General Electric, 2009

Business thrives where society thrives.
Peter Sutherland, former Director-General of the WTO, former
Chairman of BP, and Chairman of Goldman Sachs International, 2007

We are not being served as businesses by having significant problems
now and in the future by a lack of social cohesion.
Paul Polman, Chief Executive of Unilever, 2012

It is tough running a large company today. Not only are the economic conditions challenging, the decline of trust in society's most powerful institutions outlined in Chapter 3 has been even more dramatic when it comes to free enterprise.

One of our most unsettling poll findings for corporate executives – in addition to the documented retreat from globalization – has been the parallel decline in the unquestioned belief in the free enterprise system.

When GlobeScan released its first international poll exploring views of free enterprise in 2005, France was alone among the 20 nations surveyed in having a majority of its citizens disagreeing that, "The free enterprise system and free market economy is the best system on which to base the future of the world." Some thought-leaders in France were so concerned about these poll results that they launched a government commission aimed at helping to foster a more positive view of the free market. They seem to have succeeded in that France was the only country with an improved view of the free market between 2005 and 2007.

However, as Figure 28 shows, the 2005 French result was not an aberration but a leading indicator of things to come. Even before the massive market

FIGURE 28   The free market system is the best system on which to base the future of the world

"Agree,"* average of 11 tracking countries,** November 2001–February 2015

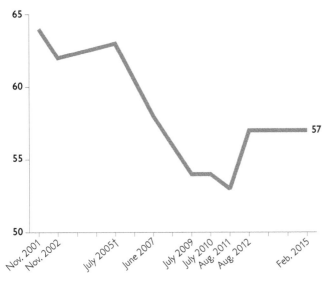

*"Strongly" and "somewhat agree"

**Tracking countries include Chile, China, France, Germany, India, Indonesia, Mexico, Nigeria, Turkey, the UK, and the USA

†Question not asked in Chile in 2005

failure called the "subprime credit crunch" came along in 2008, we discovered significant declines in free market support in nine of the 17 countries we tracked between 2005 and 2007.

While the free market system had actually lost majority support in only three countries (Turkey, France, and Chile), by June 2007 these findings suggested the gilt was slowly falling off the free enterprise lily. We advised business leaders at the time that they should do something dramatic to turn this trend around or they would pay an ever higher price for their license to operate and grow.

Perhaps with the help of the Great Recession, the decline in support for the free enterprise system slowed in the 2009 to 2011 period, as can be seen in Figure 28. The biggest surprise in the 2010 results was in the USA where there were historically low levels of support for free market capitalism. In fact, American support was so low that, for likely the first time in history, free market capitalism enjoyed more support in China and India than it did in the USA. Americans with incomes below $20,000 were particularly likely to have lost faith in the free market, with only 44% of them saying it was the best system for the future. American women also became much less positive, with just over half backing the free market in 2010. *The Economist* reported our conclusion that, "American business is close to losing its social contract with average families."[1]

The prolonged recession seems to have moderated this unprecedented decline in trust in the free enterprise system, with GlobeScan's 2012 and 2015 results showing an improved and stabilized 57% of citizens across 11 tracking countries saying the free enterprise system is the best on which to base the future of the world. But unless the free market system delivers a rebound in economic indicators soon, this may well turn out to be a temporary pause in a continuing fall in support.

I have often said if reluctant management teams didn't get proactive on CSR, it would only be replaced by something their CFO liked even less. These declining views on free market capitalism certainly qualify, and should mobilize even ultra-orthodox capitalists into action. Capitalism's social license needs to be renewed.

The old-school "business makes money; government spends it" mind-set outlined in Chapter 7 very much describes the way business has thought about broader ecological and societal services until relatively recently – largely externalizing these aspects from its decision-making and assuming that governments were looking after them. But this simplistic view is fast fading in today's world of failed states, suppliers' factories collapsing on workers, climate instability, and looming water crises in many countries.

Multinational companies are waking up to the fact that there are only very imperfect global governance mechanisms to deal with the increasing array of transboundary challenges that will have material effects on their business. As a result, leadership companies are beginning to act within the framework of sustainable development.

In fact, the increasing number of proactive "corporate sustainability" initiatives are beginning to define the next stage of corporate evolution. These initiatives are finding business justification because they help ensure the physical and social preconditions required for doing business (e.g., healthy workers, stable climate, sustainable water supply); and this risk-reduction business case is proving convincing to leading global companies such as Unilever, Patagonia, Interface, Marks & Spencer, Nestlé, Natura, Nike, and GE (General Electric). Figure 29 shows how the GlobeScan and SustainAbility

1   "Capitalism's Waning Support," *The Economist*, April 7, 2011.

FIGURE 29   Ranking of top eight leadership companies, 1997–2015

	2015	2014	2013	2012	2011	2010	2009	2007	2006	2005	2004	2002	2001	2000	1999	1998	1997
Unilever	1	1	1	1	1	5	7		6	6	8						
Patagonia	2	2	2	5	6	8	8										
Interface	3	3	3	2	3	2	1	1	2	2	3	4	4	3	3	3	7
M&S	4	4	5	6	5	4	6										
Natura	5			8													
IKEA	6																
Nestlé	7																
GE	8	6	6	3	2	2	2	2	4								
3M															8		3
Alcan									8								
Body Shop										6	6	5	6	6	8	5	
BP					7	5	4	1	1	1	2	2	2	2	1		
Dow										8	6	5	4	4			1
DuPont							5	5	5	6	3	3	4	4	6	4	
Monsanto																5	2
Nike		8	8						8								
Novo Nordisk				7				7	6	6	4	5	6		7	7	
Puma		7	7														
Shell									3	3	1	1	1	1	1	2	5
Suncor														8			
Toyota				8	7	6	3	2	7	4	5			7			
Walmart		5	4	4	4	1	4	6									

Panel of sustainable development experts has rated these and other companies over the years.

But our research suggests this is a command performance for *all* business today, not just the relatively few leadership companies. And this is even more the case in the aftermath of the financial meltdown of 2008.

Events seem to be reinforcing, validating, and expediting the pace of corporate innovation. The early thinking and actions of leadership companies quickly get forged into the fabric of corporate evolution. The driver of all this is necessity (the mother of all invention), along with rising and seemingly insatiable public and stakeholder expectations.

Public expectations of companies can be likened to American football. After a particularly good corporate initiative, the public moves the yardsticks down the field, expecting further forward movement. A few business leaders react cynically to this, saying, "No good deed goes unpunished," and use this as a reason not to continuously improve their business practices. However, most successful businesses are just as demanding of themselves for further improvement and, given that even critical NGOs need leaders to cheer onward, a number of companies have been able to capture the first-mover advantage that come with leadership. This is how progress happens.

The public understands how serious our problems are and, when they look around for the strongest hands to solve them, they see large companies as having the capacity and efficiency for putting solutions on the ground. In other words, it's "all hands on deck" and any strong set of hands that doesn't step forward will be severely judged. Just watch this play out on climate change and water over the next decade, where I predict we will witness the "outrage" factor most notably illustrated in Peter Sandman's famous "Risk = Hazard + Outrage" equation.[2] It won't be pretty. Nor will it be as productive as it would be if governments and business led the way.

As early as 2005, GlobeScan's research provided supporting evidence for three of the key elements of the business case for seriously adopting a progressive "corporate citizenship" or "sustainability" stance as a way of putting a company's "license to grow" on a firm foundation. Since that time, a veritable who's who of authoritative business advisors including Accenture, Deloitte, Goldman Sachs, Harvard Business School, McKinsey & Company, and PricewaterhouseCoopers have released data-driven case studies and reports supporting these elements.

The human resources area is one, especially for industries where attracting and retaining the best and brightest employees is paramount (e.g., finance and information technology). Companies are finding that their citizenship record is a major point of differentiation for job applicants and a major motivator for existing employees. In our surveys of corporate employees, a consistent eight in ten report being more motivated and loyal employees the more their company demonstrates its responsibility to the broader society.

The intensity of this employee motivation is, however, now declining. Figure 30 shows that the proportion of corporate employees "strongly

---

2   Peter Sandman, "Hazard versus Outrage in the Public Perception of Risk," in Vincent T. Covello, David B. McCallum, and Maria T. Pavlova (eds.), *Effective Risk Communication* (New York: Plenum, 1989), pp. 45-9.

FIGURE 30   The more socially responsible my company becomes, the more motivated and loyal I become as an employee
Average of 14 tracking countries,* November 2001–February 2013

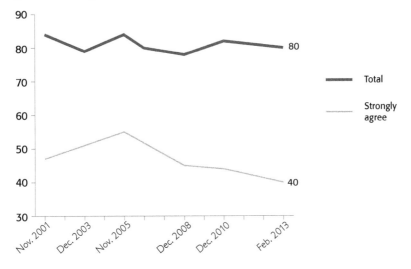

*Includes Australia, Brazil, Canada, Chile, China, France, Germany, Mexico, Nigeria, Russia, South Korea, Turkey, UK, and USA

2010: Not asked in Australia, Brazil, Canada, France, and Germany.

2005: Not asked in Brazil, Chile, China, Mexico, Nigeria, Russia, South Korea, and Turkey.

2003: Not asked in Nigeria and South Korea.

Subsample: People who work for a company of 1,000+ employees

agreeing" with the statement has declined from 55% in 2006 to 40% in 2013. Responses to other questions suggest this is due to increasing employee dissatisfaction with their company's CSR initiatives.

The second element might be called, "The best defense is a good offense." In managing inevitable future risks of reputational harm, companies that have built a buffer zone of goodwill bounce back faster.

This view was widely acknowledged as early as 2006, according to a survey of 950 CEOs across 11 countries by Weber Shandwick/KRC Research. Of responding CEOs, 79% said that a strong CSR record enables a company to recover reputation faster, postcrisis. There is evidence that this worked in BP's favor following its devastating Texas refinery explosion and Alaska pipeline corrosion problems of 2008. However, BP had not put enough credits in the bank of public opinion to withstand the reputational impact of its 2010 Gulf of Mexico drilling platform explosion and massive oil spill.

The third well-established business case for proactivity is that enlightened corporate citizenship can become a point of competitive advantage to leadership companies – when they do it right. GE is probably the best case in point.

When GE launched its "ecomagination" initiative in 2004, it identified a set of its technologies that had environmental and sustainability benefits (e.g., wind turbines and superefficient aircraft engines) that it set out to grow from a base that year of US$6.2 billion in posted sales. After two years, 2006 sales of its green technologies had doubled to US$12 billion. And their order book has continued to grow. In 2009, they reported green technology sales of US$18 billion. Interestingly, a respected environmental group, the World Resources Institute, helped GE develop this initiative.

Because the business case for corporate citizenship or corporate sustainability initiatives has been fairly well established in many sectors, it is clear that there will be ever more ambitious corporate initiatives to address broader societal challenges. In fact, Unilever's "Sustainable Living Plan" is more than that – it's the company's corporate strategy. However, the same cannot be said for business initiatives branded as CSR.

While CSR has marked an important stage in the evolution of free enterprise, CSR as practiced over the last decade is essentially dead. By this I mean first-generation CSR conducted as a voluntary add-on activity of business, mainly aimed at incremental improvement of internal business indicators such as recycling rates, CO_2 emissions, employment equity, and even philanthropic giving and relations with host communities.

GlobeScan's research shows that, while some of the best corporate work has been done over the past decade, the public's view of industry performance on CSR has not kept pace with their expectations.

Figure 31 shows what we call the "Accountability Gap." The top line is a composite measure of public expectations of business engagement on ten specific areas of responsibility, showing a holding trend from 2001 to 2011, then slowly edging downwards to 2015. The lower line is a composite net score of the global public's rating of the CSR performance of ten different industry sectors, showing a deteriorating view over the period to 2013, then a slight uptick in 2015. Based on over 60,000 interviews with the general public across 15 countries, it's a compelling picture of unmet expectations.

Without closing this gap with more impressive actions, industry is vulnerable to the rising call by NGOs for corporate accountability mechanisms

FIGURE 31 Expectations vs. performance gap
Average of 20 tracking countries,* December 2000–February 2015

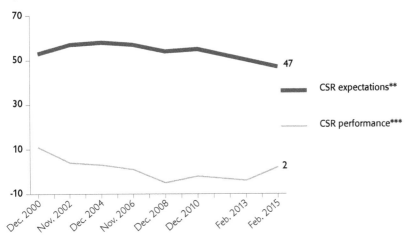

*Tracking countries include Argentina, Australia, Brazil, Canada, Chile, China, France, Germany, Greece, India, Indonesia, Italy, Mexico, Nigeria, Russia, South Korea, Spain, Turkey, UK, and USA. Not all countries were asked in all years.

**Aggregate net expectations of up to ten responsibilities of large companies (not all responsibilities were asked in each country each year)

***Aggregate net CSR performance ratings of ten industries (not all industries were asked in each country each year)

including legislation, mandatory reporting, third-party verification, and so on. Making corporate responsibility mandatory now enjoys the support of over half of global citizens, as can be seen in Figure 32.

Starting in 2002, GlobeScan has asked people around the world whether they agree or disagree that, "Our government should create laws that require large companies to go beyond their traditional economic role and work to make a better society, even though this could lead to higher prices and fewer jobs." Figure 32 shows the rising pressure on governments to force a further evolution of business beyond its traditional economic role. It's a popular mandate for making CSR mandatory.

The research suggests that things will not follow the present course for long. Citizens in industrialized countries especially are slowly losing interest in companies' responsibility claims, seeing them increasingly as public relations exercises without enough honesty (Fig. 33).

CSR will likely go in one of two directions or, more likely in today's world, in two directions at the same time – more mechanisms of accountability and governance over corporate behavior (especially aimed at minimum

FIGURE 32   Need laws requiring CSR despite risk of higher prices/fewer jobs
"Agree,"* average of 14 tracking countries,** November 2001–February 2013

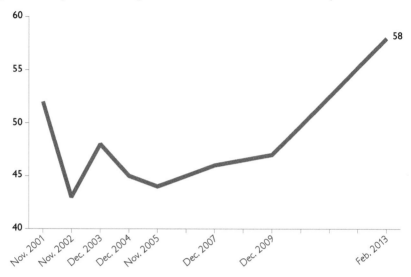

*"Strongly" and "Somewhat agree"
**Tracking countries include Australia, Canada, Chile, China, France, Germany, India, Indonesia, Italy, Mexico, Nigeria, Russia, the UK, and the USA.
Sample methodology changed between December 2007 and December 2009 in China, India, Indonesia, and Mexico.
There is no data for Italy in February 2013.

standards), as well as what one might call "next-generation" corporate initiatives.[3]

Most companies will continue to lag behind on CSR, increasing NGOs' success in campaigning for governments to introduce more coercive accountability measures. The government of India, for example, has made it compulsory for listed companies to report on their CSR programs annually. A number of NGOs regularly conduct major "name and shame" campaigns against companies talking a good line but not acting with enough commitment. These campaigns can inflict major reputational harm on targeted companies.

At the same time, however, we are predicting the emergence of what can be called "Version 2.0" corporate initiatives, moving out from strong internal programs to take on much more visionary global sustainability objectives

3   See *Changing Tack: Extending Corporate Leadership on Sustainable Development*, http://theregenerationroadmap.com/reports.html#/changing-tack.html.

FIGURE 33   Interest in vs. credibility of CSR communications
Average of ten tracking countries,* November 2001–January 2012

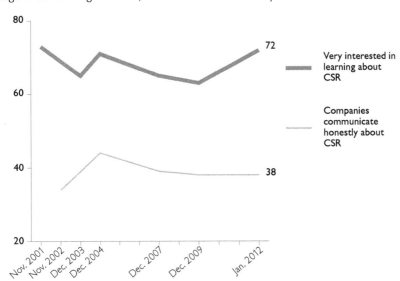

*Tracking countries include Australia, Canada, Chile, China, Germany, Indonesia, Russia, Turkey, the UK, and the USA.

that will capture people's imaginations and forcefully demonstrate that business can be very much part of the solution to global challenges.

The business case for these next-generation initiatives will be partly based on the need for a more certain business environment than governments are providing today. Already we're seeing coalitions of major companies asking European governments to set aggressive long-term targets for carbon emissions so industries have the certainty they need to make 30-year investment decisions. Another (New York-based) initiative focuses on the looming global water challenge.[4]

The tracking data presented in Figure 28, showing the decline (until recently) in the unquestioned support for the free market system over the decade, is exactly where no business person wants things to go.

The history given in Chapter 7 demonstrates how much corporate thinking and action has evolved over the career span of my generation. However,

---

4   The CEO Water Mandate seeks to make a positive impact with respect to the emerging global water crisis by mobilizing a critical mass of business leaders to advance water sustainability solutions – in partnership with the UN, civil society organizations, governments, and other stakeholders.

more significant change is needed and needed urgently if business is to regain its stature in the world.

In the midst of the 2009 economic downturn, Philips's Chief Executive Gerard Kleisterlee said, "An economic crisis is a period when you should step back and think: is this a moment to make some fundamental changes?"

So what is the business "old-think" in today's context that will need to be put off, and what are the new ideas coming up through the ranks? What will regain business's social contract sufficiently to ensure a relatively free market for decades to come?

For sure, the old "business makes money; governments spend it" thinking must finally be fully retired. Also, the "dumbest idea in the world" of business focusing only on shareholder value must be replaced. And finally, many have argued, so must viewing CSR or sustainability as a tack-on activity unrelated to core business.

As for the up-and-coming ideas that will likely be adopted and be successful in reinvigorating the free enterprise system, I see three incremental ideas and a couple of big ones.

First, many of the next-generation sustainable development initiatives that we see coming along in large companies will eventually take the form of social intrapreneurships (i.e., entrepreneurialism within an existing company). In other words, rather than continuing as staff functions within companies, the sustainable development function will evolve into profit centers with truly win–win business concepts emerging, such as GE's ecomagination.

A global infrastructure company with which GlobeScan works has launched a new business unit aimed at helping cities become more sustainable by offering a whole range of appropriate technologies and services (e.g., to reuse water and provide mobility and renewable energy). A major petroleum company is looking to launch a new business unit aimed at helping its customers use energy more efficiently. And increasing numbers of corporate affairs departments are being seen internally as delivering real shareholder value as they successfully manage brand reputation through good works not just words.

Second, as covered in greater detail in Chapter 10, partnerships between business organizations and NGOs are showing themselves to be very effective in dealing with societal challenges. And our research shows these partnerships also significantly improve the reputations of participating companies. Whether one-on-one partnerships (such as GE and the World Resources Institute, or Starbucks and Conservation International) or collaborations between groups of companies and NGOs (such as the Global Water Challenge convened by the UN Foundation, Coca-Cola and the World Wide Fund for Nature), these partnerships will play a role in regaining trust in business while at the same time effectively addressing key problems.

Groups such as the Prince of Wales' International Business Leaders Forum in the UK have not only championed such partnerships but also trained participants to help ensure more of these partnerships will be successful in spite of the organizational culture differences between for-profit and not-for-profit groups.

Third, the surging growth of a segment of business called social enterprises will also help rebuild business's social contract. The UK government reported that fully one in ten new business start-ups there in 2005 were businesses focused on social benefit rather than personal wealth creation.

Perhaps some of the best examples of social enterprises come from South Asia. The most famous is the Grameen Bank in Bangladesh, the first social enterprise to achieve significant impact and global recognition. Founded in 1976, this "bank for the poorest-of-the-poor" has provided small loans to over 8 million borrowers, 97% of whom are women. Another social enterprise in India has provided internet access to over 2 million small farmers so they can check commodity prices and choose the best time to sell their grains, resulting in significantly higher family incomes.

Helping successful social enterprises expand and prosper will be key to maximizing their contribution. Unless they "get to scale," they will be seen to be at the margins rather than key to meeting society's challenges and a tribute to business discipline.

During 2013, three different initiatives were launched focused on giving small and medium-sized social enterprises more innovative futures than being acquired by or themselves becoming publicly listed companies focused only on shareholder value. Together, these initiatives have the potential of vastly expanding the already growing trend called impact investing.[5]

In the UK, the Social Stock Exchange opened in London to enable social enterprises to be vetted and matched with ethical or impact investors. In Singapore, the Asia Impact Investment Exchange was launched to do the same. And in Toronto, the SVX (Social Venture Connexion) began enabling

---

5   Impact investors are willing to accept lower financial returns in order to invest in companies focused on providing a measurable social good in a way that also makes a profit.

impact ventures and funds to raise capital from CAD$100,000 to $10 million from accredited impact investors.

These are all important but incremental steps toward fueling the kind of innovation that will help secure free enterprise's future. However, bigger ideas and changes will also be needed in order to leverage change across all companies, not just leadership ones. These changes will be necessary to address the "laggard" or "free-rider" issue by locking in societal purpose and responsibility in all companies; and to ensure that business decisions are made within a longer-term context than simply the next fiscal quarter. A recent survey of CEOs of large companies found more than three-quarters (79%) of them report having the most pressure to deliver financial results within two years; and while 73% of them said their management teams should be planning their strategy three or more years out, only half were doing so.[6]

There are a couple of ways in which these big ideas might be established, but, given the strength of relevant public opinion trends (let alone the needs of society and the biosphere), I think it is likely they will be established over the next 25 years.

The easiest and most effective way of ensuring the free enterprise system operates in the best long-term interest of people and the planet is by governments getting back to doing their job of setting the long-term direction of human society (through effective citizen participation channels) and ensuring responsible compliance by all actors, especially companies.

Governments could most clearly do this by amending the laws and regulations whereby companies are incorporated and granted the right to operate with limited financial and legal liability. It can be argued that society is not asking enough from companies in return for these substantial benefits. Requiring them to live up to a set of broader responsibilities to our society and the biosphere would be reasonable. While business lobbyists would mount a hue and cry, I have no doubt most businesses could readily adapt and prosper under such a new social contract.

There is already an interesting model of this approach in the Benefit Corporation initiative (or "B Corp"), developed in the USA. It is aimed at certifying enterprises willing to be accountable for their broader societal impacts. The key requirement of B Corp certification is that a company must change its corporate objects to be not only accountable to its shareholders

---

6   "Short-termism: Insights from Business Leaders" report by McKinsey, December 2013.

but also to all its stakeholders, including its customers, employees (past and present), its host communities, and suppliers. From a sustainability viewpoint, one could add future generations of customers to this list, as well as other species and the biosphere.

The Benefit Corporation would be a good model on which governments could build a fundamentally new definition of business with its responsibilities to society formalized and made integral to its license to operate. Only such an approach will ensure *all* businesses will make sustainability and ethics central to their operations, or be made accountable under law. With a growing number of small and large companies, including Natura and Patagonia, voluntarily becoming Benefit Corporations, this approach may not be as revolutionary as it may first sound.

The current pattern of a few leadership companies with hundreds of thousands of free-riders or outright laggard companies will not get us to where we need to go. All businesses need to commit to giving more back to society in return for being considered "persons" under the law and enjoying the limited legal and financial liability society provides them.

As long as greed and narrow self-interest, rather than societal interest, are seen to drive the free enterprise business model, broad societal support will continue to languish at historically low levels. The large role corporate money plays in politics in many countries makes it unlikely that many politicians will step up to changing the societal bargain inherent in corporate letters patent. So it is more likely that other processes that do not require governmental leadership will be more successful in speeding the evolution of the free enterprise system. But even an Indian government approach of requiring companies to annually and publicly report on their corporate responsibility would be better than nothing.

Happily, there are two other hopeful trends under way that hold promise: the rise of societal branding among leadership companies, and the growing number of "complex coalitions" (or collaborations) among many different actors aimed at systemic changes.

There is a rapidly growing number of companies that are adopting a "societal purpose," then investing at the nexus of their corporate brand, their corporate reputation, and their corporate sustainability initiatives to both make a positive contribution to the world and drive their business forward.

Today, every business needs to develop or rediscover its larger societal purpose. What's it for, in addition to making a profit by delivering needed products and services? (A surprising number of successful companies started with such a visionary concept.) Once a company defines its societal purpose, it then needs to find a way of making a profit by delivering on it, ideally using a business model that ensures continuous improvement. Innovative companies are good at putting all this together in a way that even investors appreciate.

The following letter was published by the *Financial Times* on October 17, 2012, written in response to an article published six days previously:

Companies must find their inner societal purpose

Sir,

Michael Skapinker's article "Companies are facing a new type of opponent" (October 11) builds very well on Simon Zadek's keen observation that conflict today stems increasingly from the gulf between rich and poor within countries.

Mr. Skapinker goes on to argue quite effectively that this has created a new opposing force to free enterprise, as demonstrated by seemingly random and unexpected uprisings at mines in South Africa, at Foxconn in China and during last year's riots in Britain (not to mention Occupy Wall Street).

This phenomenon is underscored by the poll we conducted for the BBC World Service earlier this year, which revealed that majorities in 18 of 24 countries see the economic system in their country as unfair in distributing economic benefits and costs. The fact that companies are increasingly being targeted by these "new opponents" is understandable given another finding from the same poll – that free enterprise as currently practiced is progressively losing its appeal. While one in two citizens across the 24 countries believes flaws in the free market system can be fixed through reform and regulation, fully one in four now sees it as fatally flawed and that a new economic system is needed.

We would argue that the best defense to all this is a good offense. Big companies first need to manage their reputation proactively among their stakeholders to avoid being targeted; and second, they need to rediscover an authentic societal purpose at the heart of their enterprise from which to demonstrate the efficacy of free enterprise in meeting the real needs of the majority of people.

I used to joke in client presentations that those chief financial officers and other executives who continued to oppose corporate social responsibility initiatives by their companies would one day awake to discover that CSR had been replaced by something they would like even less. Well, this is it.

Doug Miller
Chairman and CEO
GlobeScan Incorporated
Toronto, Canada

Another "big idea" for turning corporations into forces for good comes from business itself. It follows a trend among business and NGO leaders who increasingly acknowledge the possibility that governments will never truly show up to play a serious role in securing a sustainable future. In this case, the idea was developed by the WBCSD, which brings together some 200 international companies "with a shared commitment to a sustainable future through economic growth, ecological balance and social progress."

In a major project[7] grappling with the challenge of describing a world well on the way to sustainability by the year 2050, as well as a pathway leading to that world, the WBCSD called for "complex coalitions" involving individuals and organizations from all sectors with critical knowledge and capabilities. These coalitions would be formed at the local, regional, national, and international levels and would aim to identify and prepare for risks and challenges before they have an impact. WBCSD envisaged such complex coalitions developing sophisticated early warning systems as well as ongoing risk-monitoring and management systems, taking advantage of the wealth of diversified knowledge, perspectives, and capabilities of its diverse members. More specific coalitions could then form to address specific challenges.

While the WBCSD as yet has been unable to create a real-life example of such a complex coalition, one could imagine a set of corporate, NGO, multilateral, academic, and governmental actors that could bring an impressive array of knowledge and capability to a problem such as the sustainable supply of potable water in Africa. In today's world full of dysfunctional governance and mistrust for traditional actors, such a complex coalition focused on climate change could well outperform the international diplomatic process in truly addressing this global challenge.

An early example of this kind of complex coalition (or collaboration) was initiated by the President of Iceland, Ólafur Ragnar Grímsson, in 2013. Called the "Arctic Circle," its mission is to facilitate dialogue among political and business leaders, environmental experts, scientists, indigenous representatives, and other international stakeholders to address issues facing the Arctic as a result of climate change and melting sea ice.[8]

---

7   "Vision 2050: The New Agenda for Business," http://www.wbcsd.org/pages/edocument/edocumentdetails.aspx?id=219.

8   See http://www.arcticcircle.org.

All of this is the order of magnitude of new ideas and actions that will be necessary to fully renew industry's social contract. Leadership companies that implement these new ideas ahead of their competitors, and very skill-fully, will do very well by doing good. Late adopters who hold back from change will be pulled by events to pay a much higher price for no real ben-efit other than simply keeping up with the pack or meeting new regulatory requirements. To aid progress, early mover advantage should be enshrined in any new government regulations.

Perhaps a final element that will ensure the renewal of business's social contract with society is the emergence of a new breed of corporate lead-ers. Virgin's Sir Richard Branson and Jochen Zeitz, the Chairman of PUMA, are two examples. Together they are pulling together what they call "The B Team" – a group of global business leaders who will together look to trans-form the future of business and use entrepreneurial skills to help solve criti-cal social and environmental challenges.

There is also some evidence that this reconception of free enterprise is under way among business school students. These up-and-coming busi-ness leaders know that the business context is changing rapidly, and they recognize that the only way to predict the future with enough certainty is to help *create* it by adopting ahead-of-the-curve business models, technolo-gies, and approaches. An increasing number are choosing business as their vehicle for improving the world rather than for amassing personal wealth.

Ray Anderson, visionary CEO of US carpet-maker Interface Inc. (which has set out to be the world's first truly sustainable company by 2020), put the business case this way in 2007, well before the global financial crisis:

> The status quo is a very powerful opiate and when you have a system that seems to be working and producing profits by the conventional way of accounting for profits, it's very hard to make yourself change. But we all know that change is an inevitable part of business. Once you have ridden a wave just so far, you have to get another wave. We all know that. For us, becoming restorative has been that new wave and we have been riding it for 13 years now. It's been incredibly good for business.[9]

At the end of the day, it doesn't really matter how corporate initiatives are labeled as long as they are substantive. The six things required for success in

---

9   Ray Anderson on conquering Mount Sustainability: http://www.greenlivingonline.com/article/green-living-interview-ray-anderson.

this next period, as identified in *Changing Tack*, are: vision, ambitious goals, a core offer, a meaningful brand, transparency, and societal advocacy.[10]

Sustainable development will be the carrying theme for many next-generation initiatives, not only because of its compelling business case but because, unlike CSR, sustainability has the benefit of the laws of physics on its side. It requires measurable action.

Everyone wants an economy that produces sustainable wellbeing without plundering the planet or savaging human dignity and community. The difference today is that people think that we can actually achieve this.

We humans seem to resist change until the last possible moment. But once we believe that a particular change is both necessary and achievable, leaps of progress happen. This is the kind of time we are living in, and companies have demonstrated their exceptional capacity to change when it is necessary.

Summary

- One of the most unsettling poll findings for corporate executives – in addition to the documented retreat from globalization – has been the parallel decline in the unquestioned belief in the free enterprise system. Capitalism's social license needs to be renewed.

- Multinational companies are also waking up to the fact that there are only very imperfect global governance mechanisms to deal with the increasing array of transboundary challenges that will have material effects on their business. As a result, leadership companies are beginning to act within the framework of sustainable development.

- As early as 2005, GlobeScan's research provided supporting evidence for three of the key elements of the business case for seriously adopting a progressive "corporate citizenship" or "sustainability" stance as a way of putting a company's "license to grow" on a firm foundation: attracting and retaining the best and brightest

---

10 See *Changing Tack: Extending Corporate Leadership on Sustainable Development*, http://theregenerationroadmap.com/reports.html#/changing-tack.html.

employees, building reputational resilience in an uncertain world, and capturing competitive advantage.

- A key external driver is the rising and seemingly insatiable public and stakeholder expectations of companies. They understand just how serious our challenges are and, when they look around for the strongest hands to solve them, they see large companies as having the capacity and efficiency for putting solutions on the ground.

- GlobeScan's research shows that, while some of the best corporate work has been done over the past decade, the public's view of industry performance on CSR have not kept pace with their expectations, resulting in an "Accountability Gap."

- Without closing this gap with more impressive actions, industry is vulnerable to the rising call by NGOs for corporate accountability mechanisms including legislation, mandatory reporting, third-party verification, and so on. Making corporate responsibility mandatory now enjoys the support of over half of global citizens.

- Governments could most clearly do this by amending the laws and regulations whereby companies are incorporated and granted the right to operate with limited financial and legal liability. It can be argued that society is not asking enough from companies in return for these substantial benefits. Requiring them to live up to a set of broader responsibilities to our society and the biosphere would be reasonable. The Benefit Corporation initiative provides an interesting model for such an approach.

- CSR will likely go in one of two directions or, more likely in today's world, in two directions at the same time – more mechanisms of accountability and governance over corporate behavior (especially aimed at minimum standards), as well as what one might call "next-generation" corporate initiatives.

- The business case for these next-generation initiatives will be partly based on the need for a more certain business environment than governments are providing today.

- There is a rapidly growing number of companies that are adopting a "societal purpose," then investing at the nexus of their corporate brand, their corporate reputation, and their corporate sustainability initiatives both to make a positive contribution to the world and to drive their business forward.

- As long as greed and narrow self-interest, rather than societal interest, are seen to drive the free enterprise business model, broad societal support will continue to languish at historically low levels.

9
The rise of the ethical consumer

People are judging us increasingly on the quality of our character as much as the quality of the products we serve.

Muthar Kent, CEO of Coca-Cola, December 2009

Businesses across the world are coming to see that principles and profits are two sides of the same coin.

Ban Ki-moon, Secretary-General of the UN, 2010

Over the last 20 years, the "Five Ps of Marketing" have driven the creation of the largest consumer marketplace the world has ever seen.

Product, price, place, promotion, and people have focused the minds of marketing executives the world over.

Does our product or service meet the needs of our customers? Is the price competitive and profitable? Do we have good distribution channels, retailers, and product placement? Are we using the right mix of communication and endorsement to promote our products and services to customers? How about our sales and service people – are they treating our customers well?

The belief has been that if you get these fundamentals right, your business will succeed.

In fact, the research suggests that the Five Ps are no longer sufficient to ensure success. Today there is a sixth P: let's call it "purpose" – the broad societal good the company and its products and services are meant to help accomplish; or call it "principles" – the standards of moral or ethical decision-making used in the business.

This sixth P is needed to respond to one of the most noteworthy trends that we've seen over the past decade: the inexorable rise of a consumer segment variously called the "responsible consumer" (by the UN Environment Programme), the "conscience consumer" (by Unilever), the "sustainable consumer" (by Consumers International), or the "ethical consumer" (by the UK magazine of the same name).

What sets this group of consumers apart from their peers is that their social and environmental concerns as citizens are reflected in their actions as consumers much more consistently than other segments of the marketplace.

GlobeScan has been tracking the growth of the ethical consumer over the last decade-and-a-half across both industrialized and emerging economies, just as it tracked the so-called "green consumer" in the early part of the 1990s in North America. Not only has ethical consumerism maintained its momentum through the worst recession in modern history, it has done so in both wealthy and non-wealthy countries, unlike the 1990s.

It is clear that the Great Recession has undermined confidence across industrialized countries and prompted citizens to rethink life priorities. At the same time, urban citizens of emerging economies such as China and India are having to endure environmental conditions that are greatly increasing their personal health concerns.

Back in October 2007, prior to the global financial meltdown, there was clear evidence of a surge in ethical consumerism when I presented at an event put on by the Prince of Wales' International Business Leaders Forum in London. In the audience were chief executives of a number of global companies including Coca-Cola, Chevron, BMW, Accenture, and Burson Marsteller. The event was focused on how businesses were addressing the challenges of the new millennium and in particular how they were making the business case for taking innovative and industry-leading efforts in corporate responsibility.

In my remarks I outlined how the results of our 30-country research with consumers, employees, and shareholders supported the elements of the business case "for doing the right thing" that many in the room had successfully made in their companies. The benefits include attracting and retaining the best and brightest employees, staying ahead of the legislative curve, and positioning themselves in the marketplace both to receive investment from ethical investors as well as to provide future competitive advantage in the consumer marketplace (see Chapter 8).

I then told the audience that we had just discovered a new element of the business case that had arrived on the scene. I showed them the increase between 2002 and 2007 in the size of our "ethical consumer" segment across G7 countries. When I suggested that this segment was already at levels that they would be picking up in their own market research, a number of chief executives in the audience nodded affirmatively.

FIGURE 34 Rewarded/punished companies seen as socially responsible/
irresponsible
"Have done," average of 14 tracking countries,* December 2000–February 2015

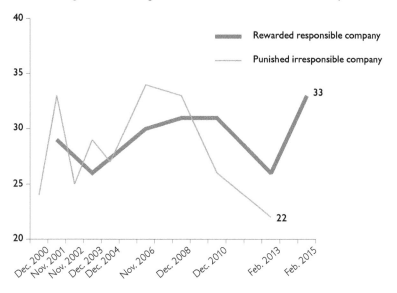

*Tracking countries include Australia, Canada, Chile, China, France, Germany,
Indonesia, Italy, Mexico, Nigeria, Russia, Turkey, the UK, and the USA.

There is no data for Italy in February 2013.

But that was in 2007 at the height of the "bubble economy." With the
onset of the Great Recession a year later, conventional wisdom would have
predicted that ethical consumerism would implode and disappear. As can
be seen in Figure 34, the withering economy did reduce the percentage of
consumers punishing or rewarding companies through their purchases or
advocacy. But the impact was far from an implosion and far from that seen
in past economic downturns.

There was an immediate reversal in the proportion of consumers punishing irresponsible companies (which had been surging). But the more
interesting group from a commercial perspective – those rewarding ethical business practices and products – continued to hold across the world
and expand in some markets for a couple of years, before tailing off as the
recession began to settle in for the long haul. This downward trend has now
reversed, with 2015 results showing the highest level of rewarding behavior
in 15 years of tracking.

In other research we have done for a major household products manufacturer on their green product offerings in the USA, we saw the size of their green consumer segment double between 2007 and 2009.

This tenacity of ethical consumers is significant because it goes against the whole thrust and weight of the consumer society as it has been practiced over the last 30 years, which has encouraged people to see themselves as consumers above citizens, seeking satisfaction and salvation in consuming ever greater volumes of stuff. The trillions spent on advertising made people feel fulfilled through consumption. Politicians made people feel patriotic by shopping (most famously, George W. Bush following 9/11). Even the consumer movement through much of this time encouraged people to be "smart consumers" focused on quality and price. The only activism they encouraged was pushing back on manufacturers that didn't deliver on the promise of more (quantity and quality) for less. The mantra seemed to be "don't leave home without your credit card, but do leave your values at home."

I had an interesting encounter with the global advertising industry on a panel at a sustainable consumerism conference organized by the UN Environment Programme in Paris in 2003. After I presented the findings of our first global poll that identified and measured the ethical consumer segment, the representative of the Advertising Industry Association gave a rather old-school talk positioning his industry as part of the solution to sustainable development. In a breakout group discussion following our presentations I suggested that his industry wouldn't be a real part of the solution until it admitted to being a big part of the problem. He flat-out refused to admit to being part of the problem, using the curious argument that advertizing didn't actually encourage people to buy a particular product, it just gave them information on which they could base a purchase decision. I replied that I was sure his major-spend clients would be interested to hear him admit that, but regardless, it is clear that people surrounded by pervasive advertising felt they needed to buy *something*! Hence the problem.

So the fact that one in five or more citizens, in both rich and emerging economies, are refusing to define themselves narrowly as consumers and are integrating their values as citizens into their purchase decisions to an historical extent, is significant. No wonder the likes of Unilever and Procter & Gamble have set off to take competitive advantage of the ethical consumer phenomenon.

FIGURE 35   I can make a difference as a consumer in corporate behavior
"Agree," OECD vs. non-OECD countries,* November 2001–February 2015

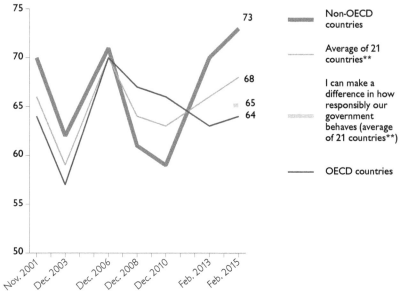

*OECD countries include Australia, Canada, Chile, France, Germany, Greece, Italy,
Mexico, South Korea, Turkey, UK, and USA; non-OECD countries include Argentina,
Brazil, China, India, Indonesia, Kenya, Nigeria, Peru, and Russia.

**Includes Argentina, Australia, Brazil, Canada, Chile, China, France, Germany, Greece,
India, Indonesia, Italy, Kenya, Mexico, Nigeria, Peru, South Korea, Turkey, UK, and USA.
Not all countries were asked in all years.

What might be going on here? GlobeScan's research shows that an increasing number of people believe their ability to influence companies to help
solve world problems is greater than their influence over their governments
to do the same. This fundamental shift, from looking to governments to
looking to companies to change the world, hasn't been seen before, and it is
in the process of changing everything to do with running a large company.

Figure 35 shows consumers' surging sense of empowerment across
emerging markets (non-OECD countries) from 2010 to 2015 especially,
while it slowly declines in OECD countries, but still at healthy majority levels. It also shows people's lower sense of power to influence their government's behavior.

Our long-time research partner in Brazil, Fabián Echegaray of Market
Analysis, first developed this thesis, supported by his research among
Brazilian consumers. He postulated that in part because of their frustration
with the poor leadership and low efficacy of governments to actually solve

the significant problems that face us, people are taking their concerns as citizens into their behavior as consumers. In the process they are rewarding companies that are early adopters of more enlightened business models that maximize the social and environmental benefits of their processes, products, and services.

Who are the ethical consumers? People in this segment are striving for consistency between their concerns and their behavior. They are essentially voting with their dollars, pounds, and yuan to help establish their values and aspirations in the world. They also tend to be more educated consumers with more disposable income than other segments, and more likely female (who still tend to do the household shopping). And as further reinforcement, ethical consuming is becoming the cool thing to be seen to do.

All of this makes the ethical consumer segment important beyond their numbers, and something that gets industry attention very quickly. It also helps advance the adoption of sustainable development by more businesses, given the potential market share advantage to them. And most interesting of all, ethical consumers are equally represented in emerging economies as in industrialized countries (for likely the first time in history).

The early growth in ethical consumerism led to new market phenomena such as Brand (RED), the initiative of U2's lead singer, Bono, that by 2010 contributed US$50 million to the UN Aids Programme due to the large number of consumers choosing to pay a premium for "RED" products offered by companies such as American Express and Gap. Another example is supermarkets in the UK, who have been fighting with each other for years over who has more free-range eggs, organic food, and fair-trade products on their shelves.

In 2007, the US consumer products giant, Procter & Gamble, set out to sell US$30 billion of green products over the next five years, and changed its corporate mission statement for only the second time in 110 years to include a responsibility for product impacts on future generations.

The early mover in the automotive sector, Toyota, saw their Prius hybrid gas–electric automobile become a green icon worldwide that fueled their reputation and growth until both were undermined by a number of massive quality recalls and competing products from other manufacturers. Even Walmart, that years ago would have been voted "least likely to succeed" in sustainability, has taken remarkable steps since 2009, including their initiative to create a sustainability index for every product they sell, which is having a significant impact on the way their huge number of suppliers operate.

Most recently, Unilever has launched its "Sustainable Living Plan" that has been voted the best corporate sustainability initiative by an authoritative panel of sustainability leaders across 60 countries.[1] Unilever's ambition is impressive. They are setting out to halve the environmental footprint of their products, source 100% of their food products from sustainable sources, deliver potable water to 1 billion people, and improve the lives of 500,000 family farmers by including them in their supply chain. But most importantly, they are beginning to apply their marketing know-how to encourage consumers to adopt more sustainable behaviors.

Case study: Procter & Gamble

To demonstrate the materiality of the ethical consumer phenomenon to major businesses we can look at the example of consumer products company Procter & Gamble (P&G). This is a company that knows very well how challenging yet ultimately rewarding the ethical consumer segment is.

P&G began their involvement with the green consumer segment back in the early 1990s during the last "green wave" of environmental concern. Back then they were unsuccessful with it, like many other companies. Most green offerings at the time were about 10% more expensive than their regular product formulation. When the green consumer market collapsed in 1992, most concluded that it was because of the worsening economy and people were not prepared to pay a premium for green attributes.

To their credit, P&G kept working on greening their product formulations, including fresh research and focused innovation. In 2010, sensing the time was right, they launched "Future Friendly," a multi-brand, multi-platform initiative to:

- Introduce what they call "sustainable innovation products" (SIP), which are products with a significantly reduced (>10%) environmental footprint versus previous or alternative products

- Engage with their consumers to reduce their collective environmental impact

- Continue to grow their social responsibility efforts.

After setting ambitious targets for this initiative, they quickly increased their goals further. Their revised 2012 goals include:

---

1   The 2015 Sustainability Leaders survey report from GlobeScan and Sustain-Ability can be downloaded from http://www.globescan.com/component/edocman/?view=document&id=179&Itemid=591.

- Develop and market at least US$50 billion in cumulative SIP sales. By the end of the second quarter of 2012 P&G reported they had already exceeded their goal, recording US$52 billion in cumulative SIP sales.

- Deliver a 20% reduction (per unit of production) in CO_2 emissions, energy consumption, water usage, and disposed waste from P&G plants, leading to a total reduction over the decade of at least 50%. By mid-2012, P&G operations reported a 71% reduction in waste disposed, 22% reduction in water usage, 16% reduction in energy usage, and 14% reduction in direct CO_2 emissions.

- Enable 300 million children to "Live, Learn and Thrive," and prevent 160 million days of disease from unclean water and save 20,000 lives by delivering 4 billion liters of clean water through P&G's "Children's Safe Drinking Water" program. By 2012, P&G surpassed their goals by reaching 400 million children, they prevented over 170 million days of disease, delivered 4.22 billion liters of clean water, and saved over 22,000 lives as a result.

Of course this isn't the first time in history there has been a surge in ethical consumerism. The green consumer movement of 1988–92 transformed the consumer marketplace for a few years in Europe and North America. It's important to look at why that movement lasted such a short time back then in order to understand the current situation better.

GlobeScan (when it was still called Environics International) was conducting consumer research in North America throughout the green consumer phenomenon of the late 1980s and tracking it on a quarterly basis, so we had a ringside seat on something that had a huge impact on the marketplace. Thousands of green products were launched, scores of books and magazines were published (including the first *Green Consumer Guide* by John Elkington and Julia Hailes in the UK), and companies were competing to out-green each other. All this came crashing to the ground in 1992. What happened? For many it was "the economy, stupid" – that irreverent catch line of the Clinton presidential campaign in the USA. This view of the recession got everyone focused on the economy and, by conventional wisdom, caused the implosion of the green consumer marketplace. In other words, a "need-to-have" goal pushed a "nice-to-have" goal off the agenda. This can be seen from Canadian public opinion through the 1990s, with regular purchasing of green products falling significantly between 1993 and 1999 (Fig. 36).

FIGURE 36   Canadian consumption of green products (self-reported) 1990–1999

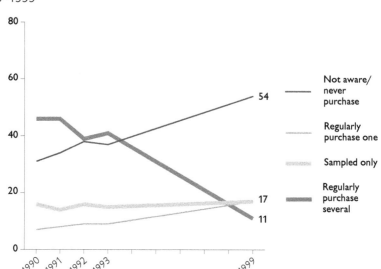

Clearly there is a relationship between economic worries and reduced concern for the environment, but GlobeScan's more recent evidence suggests it is much weaker and of shorter duration than conventional wisdom suggests.

GlobeScan's research revealed that a more significant factor in the 1992 fall-off in green consumerism was an implosion of trust by consumers in the product and service offerings. Every new product just happened to cost at least 10% more than the alternative and worked significantly less effectively. Indeed, there were many examples of outright marketeering, the best example of which was baking soda being relabeled as a "green" product.

The key lesson for the current rise of the ethical consumer is the essential need for quality assurance and independent verification of product claims in order to retain consumer trust.

The best way to accomplish this is for companies already in the ethical space, and doing it well and comprehensively, getting together and choosing an authoritative label with third-party verification (ideally by an NGO or scientific organization) in order to lock in their competitive advantage and safeguard themselves against market implosion due to consumer distrust and opportunism.

One of the best examples of such a labeling system (in addition to the Rainforest Alliance label) is the Fairtrade label, a major focus for the ethical consumer segment and a well-known and significant phenomenon in many developed countries particularly in the coffee, chocolate, and banana categories. We've done research for a number of "green" product labels in different countries over the years and they all test very well in the sense that they are well regarded by consumers and are trusted to differentiate green products for the consumer. However, there is frequently low awareness of these labels because insufficient marketing muscle is put behind them to achieve the high levels of awareness that generate market pickup. The Fairtrade label is a notable exception in that it enjoys high public awareness, especially in European countries. Back in 2006, I spoke publicly on numerous occasions,[2] identifying the Fairtrade label as the brand that I expected to grow the most in the coming period given the ethical consumer phenomenon that our research had revealed.

By wonderful happenstance an opportunity developed for GlobeScan a couple of years later to do multi-market research for Fairtrade International, the organization that coordinates this mark worldwide. This research certainly has validated the trends that we saw in our own research and reinforces the learning over the years that awareness is everything when it comes to these labels.

The continuing market success of Fairtrade-labeled goods across developed countries especially is a testament to the abiding strength of the ethical consumer segment, and has proven to a number of global companies that attracting and retaining these consumers is material to their future success.

Even through the crushing economic downturn and crisis of 2008 and 2009, Fairtrade-labeled products across the world enjoyed continued success albeit not at the usual levels of 12% per annum growth they enjoyed in 2007. But this was in the midst of a market in which most product sales in the categories covered by Fairtrade had declined by double-digit percentages. In 2012, sales volumes of Fairtrade-labeled products rose 27% across the world. This underscores both the abiding power of this new market segment and suggests that, as long as the certification works effectively in retaining consumer trust, the ethical consumer is here to stay.

How big a phenomenon is it now? Determining the "real market" size of the ethical consumer segment is a challenging assignment. The challenge is that there is a "halo effect" of consumers telling pollsters they will pay

---

2   Most notably at the UN Environment Programme's 2006 Sustainable Consumerism Conference in Berlin, in addition to many client presentations.

for social or environmental attributes but never actually do so. However, the drop-off is not as large as some believe or claim – usually to justify not introducing products with improved benefits into the market. (My favorite expression of this point of view is from a drinks industry client who, 20 years ago, claimed that our self-reported purchase intention numbers were "all froth and no beer.")

GlobeScan has triangulated its research with clients' actual sales numbers for enough years to have developed a formula for converting self-reported behavior intentions expressed in consumer surveys into real market numbers. Without giving away trade secrets, I can report that the real market numbers are today in the range of 10–15% (depending on the product category) in a number of industrialized and emerging economies. This is about half the size of the ethical consumer segment that we calculate based on consumers' stated intentions through surveys – but still large enough and growing quickly enough to entice some major players (such as Unilever and Procter & Gamble) to take it seriously. As Joel Makower said in his 1990 book *The Green Consumer:*[3]

> The marketplace is not a democracy; you don't need a majority opin-
> ion to make change. Indeed, it takes only a small portion of shoppers
> – as few as one person in ten – changing buying habits for companies
> to stand up and take notice.

GlobeScan's client-specific research repeatedly confirms – whether it's a green consumer product, a green electricity offer, or other sustainability product or service – that at least 10% of the market now actively choose products with sustainability attributes. In the case of one US client, the size of their "active green consumer" segment grew 50% between 2008 and 2010 – and of course their sales figures confirm this. This has had a big impact in terms of their market share and value creation.

But it's not only leading consumer companies who are recognizing the growth and importance of ethical consumption. It's interesting to see that even the mainstream consumer protection movement has identified and is responding to this theme.

Thirty years ago, the modern consumer movement began encouraging people to become active consumers, meaning consumers who would stand up to the companies to demand higher quality, better pricing, and other attributes that at the time were critical to the development of an orderly

---

3   This was the US version of the landmark book by John Elkington and Julia
     Hailes, *The Green Consumer Guide* (Gollancz, 1988).

and responsible consumer marketplace. While this thrust is still under way in some of the emerging economies such as China and India, there is today a new active consumer movement happening from the ground up that consumer associations around the world have recognized and are responding to.

Consumers International, "the global voice for consumers," represents 220 consumer unions, consumer reports. and other consumer associations across the world, with over 4 million members in total. I had the pleasure of presenting to the International Board of Consumers International in London in 2007, at which time they adopted a new long-term strategy that included aggressively promoting what they called "sustainable consumers;" in other words consumers that would act in the marketplace with their intention of improving the environment and improving social conditions in their country and in the country of origin of their products and services. Consumers International has been very active ever since, including working with governments and international agencies to put in place the product testing and consumer protection measures needed for a well-functioning ethical marketplace.

Will the current ethical consumer phenomenon achieve truly game-changing proportions and last more than a few years, unlike the experience of the 1990s? To answer this I go back 20 years when we convinced a forest company to build their next pulp mill in Los Angeles (using large quantities of recycled paper) rather than in the Pacific Northwest (using harvested wood pulp). To do so, they had to be convinced that the recycling behavior of that time was deeper and more mature than that of 20 years earlier (in the 1960s) when it came and went and wasn't a big market force. We were able to convince them, through research findings, that recycling behavior was real and going to be sustained.

GlobeScan's data and instincts as pollsters say the same thing today about the ethical consumer phenomenon. It has momentum and endurance, especially around key drivers of consumer concern such as climate, water, and energy.

Part of the reason for our confidence in the enduring strength of the ethical consumer is that our analysis shows they aren't alone. There is an equally large segment of consumers who also think holistically about the challenges we face, have just as developed concerns as citizens, yet are not currently acting on these concerns in the marketplace. What holds some of them back is not feeling powerful as individual consumers; but they do feel very collectively empowered acting in concert with other consumers. Others in this

FIGURE 37 Have rewarded companies seen as socially responsible
OECD vs. non-OECD countries,* August 1999–February 2015

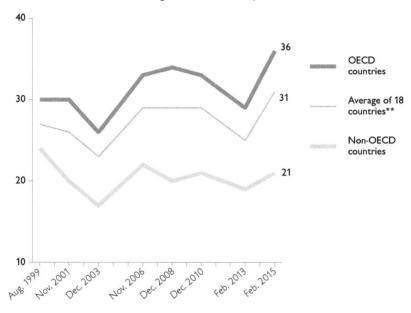

*OECD countries include Australia, Canada, Chile, France, Germany, Greece, Mexico, South Korea, Spain, Turkey, UK, and USA; non-OECD countries include Argentina, Brazil, China, India, Indonesia, and Nigeria.

**Includes Argentina, Australia, Brazil, Canada, Chile, China, France, Germany, Greece, India, Indonesia, Mexico, Nigeria, South Korea, Spain, Turkey, UK, and USA. Not all countries were asked in all years.

segment hold back because they don't want to be the "chump" that does the right thing in the supermarket while many others continue to buy products that are damaging to the planet and society. We have called this segment the "Demanding Regulators" because their analysis leads them to believe that stronger legislation or wholesale "choice editing" by manufacturers (i.e., removing more damaging products from shelves) is the most effective way forward. As the profile of ethical products and ethical consumption grows, consumers in this segment will increasingly become active as ethical consumers.

In the aftermath of the global financial crisis, when the public is calling for greater oversight and involvement in the economy by their governments, it will be interesting to see how the Demanding Regulators segment – in most countries every bit as big as the ethical consumer segment – will begin to respond to opportunities to be consistent between their concerns and their actions. Consistency is something that psychological literature suggests is a human need.

But the real tipping point in the consumer marketplace will come, I would predict, when the survival instinct of the species gets more fully activated and engaged; probably well before 2020 and probably linked to the water and climate issues.

In the meantime, those of us who work closely with leading companies know how much is already changing "under the hood" with greener product formulations and more ethical supply chains – progress that is seldom communicated to the casual consumer (for fear of attracting vocal critics). Many years of hard work in the automotive industry, for example, is only now becoming evident to consumers through the launch of many more vehicles with electric or highly efficient diesel engines. Indeed, any consumer-facing companies not readying themselves for this tipping point may well not survive into the 2020s.

Certainly scientists are suggesting that the planet is going to continue to talk to humans about climate change, through things such as 100-year droughts, mile-wide tornadoes, species extinctions, and Texas-sized icebergs. This, together with the rising concerns about water availability and quality, will ensure a steady deepening of ethical consumerism.

A closer look at GlobeScan's latest research into ethical consumption shows a significant uptick in the percentage of consumers in OECD countries rewarding socially responsible companies with their business or advocacy (Fig. 37).

Where might such renewed ethical consumer shifts first manifest? And how might companies and governments take advantage of the inherent opportunities?

Conventional wisdom has it that Western democracies are the global hegemons when it comes to influencing lifestyles and consumer behavior; and indeed Figure 37 shows OECD consumers continuing to lead. But there is evidence to suggest we are closer to the day when a new "Asian modernity" might sweep the world, as the increasing empowerment of non-OECD consumers suggests (Fig. 35).

GlobeScan's most recent global research on consumerism, conducted in early 2014 together with the US brand consultancy BBMG, has identified a significant market segment we call the "Aspirationals" that is well

FIGURE 38   Percentage of population who are aspirationals
21 countries, 2014

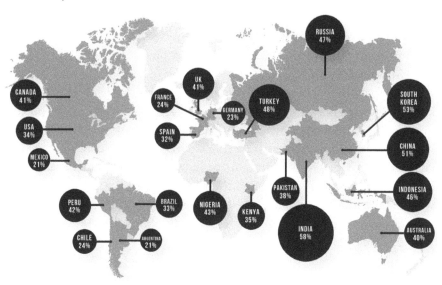

distributed across 21 countries studied,[4] but overrepresented in China and India (Fig. 38). The size and profile of this psychographic segment suggests they will very much determine what the future looks like (the percentages presented in this figure have not yet been adjusted to "real market numbers").

Aspirational consumers are characterized by their love of shopping and style, desire for responsible consumption, and trust in brands that act in the best interest of society. They are empowered, young, and urban shoppers.

Given their numbers (51% of Chinese, 58% of Indian, and 34% of American consumers), Aspirationals are a significant market segment. Given their high level of social engagement both on- and offline, they are more likely than others to shape the societal norms in their countries – they are a cultural force. And given their upward mobility, they are in the process of uniting style, social status, and sustainability values to *redefine consumption* and modernity.

While Aspirationals are defined the same worldwide – built on how consumers answer an extensive set of attitudinal and behavioral questions

4   GlobeScan and its national research partners interviewed random samples of 1,000 consumers in each country in person or by telephone during January to April 2014. The national results are considered accurate to within 3.5%, 19 times out of 20.

– the segment clearly manifests differently in different markets. In emerging economies, Aspirationals are currently more consumed by consumption, caught up as they are in burgeoning markets and new wealth. Yet their higher environmental and social concerns have them looking for and responding to more responsible choices.

In industrialized countries, Aspirationals tend more toward post-material values and behaviors. Some are looking to get their consuming behavior consistent with their concerns as citizens (e.g., buying electric cars); others are motivated by doing more with less (e.g., using car-sharing services).

As with other consumers, peer identity and group norms are key motivating factors for Aspirationals. They are actually quite a tribal lot. This is especially true in key Asian markets such as China where conspicuous consumption and social "face" are both important and explicit. Easier to miss is the other side of the Chinese mind-set – a strong, long-term, collective aspiration toward social and environmental progress.

Above all, Aspirational consumers everywhere want to be part of the solution, and they are ready to let companies lead. So, opportunity clearly knocks.

Wherever they are in the world, Aspirationals could well be the best thing we have going for solving some of our intractable global challenges. So what's really needed is for progressive companies and governments to treat this consumer segment as the precious resource that it is. And this is beginning to happen.

Opportunities

How might a business or government act if it wanted to convert the Aspirational segment's latent demand into real solutions for our global challenges, our global economy, and their own bottom line?

1. **"Sharing economy" solutions.** Market offers within what has been variously called the sharing, collaborative or "We" economy are particularly well suited to Aspirationals in both emerging and industrial economies.

    In emerging markets, sharing a car, washing machine, or other major appliance delivers the consumer benefit sooner than they could have managed on their own, while greatly reducing its footprint (in both ecological and household budget terms). But they need to be stylish offers such as BMW's electric "i Series" automobiles.

In industrial economies, a key selling feature of sharing is getting to use a higher-quality car, appliance, or tool than a consumer would buy themselves, without the hassle of ownership.

The Aspirational segment is key not just for changing cultural norms to be more conducive to sharing, but by making it "cool" (as urban "Millennials" have done for car-sharing services such as Zipcar).

2. **Collaborative consumer engagement.** Aspirationals respond enthusiastically to opportunities for meeting people like themselves and taking collective action. Brands that find ways to leverage individual actions into collective impacts across their entire consumer base can create the modern equivalent of "brand loyalty."

   Unilever's "Project Sunlight" is an excellent case in point. Focused on instilling more sustainable behavior by parents and their children across the world, the initiative recorded 83 million "Acts of Sunlight" recorded by consumers on its website after only six months. Other corporate platforms that are well positioned to engage Aspirationals include British Telecom's "Better Future," Hewlett-Packard's "Living Progress," McDonald's "Together for Good," Marks & Spencer's "Plan A," and The Walt Disney Company's "Be Inspired."

3. **Start in Asian markets.** Entrepreneurs and intrapreneurs with clean technology solutions for consumers will get earlier traction in emerging markets in the foreseeable future.

   Research suggests serious amounts of yuans and rupees are being and will be spent on people- and planet-friendly choices, even if that's not the case just now for dollars and pounds. Asia is where the cleantech market is alive and well today.

4. **A nudge from government.** Finally, there is a clear opportunity and role for governments at all levels to harness the potential of Aspirationals. While not essential, well-focused government interventions and leadership always help to mobilize a latent consumer readiness to act in new ways. People know that government and business institutions can leverage larger change than they can as consumers; the public needs to see these institutions playing their part.

In conclusion, we believe Aspirationals provide the opportunity for unlocking the market for sustainable product and service offerings, and to propagate the new business models needed to propel economies forward.

Brands and companies that successfully tap the power of this segment will be big winners. And in so doing, they will help redefine modernity in more sustainable terms and thereby help address humanity's challenges. They should grasp the opportunity.

Summary

- GlobeScan's research suggests that the "Five Ps of Marketing" (product, price, place, promotion, and people) are no longer sufficient to ensure business success. A sixth P is needed: let's call it "purpose" – the broad societal good the company and its products and services are meant to help accomplish; or call it "principles" – the standards of moral or ethical decision-making used in the business.

- This sixth P is needed to respond to one of the most noteworthy trends that we've seen over the past decade: the inexorable rise of the ethical consumer.

- The rise of ethical consumerism right through the Great Recession is significant because it goes against the whole thrust and weight of the consumer society as it has been practiced over the last 30 years, which has encouraged people to see themselves as consumers above citizens, seeking satisfaction and salvation in consuming ever greater volumes of stuff.

- So the fact that one in five or more citizens, in both rich and emerging economies, are refusing to narrowly define themselves as consumers and are integrating their values as citizens into their purchase decisions to an historical extent, is significant.

- The continuing market success of Fairtrade-labeled goods is a prime example of the strength of this market segment, as are the significant moves by major companies including Unilever and Procter & Gamble to take competitive advantage of the ethical consumer phenomenon.

- GlobeScan's most recent global research on consumerism, conducted with the US brand consultancy BBMG, has formulated a more powerful way of identifying consumers who will actually buy more human- and planet-friendly products – a significant market segment we call the Aspirationals. These consumers are characterized by their love of shopping and style, desire for responsible consumption, and trust in brands that act in the best interest of society. They could well be the best thing we have going for solving some of our intractable global challenges.

- How might companies and governments take advantage of the inherent opportunities? First and foremost, progressive companies and governments need to treat this consumer segment as the precious resource that it is, collaboratively engage them, and offer them "sharing economy" solutions, perhaps starting in Asian rather than Western markets. And a well-designed nudge from governments would help too.

- Brands and companies that successfully tap the power of ethical consumers will be big winners. And in so doing, they will help redefine modernity in more sustainable terms and thereby help address humanity's challenges. They should grasp the opportunity.

10
A civil society renaissance?

Never doubt that a small group of thoughtful, committed citizens can change the world; indeed, it's the only thing that ever has.

Margaret Mead, American anthropologist

Business, labour and civil society organizations have skills and resources that are vital in helping to build a more robust global community.

Kofi Annan, former Secretary-General of the UN, 2001

The relative decline in the public's regard for the nation-state, demonstrated in part by declining levels of trust in national governments over the last decade, has led to another important phenomenon in the world: the rise of non-state actors.

From al Qaeda to Walmart and the Gates Foundation to Transparency International, non-state actors are playing increasingly pivotal roles in the world; roles that governments once played. The most trusted category of non-state actors is known collectively as "civil society."[1] Made up mainly of NGOs and social movements, these groups have more power in today's soft-power world than they've ever had before (Fig. 39).

It can be argued that government bureaucrats and their political masters share some of the blame for this phenomenon. They've become increasingly ineffective at delivering on their critical roles in society, especially in the areas of moral leadership and addressing long-term problems.

As a result of these and many other factors, the legitimacy of governments has been badly eroded, and bureaucrats and politicians have become some

---

1   According to Wikipedia, "Civil Society is the arena outside the family, the state, and the market where people associate to advance common interests."

FIGURE 39　Net trust* in institutions
Average of 24 countries,** 2014

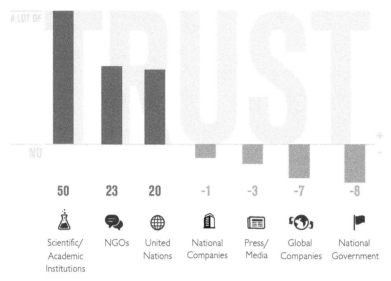

Scientific/ Academic Institutions	NGOs	United Nations	National Companies	Press/ Media	Global Companies	National Government
50	23	20	-1	-3	-7	-8

*"A lot of trust" and "Some trust" minus "Not much trust" and "No trust at all"
**Includes Argentina, Australia, Brazil, Canada, Chile, China, France, Germany, Ghana, Greece, India, Indonesia, Israel, Kenya, Mexico, Nigeria, Pakistan, Peru, Russia, S. Korea, Spain, Turkey, the UK, and the USA.

of the least-trusted leaders, far less respected than NGO leaders or even business leaders.

The 2003 World Economic Forum Poll across 15 countries explored public trust in a range of different leaders, and found NGO leaders were most trusted (Fig. 40).

In 2010, GlobeScan found three in five citizens across 20 countries believed that business leaders offered better leadership for the future than today's political leaders.

But the continuing decline of the nation-state and rise of non-state actors will also be due to the characteristic powers of nation-states becoming less relevant in the world as it is evolving.

The ability to raise an army and declare war has long been a defining power of the nation-state. But in tomorrow's soft-power, war-weary world, this will no longer necessarily be an advantage nor a defining element of effective power, as we've already seen in the last decade. Independent experts suggest that the so-called "war on terror" is most effectively fought through improved policing in failed states and regions rather than with armies.

FIGURE 40 Trust in leaders

"A lot" and "Some trust," average across all 15 countries surveyed,* November 2002

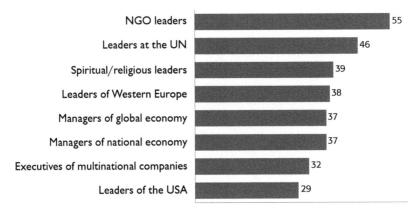

NGO leaders	55
Leaders at the UN	46
Spiritual/religious leaders	39
Leaders of Western Europe	38
Managers of global economy	37
Managers of national economy	37
Executives of multinational companies	32
Leaders of the USA	29

*Countries include Argentina, Canada, Germany, India, Italy, Japan, Mexico, Netherlands, Nigeria, Qatar, Russia, S. Korea, Turkey, the UK, and the USA.

Similarly, the nation-state's power to issue passports and levy taxes may become less relevant in future, as it has already begun to do in the EU. A question that GlobeScan has been asking since the turn of the century is portrayed in Figure 41, showing a marked upward trend in the percentage of citizens across 16 countries who agree they see themselves "more as a global citizen than a citizen of my country," especially in non-OECD countries. If this trend continues, which nation-state will be able to issue a global passport?

While nationally levied taxes will clearly continue for a very long time, the current international negotiations toward globally harmonized carbon taxes, or other "global economic instruments" such as tradable emission permits, suggest that even this power may migrate to extra-state bodies in the future, as it has been doing in the EU. The renewed promotion (by France and others) of a Tobin Tax on international financial transactions is another example, where tax revenue would go to support global governance bodies.

The increasing array of multinational processes and negotiations aimed at creating extra-national laws or treaties to address the growing number of global and transboundary problems presents an additional challenge for the nation-state. While these global processes are often "controlled" by nation-states via the UN or its array of sister global institutions, it is likely that every success will be attributed by the public to the UN and every failure of negotiations will be blamed on certain intransigent nation-states. In

FIGURE 41   I see myself more as a global citizen than a citizen of my country
"Agree," OECD vs. non-OECD countries,* December 2000–February 2015

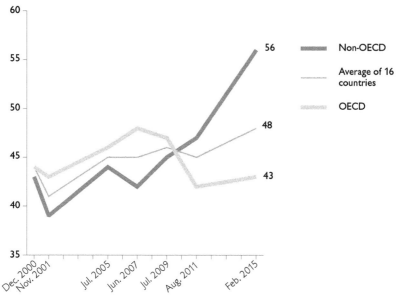

*OECD countries include Canada, Chile, France, Germany, Mexico, Spain, Turkey, UK, and USA;
non-OECD countries include Brazil, China, India, Indonesia, Kenya, Nigeria, and Russia.

Not all countries were asked in all years.

our judgment, all of this will continue to slowly erode the legitimacy and power of the nation-state.

While it is obviously decades too early to see the real demotion of the nation-state to second-tier actor, it is clear that the power and legitimacy of non-state actors is very much a force in today's world.

When GlobeScan asked 20,000 citizens around the world in the summer of 2008 who was winning the war on terror, al Qaeda or the USA, almost half (47%) said neither side was winning. Only one in five (20%) thought the USA was winning, and 10% said this non-state actor with no fixed address was beating the world's mightiest nation-state. While the 2011 killing of Osama Bin Laden by US special forces may have moderated this view, few would argue with the declining efficacy of armies, and therefore nation-states, in the 21st century.

OK, so NGO leaders are trusted, but how involved should they be in important international negotiations? GlobeScan asked people in G20 countries in November 2001 whether they agreed that, "Leaders of major environmental and social non-government organizations should be excluded when

FIGURE 42   Unelected NGO leaders should be excluded from official globalization negotiations
Average of G20 countries,* November 2001

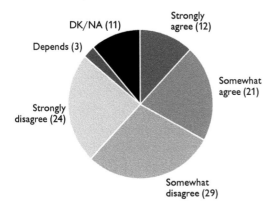

DK/NA (11)

Strongly agree (12)

Depends (3)

Somewhat agree (21)

Strongly disagree (24)

Somewhat disagree (29)

*Countries include Argentina, Australia, Brazil, Canada, China, France, Germany, India, Indonesia, Japan, Mexico, Russia, S. Africa, S. Korea, Turkey, the UK, and the USA.

government leaders negotiate globalization agreements, because they are not widely elected," a majority of 53% disagreed, indicating a strong constituency for NGOs at a time when police lines were keeping their members from participating in multilateral negotiations and meetings (Fig. 42).

My favorite civil society story is from the World Economic Forum's annual meeting in New York in 2002, where I participated in a round-table discussion on globalization. Niall FitzGerald, then Chief Executive of Unilever, was the discussion starter at our table. He gave a wonderfully balanced and thoughtful assessment of the state of globalization. After he was finished, an NGO leader from the global South leaned over to me and asked, "What NGO is he from?"

A few years later I was able to share this story with Niall when he was Chairman of Reuters. He listened with delight, and when I had finished he said, "That's good!" I agreed that it is very good to be able to blur the lines between two worlds seemingly at odds. While Niall is not alone in being able to do this, there are still too few business or indeed NGO leaders like him. In my judgment this is the major limiting factor keeping civil society from playing a larger role in the world because it keeps operational partnerships between business and NGOs from coming to scale – something I would suggest the world needs in order to move forward.

Fortunately, there are a good number of senior leaders who have switched between NGOs and the corporate world. Gerd Leipold, a previous Executive

Director of Greenpeace International, started his career in the corporate world of accounting. Helio Mattar, one of the seven *éminences grises* who created the World Social Forum, used to run General Electric Brazil, and now runs the Akatu Foundation focused on conscious consumption. I went from being a junior executive at 3M Company to being a founding director of Friends of the Earth Canada/Les Amis de la Terre, back in the 1970s. Countless NGO up-and-comers have moved the other way, being hired by global companies to help them be more effective with stakeholder relations.

Perhaps this is why, from my own observations, when corporate and NGO leaders meet to discuss global problems there is usually significant agreement on the key points of causes and solutions. It is when government leaders then join the discussion that things can break down, mainly I think due to what Buddhists would call the "habit energy" of past ways of talking with governments, back in the old paradigm when nation-states had the moral authority to tell everyone else what to do.

In the continuing absence of effective international governance and adequate global institutions, I predict the emergence of multi-sectoral "coalitions of the willing" focused on specific issues – numerous non-state actors working in concert with some nation-states and relevant UN agencies to achieve desired ends.

Given the negative connotations of "coalitions of the willing" because of the term's highly publicized first use by the Bush administration to give legitimacy to its invasion of Iraq in defiance of the UN, I prefer to use the equivalent Arabic term *tahalouf* – a more fitting name for this important element of future global governance.

The first major *tahalouf* at a global scale was the International Campaign to Ban Landmines. Launched in 1992 by a coalition that ultimately involved 1,400 civil society organizations in 80 countries, it attracted the active partnership of the Canadian government in helping to bring other nation-states to the table. The process culminated in December 1997, when 122 countries signed the Anti-Personnel Mine Ban Convention in Ottawa. For the first time in history, a conventional weapon in widespread use had been comprehensively prohibited, and it only took five years. This unique initiative received appropriate recognition when it was awarded the 1997 Nobel Prize for Peace. The Nobel Committee recognized not only the achievement of the ban, but also the promise of the model created by the ban movement. The committee concluded: "As a model for similar processes in the future, it could prove of decisive importance to the international effort for disarmament and peace." I would argue the model has even broader applications.

One of the more recent *tahaloufs* is the Global Water Challenge. Formed in 2007, its mission is to generate a global movement to meet the urgent need for universal access to safe water and sanitation by spurring collective awareness and investment in innovation by corporate, public, and non-governmental actors. The founding partners included Coca-Cola and the World Wide Fund for Nature. The first meeting was hosted by the US State Department, and the initiative has been greatly assisted by Ted Turner's UN Foundation.

An early Challenge success has been enlisting the Washington lobbying efforts of its member companies (including Dow, Procter & Gamble, and Levis as well as Coca-Cola) to help ensure passage of the US Water for the Poor Act in 2007. The Act allocates US$300 million a year to assisting developing country governments to improve water infrastructure and education. Perhaps their most promising initiative is identifying social entrepreneurs and technologies in need of venture capital to achieve their potential impact on improving access to water and sanitation, and then finding matching sources of private capital for them.

More recently, the Global Water Challenge has initiated RAIN (Replenish Africa Initiative) to improve access to safe water for 6 million people in Africa by 2020. RAIN is backed by an 11-year commitment by TCCAF (the Coca-Cola Africa Foundation) and made possible through the support of more than 140 partners who provide development expertise and additional resources required to implement the projects sustainably. To date, RAIN has made investments to reach 2 million people with sustainable, safe water access in 37 of Africa's 55 countries by the end of 2015. In addition to safe water and sanitation access, RAIN's 2020 commitment will deliver programming to uplift women, youth, and their families by creating employment opportunities through water, providing training in water and business management, and supporting water enterprise.

While they themselves see their work as only a stepping-stone toward universal access, the Global Water Challenge in my judgment has the potential to generate the magnitude of action necessary to achieve the UN's Millennium Development Goal of halving the number of people without access to sanitation services. Certainly governments have been unsuccessful in doing it on their own.

Part of the potency of civil society is its very diversity and vastness. The Union of International Associations in Brussels, the major authority on global civil society since it began cataloging the field in 1907, has 130,000 entries in its 2012 catalog of international associations of civil society organizations alone. Some of these associations in turn have thousands of member NGOs each, and many associations have hundreds of NGO members.

Back in 2003, Professor Mary Kaldor at the London School of Economics estimated that over 20 million people were involved in civil society organizations worldwide, including members of social movements, the least structured of such organizations. Enabled by the internet, social movements burst onto the scene in the 1990s mainly to fight against economic globalization (e.g., the World Social Forum, Third World Network, etc.). They have since grown so quickly that by 2015 one of them on its own – avaaz.org – claims 40 million members across 190 countries. This online community campaigns on a range of issues including human rights, climate change, and access to water.

Figure 39 shows that the most trusted societal institutions are scientific and academic institutions and NGOs. The latter finding is corroborated by the annual Trust Barometer produced by public relations firm Edelman (which doesn't rate scientific or academic institutions). Their 2014 online consumer survey across 27 countries found: "NGOs remain the most trusted institution globally."[2]

Global NGOs have never had the trust they have today, and therefore the soft power. In part, this is because they are values-driven organizations in an increasingly values-driven world. They are also non-state actors in a world looking for alternatives to governments that are seen to be unresponsive, ineffective, or corrupt. Finally, it is because the issues they are addressing – poverty, human rights, environmental preservation – are transboundary in nature (and thus poorly suited to being solved by nation-states) and have issue constituencies larger than ever before.

GlobeScan has tracked what the global public sees as the most serious global problems for the last 15 years. In Figure 43, only the percentage of people who say a problem is "very serious" is shown. Until recently overtaken by growing concern over terrorism, extreme poverty has had particular salience among the global issues we have been tracking, peaking in 2009/10.

The main point from this chart is that, seven years into the Great Recession with no real economic recovery in sight, the state of the global

---

2   See http://www.edelman.com/insights/intellectual-property/2014-edelman-trust-barometer/.

FIGURE 43 Seriousness of global problems
"Very serious," average of 17 tracking countries,* December 2000–February 2015

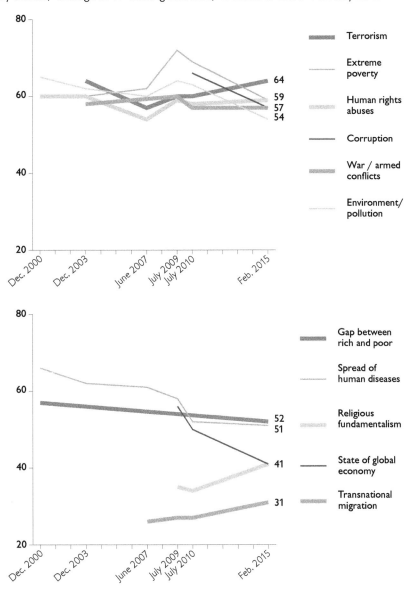

*Tracking countries include Brazil, Canada, Chile, China, France, Germany, India, Indonesia, Italy, Kenya, Mexico, Nigeria, Russia, Spain, Turkey, UK, and USA.

economy is seen as a significantly less serious concern to people than many of the issues addressed by NGOs, including extreme poverty, human rights abuses, environmental pollution, and the gap between rich and poor.

In fact, we saw poverty take off as an issue following September 11, 2001, as covered in Chapter 11. Now that the war on terror has returned as the war on ISIS, there is a need for more inspired leadership to define a replacement focus of concerted global action. This is a huge opportunity for civil society, and global NGOs in particular, to outline a compelling whole-system approach to the problem of terrorism, with a heavy emphasis on reducing poverty and injustice.

Another opportunity for civil society to contribute to positive change in the world, where NGOs and companies could work effectively together, is the area of fairer trade. "Fairtrade" is both the kind of international trade most people want and the brand name used to designate products for which the producers in developing nations are guaranteed fair prices. Our research suggests it has one of the largest growth potentials of any brand in the world.

As outlined in Chapter 9, consumers in both rich and poor countries are looking past price and quality to the practices and ethics behind the products they purchase. Fairtrade products are already enjoying some of the largest sales growth in the food category in many European and North American markets, continuing through the Great Recession.

While NGOs are often focused on gaining over 50% popular support for their campaigns, shifting purchases by only a couple of percentage points from traditional products to Fairtrade-branded products will be all that is necessary to interest leading companies in helping to expand the trend to ever higher percentages, with material effects on poverty alleviation and the quality of life in developing countries – helping create a more secure and peaceful world.

The coffee category is already showing the way. After pioneering promotion and selling efforts by NGOs and small coffee retailers, the growth in sales of Fairtrade coffee has recently attracted the involvement of the largest global seller of coffee: Nestlé now offers Fairtrade-certified coffee, following earlier moves by Starbucks. This mainstreaming will help reverse the long-term decline in the price paid to coffee producers. Cadbury's recent embrace of Fairtrade chocolate across its brands is doing the same in the sweets category.

❖

Another indication of the strength of civil society is that major international NGOs such as Oxfam, Greenpeace, and Transparency International have brand values as high as those of major global companies.[3]

These developments, together with the rise of philanthropy among an aging population in the West, mean that much is possible, but it is up to civil society leaders and boards of directors to rise to the challenges this opportunity presents.

A well-respected voice in the international NGO sector, Burkhard Gnärig, Executive Director of the International Civil Society Centre in Berlin, points in his recent book[4] to "the complex, slow and often ineffective global governance of most international civil society organizations" as a barrier to innovation in the sector, calling it "the sector where participatory decision-making and insufficiently empowered leaders are the norm rather than the exception."

It's not an overstatement to say that the current generation of NGO leaders, and the next, will determine the role NGOs play in the world for a long time to come. The next decade has the potential to see a great resorting of roles in society, given low levels of trust and increased demands for transparency and accountability by the public and stakeholders.

Both leading companies and NGOs have begun addressing this challenge by regularly reporting on a wide range of factors concerning their governance as well as their social and environmental impacts. Charitable foundations are also taking some significant strides in this direction and will need to take more.

Reflecting the prior efforts of business, the IANGO (International Advocacy NGO network) Accountability Charter was a promising signal that at least 25 major global NGOs were willing to step up to the inevitable legitimacy, governance, and transparency challenges that come with an expanded role. I had the pleasure of speaking at the launch event for the Charter in London in December 2006 where the signatories agreed to hold themselves to codified standards and publicly report on their compliance across nine key areas, including responsible advocacy and ethical fundraising.

But increased efficacy and professionalism within NGOs will also be necessary to live up to the opportunities. Excellent campaigning and effective partnering will be the key factors for success. Both will require the

---

3   According to the annual Edelman Trust Barometer, produced by Edelman Public Relations, New York City.

4   Burkhard Gnärig, *The Hedgehog and the Beetle: Disruption and Innovation in the Civil Society Sector* (International Civil Society Centre, 2015).

FIGURE 44   Support for environmental and social groups' actions
Average of 16 countries,* August 2012

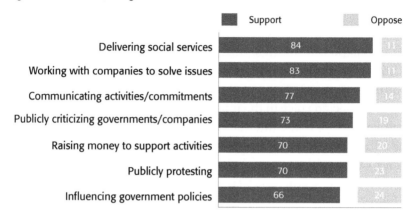

*Includes Australia, Brazil,Canada, China, Germany, India, Indonesia, Kenya, Mexico, Nigeria, Pakistan, Peru, Spain, Turkey, UK, and USA

The white space in this chart represents "Depends" and "DK/NA."

suppression of organizational ego in order to coordinate efforts more effectively with others for maximum effect. Only this will bring the impact of NGOs on issues up to the scale required. Without demonstrated efficacy, trust is not enough for NGOs to earn a broader societal role: they must demonstrate they can make a real difference on broadly held societal goals.

A good example of the needed innovation and collaboration among NGOs is the START Network, a consortium of over 20 leading humanitarian NGOs working to strengthen the humanitarian aid system. They are focused on three key initiatives: an innovative quick-response fund for humanitarian crises, building civil society's on-the-ground capacity, and building a platform for incubating innovative humanitarian solutions. As I was waiting to deliver a keynote speech at START's annual conference in London in May 2015, I was pleased to hear a number of participants speak of the need for new ground-up accountability mechanisms for their sector, whereby the very people experiencing a humanitarian emergency could rate how well the humanitarian system is meeting their needs.

In my remarks, I reinforced the need for this bottom-up accountability by reporting that, when GlobeScan last asked the public across 16 countries in 2012 why they don't trust NGOs, they mentioned NGOs' lack of impact as one of their major reasons. So efficacy is key for NGOs to demonstrate. I believe this will increasingly drive NGOs to partnerships with other organizations, including companies.

In the same 2012 survey across 16 countries, GlobeScan asked citizens their degree of support for specific NGO activities. Figure 44 shows that the public most supports the kinds of direct social service delivered by humanitarian (and many other) NGOs, as well as partnerships with business.

Partnerships with business can be particularly powerful because they link values and lofty goals directly with extensive implementation capacity. Such partnerships also deliver the added benefit of helping NGOs learn to be more businesslike and accountable. While there have been some notable successes (e.g., GlaxoSmithKline and Save the Children's partnership to save the lives of a million children; Unilever and the World Wide Fund for Nature on the Marine Stewardship Council), business leaders appear to be falling back from being interested in partnering with NGOs. There is a need for leaders on both sides to make such partnerships work, including the wider use of the social enterprise business model.

Civil society could still fail to measure up to its potential. Coming to scale must be everyone's rallying cry. Every organization can point to some examples of their positive impact, but no organization can honestly say it is making enough of a difference given the size of our challenges and the magnitude of human aspirations. Moderating organizational (and personal) egos and collaborating more with others on campaigns and services will be vital.

But at the end of the day, trust is the oxygen of the new millennium. And trust is civil society's most precious commodity. While NGO leaders have done well to retain high trust levels over the last decade, if civil society organizations stumble and lose public trust, they will lose everything.

Summary

- The relative decline in public regard for the nation-state, demonstrated in part by historically low levels of trust in national governments over the last decade, has led to another important phenomenon in the world: the rise of non-state actors.

- The most trusted category of non-state actors is known collectively as "civil society." Comprised mainly of NGOs and social movements, these groups have more power in today's soft-power world than they've ever had.

- According to the Edelman Trust Barometer, major international NGOs such as Oxfam, Greenpeace, and Transparency International have brand values as high as those of major global companies.

- NGOs also have issue constituencies larger than ever before because the issues they are addressing – poverty, human rights, environmental preservation – are transboundary in nature (and thus poorly suited to being solved by nation-states) and seen as very serious by the public.

- In 2015, seven years into the Great Recession and with no real recovery in sight, the state of the global economy is seen as a significantly less serious concern to global citizens than many of the issues addressed by NGOs, including extreme poverty, human rights abuses, environmental pollution, and the gap between rich and poor.

- All of these developments, together with the rise of philanthropy among an aging population in the West, mean that a civil society renaissance is possible, but it is up to civil society leaders and boards of directors to rise to the challenges this opportunity presents.

- In the continuing absence of effective international governance and adequate global institutions, I predict the emergence of multi-sectoral "coalitions of the willing," or *tahaloufs*, focused on specific issues – numerous NGOs working in concert with some leadership companies, nation-states and relevant UN agencies to achieve desired ends (as with the 1992 International Campaign to Ban Landmines).

- Another opportunity for civil society to contribute to positive change in the world, and where NGOs and companies could work effectively together, is the area of fairer trade.

- The next decade has the potential to see a great resorting of roles in society, given low levels of trust and increased demands for transparency and accountability by the public and stakeholders. It's not an overstatement to say that the current generation of NGO leaders, and the next, will determine the role NGOs play in the world for a long time to come.

- Civil society could still fail to measure up to its potential. Coming to scale must be everyone's rallying cry. Moderating organizational (and personal) egos and collaborating more with others on campaigns and services will be vital. Public trust must be retained. If civil society organizations stumble and lose public trust, they will lose everything.

11
War on terror to war on poverty?

In today's globalized world, if you don't visit a bad neighborhood, it
will visit you.

Tom Friedman, *New York Times*, 2003

War on anything is stupid.

Jack Kornfield, American Buddhist leader, 2007

The Obama Administration's burying of the term "war on terror" in 2013
was an inevitable result of public opinion trends over the last decade. The
fact that the same administration relaunched the war on terror as the war
on ISIS two years later was disheartening to those of us who see war as a
hugely ineffective and expensive way of trying to solve anything. The question is, what rallying cry might replace warfare and challenge humanity to
become all it can be? And who is going to lead on this?

A friend of mine with 25 years' service as a policeman tells me that the
American "war on drugs" was declared in 1904 when 4% of the American
population was addicted to heroin. (It was then relaunched by Richard
Nixon in 1971.) After a hundred years of this war, with untold billions of dollars spent and millions of lives affected through drug eradication programs
in Latin America and soft-drug-related incarceration in America, he claims
that about the same percentage of Americans are today addicted to heroin or similar drugs. After a quarter-century on the beat, my friend favors
outright legalization of all drugs, including heroin, saying it will drastically
reduce the crime rate.

Interestingly, in 2011, a high-powered UN group of eminent persons
agreed it is time for governments to find new ways to deal with the world's
drug problem. "The fact is that the war on drugs has failed, with devastating

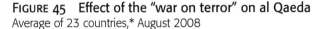

FIGURE 45   Effect of the "war on terror" on al Qaeda
Average of 23 countries,* August 2008

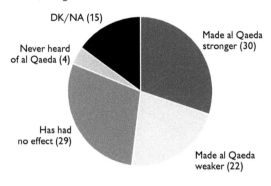

DK/NA (15)

Never heard
of al Qaeda (4)

Made al Qaeda
stronger (30)

Has had
no effect (29)

Made al Qaeda
weaker (22)

*Includes Australia, Brazil, Canada, China, Costa Rica, Egypt, France,
Germany, India, Indonesia, Italy, Kenya, Lebanon, Mexico, Nigeria,
Pakistan, Panama, Philippines, Russia, Turkey, UAE, UK, and USA

consequences for individuals and societies around the world," former Brazilian president Fernando Henrique Cardoso said at the unveiling of the report by the Global Commission on Drug Policy.[1]

Like the war on drugs, the war on terror is likely to be seen by historians as an understandable 20th-century response to the events of September 11, 2001, but a failure in both its strategy and execution.

GlobeScan's August 2008 23-nation poll for the BBC World Service (Fig. 45) revealed that, seven years after 9/11, the global public's most common view was that the USA's war on terror either had no effect on al Qaeda (29%) or indeed had made it stronger (30%). The fact that only one in five citizens in the countries surveyed (22%) thought that the war on terror had succeeded at one of its primary aims, to weaken al Qaeda, attracted a lot of media coverage worldwide.

Even in the USA, this 2008 poll found Americans divided about the success of the conflict with al Qaeda, with as many saying that it had made al Qaeda stronger (33%) as felt that it had succeeded in weakening it (34%).

These findings and recent history suggest that hard military power alone will not win 21st-century wars. The 2011 NATO withdrawal from Afghanistan

1   Along with Mr. Cardoso, the Global Commission on Drug Policy's members included former Colombian President Cesar Gaviria, former Mexican President Ernesto Zedillo, former US Secretary of State George Shultz, and former UN Secretary-General Kofi Annan.

FIGURE 46   The use of military force is the most effective way of reducing international terrorism

"Agree," OECD vs. non-OECD countries,* November 2001–February 2015

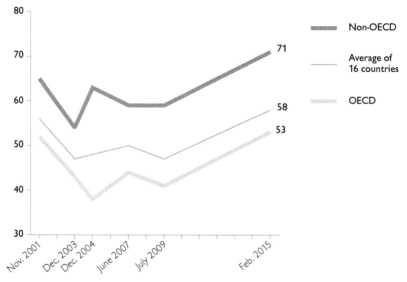

*OECD countries include Australia, Canada, Chile, France, Germany, Mexico, Spain, Turkey, UK, and USA; non-OECD countries include Brazil, China, India, Indonesia, Nigeria, and Russia.

Not all countries were asked in all years.

is another case in point. The January 2011 BBC World Service Poll found only 16% across G20 countries favored continued NATO attempts to win militarily, with most (40%) favoring "negotiating with the Taliban to include them in a new government there." Another 29% favored the immediate unconditional withdrawal of NATO forces.

Actually, until recently, there has been little evidence that many citizens around the world ever thought that a *war* on terror was the best way to address the problem of international terrorism.

GlobeScan first explored this early in 2002, when there was maximum solidarity on the subject of international terrorism. Even then, barely a majority (52%) of citizens of the industrialized countries surveyed agreed that "the use of military force is the most effective way of reducing international terrorism."

As Figure 46 shows, such support fell below 50% by 2004 and stayed there through 2009. The biggest fall occurred in America where the number believing in the effectiveness of military force dropped from 76% in 2002 to 48% in 2009.

FIGURE 47 Most important problem facing the world
Open-ended responses, USA and global respondents, July/August 2002

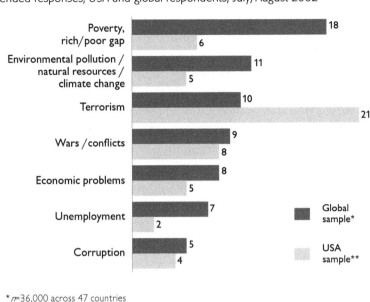

Poverty, rich/poor gap	Global: 18, USA: 6
Environmental pollution / natural resources / climate change	Global: 11, USA: 5
Terrorism	Global: 10, USA: 21
Wars /conflicts	Global: 9, USA: 8
Economic problems	Global: 8, USA: 5
Unemployment	Global: 7, USA: 2
Corruption	Global: 5, USA: 4

Global sample*

USA sample**

*n=36,000 across 47 countries

**n=1,000

Source: Gallup International/Environics International Ltd.

However, the recent military advances and acts of genocide by ISIS have raised support for military force across 16 tracking countries to its highest level recorded by GlobeScan in over a decade of tracking. This and other research findings suggest that citizens of both OECD and non-OECD countries are again supportive of military action. The historical trend suggests this will not last long.

Exploring the evolution of views over the last decade is instructive in predicting the future. In the wake of the 9/11 terrorist attacks, GlobeScan's research showed that, in addition to a genuine outflowing of grief and sympathy toward the USA, the global public's reaction was twofold: passive support for America striking back against al Qaeda bases and their Taliban protectors in Afghanistan; and active support for a renewed focus on global poverty reduction.

In a summer 2002 "Voice of the People" poll GlobeScan (then called Environics International) carried out in partnership with Gallup International, we asked 36,000 citizens across 47 countries to name what they saw as "the most important problem facing the world." The contrast between global opinion and the views of Americans was fascinating, as Figure 47 shows.

While Americans were perhaps understandably focused on terrorism, the rest of the world was focused on what some might call primary prevention against terrorism – poverty alleviation.

In these other countries, people wanted a war on poverty while America was focused on a war on terror.

This public focus on extreme poverty or the gap between rich and poor has tenaciously continued, with no end in sight. In the 2005 "Voice of the People" survey that Gallup International presented at the World Economic Forum in January 2006,[2] fully 28% of the global public spontaneously named "closing the rich/poor gap" or "eliminating poverty" as the most important issue for global leaders to address. While the question wording and country count was slightly different than in 2002, it suggests the poverty focus has not only continued but grew over the four years from 2002 to 2006.

GlobeScan's research confirms that the strength of concern and indeed self-interest about global poverty has continued. Figure 43 shows that extreme poverty held top position in our global issues table from 2007 until 2010 in terms of its rated seriousness, with seven in ten citizens rating it as "very serious" in 2009 and 2010, just ahead of "corruption," and significantly ahead of all ten other issues tested.

From all this research, we can conclude that millions of people around the world are very sympathetic with Tom Friedman's view that primary pre-vention ("fixing poor neighborhoods"), more than military force, is the best way to address the problem of terrorism.

Had America limited its military action to Afghanistan (rather than add-ing Iraq) and launched a soft-power initiative to remove the underpinnings of radicalism, the world would be a very different place today.

Rather than a world that today seems to invite the worst that people and countries have to offer, we could be closer to that very American of worlds where people are encouraged to offer up their best.

And what about today, now that ISIS has outdone al Qaeda in its brutality and ambition? GlobeScan's latest 2015 tracking (see Fig. 46) shows a majority of people (58%) now support military action to reduce terrorism. But that is not to say these same people have forgotten about poverty.

Figure 48 shows how global problems stack up differently in the minds of citizens of industrialized (OECD) and developing (non-OECD) countries in 2015. While terrorism is the most serious concern in OECD countries,

---

2   Gallup International's December 2005 "Voice of the People" survey interviewed 50,000 people across 68 countries.

FIGURE 48   Seriousness of global problems
"Very serious," OECD vs. non-OECD countries,* February 2015

OECD Countries

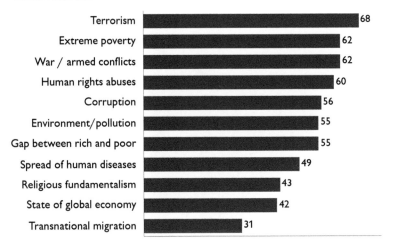

Non-OECD Countries

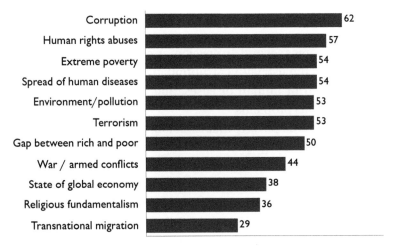

*OECD countries include Australia, Canada, Chile, France, Germany, Mexico, South Korea, Spain, Turkey, UK, and USA; non-OECD countries include China, Ghana, India, Indonesia, Kenya, Nigeria, Pakistan, and Peru.

FIGURE 49   Fairness of sharing of economic benefits and burdens
"Economic benefits and burdens have been shared fairly," OECD vs. non-OECD countries,* December 2007–February 2015

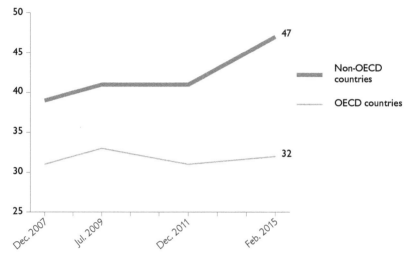

*OECD countries include Australia, Canada, Chile, France, Germany, Mexico, Spain, Turkey, UK, and USA; non-OECD countries include Brazil, China, India, Indonesia, Kenya, and Nigeria. Not all countries were asked in all years.

extreme poverty comes second. In developing countries, citizens rate terrorism halfway down the list, with corruption, human rights abuses, extreme poverty, the spread of human diseases, and environmental pollution all rated as more serious problems.

It is not only extreme poverty that is fueling conflict, it is also the widening gap between rich and poor. Even if the poor are not destitute, they cannot be constantly reminded of the relative wealth of others every day on television and in the tabloid media, without consequences.

The 2011 urban uprising by mainly poor black youths in the UK was the inevitable result of yawning inequity, leading to a broken social contract, leading to indiscriminate violence against a system in which they have no stake. Many of the youths interviewed during the unprecedented lawlessness and burning of businesses and shops across London and Birmingham justified their actions by saying it was only the rich and the police being targeted – the rich who were too rich compared with them and the police who were the instrument of the state in keeping them down.

Together with the uprisings across the Middle East, led by disgruntled youths, as well as in places such as Spain, Israel, and most notably America with the Occupy Wall Street movement, this all suggests more unrest to come. This is because, at the root of the gap between rich and poor, lies the issue of fairness and justice – the perceived lack of which generates uprisings, as human history has amply shown.

Not only do citizens of industrialized countries think their governments are being unfair with poorer countries in trade negotiations, they think their governments are not fairly distributing economic benefits and burdens within their own society. Figure 49 shows how views on economic fairness among citizens of OECD countries are stuck at very low levels, while in developing (non-OECD) countries, citizens are increasingly seeing economic fairness in their (still growing) economies.

Looking at specific countries where majorities of their citizens saw a lack of economic fairness in 2009, it appears quite predictive of mass protests that arose in 2011 starting with the Arab Spring (Egypt), the London riots (UK), and the Indignados (Spain), through to Occupy Wall Street (USA). With strong majorities of citizens continuing to see economic *un*fairness across OECD countries, the rich/poor gap will remain firmly on the political agenda in these countries, with further civil unrest likely to be seen in response to local or national conditions.

Clearly, citizens in many countries have been stirred up by fear and a sense of unfairness, in part through events and in part by political and religious leaders with questionable motives. As a wise man once said, "When people are afraid, they tend to make bad decisions." And our research suggests the war on terror along with the second (and third) Iraq war will be seen by history as mistakes.

But will a war on poverty be mounted instead of a war on terror? Certainly poverty as an issue has all the attributes needed for real progress to be achieved in our lifetime – indeed there has been much progress already, including achieving the Millennium Development Goal of halving extreme poverty between 1990 and 2015. Unfortunately, the UN estimates that 1.2 billion of our fellow humans still live on less than US$1.25 per day. Public opinion research suggests that poverty continues to have high levels of relevance, self-interest, and urgency in most countries. There are also perceived solutions available, with a growing belief that people, working together, can accomplish whatever we set out to do.

But even with today's high levels of personal commitment to help reduce global poverty and the rich/poor gap, unlocking significant amounts of money to fund such a war from national treasuries impoverished by bailouts and recession will be challenging to say the least.

The US Congressional Budget Office has estimated that US$1,300 billion will have been spent just on the second Iraq war. This is about twice what the entire world needed to spend in order to meet all the Millennium Development Goals agreed by all countries at the UN in September 2000. More than half these goals had not been fully achieved by the 2015 target.

So the easy money for a war on poverty is long gone. Some are now turning to innovative sources to fund needed poverty-alleviation initiatives including the Tobin Tax on international financial transactions and other global taxes on everything from air travel to shipping. Add to these initiatives various tax reform measures aimed at reducing the rich/poor gap through so-called "Robin Hood" taxes such as that being proposed by Warren Buffett in the USA. Where there's a will, there's a way, and it seems likely that there will be important innovations and breakthroughs. The first globally levied tax is likely to make it into the history books by the end of this decade.

Not only is money a challenge, so too is continuing public support for a war on poverty. While still supportive today, there is evidence of a rising, more bellicose us-and-them stance in some OECD countries, driven in some cases by a "fear agenda" from politicians. Who will step forward with a compelling primary prevention case for poverty reduction, education, and youth employment initiatives as the most cost-effective and enduring way to truly improve global security?

This is a real leadership opportunity for someone of the stature of a UN Secretary-General, a Pope, a Dalai Lama, or an EU President. GlobeScan's research suggests the building blocks of public understanding are clearly there for such a leader to redefine global security in a more holistic and positive manner.

To underscore the importance of all this, even in the world's richest country, nearly a quarter of American children are living in poverty.[3] Their number increased for the fourth year in a row to 22% in 2010, the highest since 1993. Child poverty was the fourth highest in 2010 since the mid-1960s, when a federal "war on poverty" was launched by President Lyndon Johnson.

But calling it a *war* on poverty is perpetuating a mental construct that is so "last century." Mobilization of resources is key, but surely "sharing the wealth" would better build on the success of the 1980s and 1990s when unprecedented wealth was created in the world. It only now needs to be better distributed.

3   US Census Bureau, 2010.

And, as for *war*, surely "no enemies" would be a rallying cry better able to send the signal that humanity needs to hear today; that we're committed to bringing everyone with us into the future with dignity and with their real needs met. As Gandhi said, "The world has enough for every man's need, but not for every man's greed."

Summary

- The Obama Administration's burying of the term "war on terror" in 2013 was an inevitable result of public opinion trends over the last decade. The question is, what rallying cry might replace warfare?

- Like the war on drugs, the war on terror is likely to be seen by historians as an understandable 20th-century response to the events of September 11, 2001, but a failure in both its strategy and execution.

- Until recently, there has been little evidence that many citizens around the world ever thought that a *war* on terror was the way to best address the problem.

- In the wake of the 9/11 terrorist attacks, GlobeScan's research showed that, in addition to a genuine outflowing of grief and sympathy toward the USA, the global public's reaction was twofold: passive support for America striking back against al Qaeda bases and their Taliban protectors in Afghanistan; and active support for a renewed focus on global poverty reduction.

- This public focus on extreme poverty or the gap between rich and poor has tenaciously continued, with no end in sight.

- Today, with ISIS outdoing al Qaeda in its brutality and ambition, GlobeScan's latest 2015 tracking shows a majority of people now support military action to reduce terrorism. But that is not to say these same people have forgotten about poverty.

- It is not only extreme poverty that is fueling conflict, but also the widening gap between rich and poor. Even if the poor are not destitute, they cannot be constantly reminded of the relative wealth of others every day on television and in the tabloid media, without consequences.

- Looking at specific countries where majorities of their citizens saw a lack of economic fairness in 2009, it appears quite predictive of the mass protests that arose in 2011 in many countries.

- Clearly, many citizens have been stirred up by fear and a sense of unfairness, in part through events and in part by political and religious leaders with questionable motives. As a wise man once said, "When people are afraid, they tend to make bad decisions."

- But will a war on poverty be mounted instead of a war on terror? Certainly poverty as an issue has all the attributes needed for real progress to be achieved in our lifetime. Public opinion research suggests that poverty continues to have high levels of relevance, self-interest, and urgency in most countries. There are also perceived solutions available, with a growing belief that people, working together, can accomplish whatever we set out to do.

- This is a real leadership opportunity for someone of the stature of a UN Secretary-General, a Pope, a Dalai Lama, or an EU President. GlobeScan's research suggests the building blocks of public understanding are clearly there for such a leader to redefine global security in a more holistic and positive manner.

12
Whither the United Nations?

The [UN] Secretariat building in New York has 38 stories. If you lost ten stories today, it wouldn't make a bit of difference.
John Bolton in 1994 before becoming US Permanent Representative to the UN, 2005–2006

More than ever before in human history, we share a common destiny. We can master it only if we face it together. And that, my friends, is why we have the United Nations.
Kofi Annan, former Secretary-General of the UN, December 1999

In February 2005, I had the pleasure of briefing the UN Secretary-General's Office on the top floor of the UN headquarters building in New York. This was one of the floors that the US Ambassador to the UN at the time, John Bolton, had once famously said that if it were removed, no one would notice any difference.

Kofi Annan's Chief of Staff at the time, Mark Malloch Brown (soon to be named UN Deputy Secretary-General), drew together members of his staff to help inform their attempt to move a "once-in-a-generation" package of UN reforms through the UN General Assembly and Security Council.

It was hard slugging for this reform package at the time, especially because of the anti-UN position of the Bush Administration – in part because of the unwillingness of the UN to sanction the 2002 Iraq invasion by the USA. My audience that day was heartened by a number of our research results (Fig. 50), especially the two-thirds majority view (66% of people across 22 countries) that the UN was playing a mainly positive role in the world, including a solid majority of American citizens (59%). After the trashing the UN had been getting in the American media, they saw this later finding surprising and reassuring.

FIGURE 50   UN influence in the world
Average of 22 countries,* December 2004

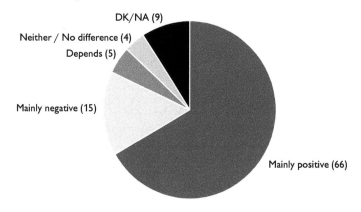

DK/NA (9)

Neither / No difference (4)

Depends (5)

Mainly negative (15)

Mainly positive (66)

*Includes Argentina, Australia, Brazil, Canada, Chile, China, France,
Germany, India, Indonesia, Italy, Japan, Mexico, Nigeria, Philippines, Russia,
South Africa, South Korea, Switzerland, Turkey, UK, and USA

FIGURE 51   Possible Security Council reforms
Average of 23 countries,* December 2004

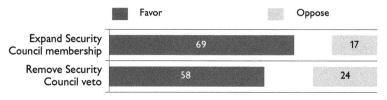

	Favor	Oppose
Expand Security Council membership	69	17
Remove Security Council veto	58	24

*Countries include Argentina, Australia, Brazil, Canada, Chile, China, France, Germany, India,
Indonesia, Italy, Japan, Lebanon, Mexico, Nigeria, Russia, Philippines, Poland, S. Africa, S. Korea,
Spain, Turkey, UK, and the USA.

The most memorable moment for me, however, was when I was asked
what our research suggested about the conventional wisdom that the UN
couldn't be at odds with an American administration and expect to succeed.
We responded that in the current circumstance, with the global public's trust
in the UN so much stronger than their trust in the Bush Administration, they
could take a contrary position to the USA on matters such as UN reform
– especially since the American public didn't agree with their President's
position on the UN. This is something that Mr. Malloch Brown took up with
some significant media success at least, through a protracted and very public spat with the much-ridiculed Ambassador Bolton.

Unfortunately, despite the best efforts of Kofi Annan and Mark Malloch Brown, their 2005 UN reform plan lies in the trash bin of history. In most people's judgment this was a much-needed modernization of a 60-year-old institution. But it failed due to a problem bigger than simply not being in tune with Washington. In my view it failed because of the stranglehold self-interested nation-states have on the organization under the UN's constitution, especially the Permanent Five Security Council members (China, France, Russia, the UK, and the USA). They were simply unwilling or unable to find agreement on a package that would have slightly eroded their power. The December 2004 BBC World Service Poll shows majority public support for even more significant reforms than those member states defeated (Fig. 51).

In the midst of all this, I had the following opinion piece published in Canada's *Globe and Mail* newspaper on March 12, 2005:

What the world wants for their UN

The current proposals for UN reform are far from meeting the expectations of either global citizens or emerging leaders worldwide.

As revealed in our BBC World Service Poll released today, two in three citizens (64%) across the 23 countries surveyed want a significantly more powerful United Nations operating in world affairs. Seven in ten (69%) want to expand the Security Council's permanent membership beyond the current five countries. And six in ten (58%) of the 23,000 citizens surveyed want the absolute veto power of permanent Security Council members abolished.

This call for the democratization of the United Nations system is even more powerfully made by leaders of civil society organizations worldwide. In a special survey of 1,000 of these leaders that we recently conducted for the King Baudouin Foundation with support from the Rockefeller and Mott Foundations, a recurring theme is the need to loosen the tight control of the UN system currently exercised by a few industrialized nation-states.

While much of the official UN structural reform debate is currently focused on extending the permanent membership of the Security Council, it is interesting that leaders of non-governmental organizations, companies, think-tanks, and academic faculties call even more strongly for an efficient and effective UN General Assembly and for making the IMF, World Bank and WTO accountable to the United Nations.

There are three key conclusions from this recent research:

- **Deep UN reform is not an option but a necessity.** Stakeholders across all sectors, especially those having existing interaction with UN agencies, are overwhelmingly dissatisfied with its operations and current impact in the world. They call for reforms aimed at greater operational efficiency, program innovation, and improved interaction with non-state actors. To govern in the 21st century, the UN must become a 21st-century organization. The good news is that stakeholders care enough to want the very best.

- **Democratizing the UN system.** A recurring theme in stakeholder responses to a wide range of questions on UN reform topics is the need to loosen the tight control of the UN system currently exercised by a few industrialized nation-states. While much of the official UN structural reform debate is currently focused on extending the permanent membership of the Security Council, it is interesting that stakeholders call even more strongly for an efficient and effective UN General Assembly and for making the IMF, World Bank and WTO accountable to the United Nations. Creating a Civil Society Forum of non-state actors is seen as equal in priority to bringing developing countries into the Security Council.

- **Emergence of the global citizen: can world government be far behind?** For the first time in history, one in five citizens around the world see themselves more as citizens of the world than citizens of their individual country. When we asked NGO leaders to choose their ideal form of global governance for the year 2020, as many said the emergence of directly elected world government as selected "a reformed and strengthened United Nations."

Clearly, we're at an historic moment in the evolution of the world governance system. The question is, will the UN leadership stop looking to signals from Washington and rather to the expansive expectations of the world's people to shape their proposals?

Clearly, the Bush years were very tough on global institutions, and the credibility of the UN certainly suffered. Colonial-style "ownership" by the USA and Europe of multilateral institutions such as the World Bank and the IMF respectively has undermined the trust in these institutions of different regions of the world. The inability to reform the governance of the IMF to reflect the growing power of non-G7 countries has most recently resulted in China creating the Asian Infrastructure Investment Bank in late 2014 that will compete with the World Bank and Asian Development Bank.

As Figure 10 shows, trust in the UN has declined slightly over the last decade, but not as significantly as other institutions. It remains one of the most trusted institutions, and far more trusted than national governments overall. But, as shown by Figure 52, the low levels of trust in the UN displayed by the Arab world and Latin America are certainly cause for concern.

FIGURE 52 Trust in UN
Net trust,* by region,** July/August 2002–February 2015

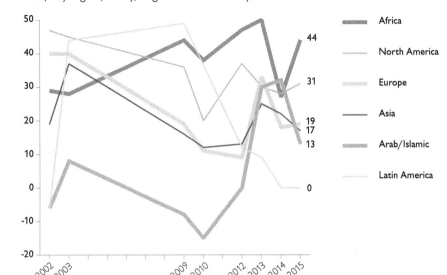

*"A lot of trust" and "Some trust" minus "Not much trust" and "No trust at all"

**Africa includes Kenya and Nigeria; Arab/Islamic includes Indonesia and Turkey; Asia includes China, India, and Pakistan; Europe includes France, Germany, Spain, and UK; Latin America includes Chile and Mexico; North America includes Canada and US.

For these and other reasons, an unreformed UN is under as much threat today than ever in its 70-year history. The current relative vacuum of global governance won't last long. One way or another, the demands of the post-superpower world for ever more effective global standards and coordinated action will be met.

This is because, increasingly, the world's greatest challenges are global in scope; especially the so-called "global commons" of our common water, food, and atmospheric resources. (Who owns the water cycle? Which nation has sovereignty over the atmosphere?)

Without very strong moral leadership on the part of the UN under current Secretary-General Ban Ki-moon on challenges such as delivering a new global climate change convention, and other serious topics such as poverty and conflict, the relevance of the institution is at risk.

The urgent requirement for international action on a range of pressing issues is giving rise to inspired diplomacy, partnerships, and mass collaboration based in part on the legitimacy of global public opinion. As detailed in Chapter 10, we are seeing the emergence of multi-stakeholder "coalitions of the willing" (*tahaloufs*) as instruments of progress, first exemplified by the International Campaign to Ban Landmines, involving non-state as well as nation-state actors. The work of the Gates Foundation and the UN Foundation are also helping to fill the void with innovative approaches. The UN Foundation's incubating of the Global Water Challenge – a global collaborative focused on water – is another good example of the new *tahalouf* genre.

It is interesting that a recent version of Shell Oil's highly respected strategic scenarios – stories of what the future global business climate might look like – includes "Blueprints" as one of their two possible future worlds. The Blueprints world is defined by the coming to scale of partnerships and collaboration among a wide range of actors that effectively marshal the forces needed to come to grips with our challenges.[1]

At the same time, as we saw in the Arab Spring uprising in Tunisia, Egypt and elsewhere, social media and the internet allows for mass mobilization of people in the streets strong enough to topple governments. It also allows for global real-time polls and online mobilization as exemplified by avaaz.org, which regularly surveys its 40 million worldwide members in order to shape its campaigns that can deliver hundreds of thousands of letters, petitions to elected officials within a week, often on global issues.

All of these examples, plus our own research, show that people around the world believe global governance is too important to leave to the inherently conflicted nation-states and somewhat ineffective UN system to sort out.

Whither the United Nations? Our research with both the global public and with global opinion leaders suggests that humanity will have some form of world government within 100 years. Whether this will be called the UN or something else won't be so important.

I'm encouraged in this prediction (which I first made in a presentation at the 2004 World Social Forum in Porto Alegre, Brazil) by the *Financial Times* columnist Gideon Rachman, who in a December 2008 column said, "For the first time in my life, I think the formation of some sort of world government is plausible." He went on to define what he meant by world government as an entity with statelike characteristics, backed by a body of laws. He pointed to the EU as a reasonable model on which to build.

---

1   See https://s00.static-shell.com/content/dam/shell/static/future-energy/
     downloads/shell-scenarios/shell-energy-scenarios2050.pdf.

FIGURE 53   Having your country's UN General Assembly representative elected by citizens

"Favor" vs. "Oppose," by country, December 2004

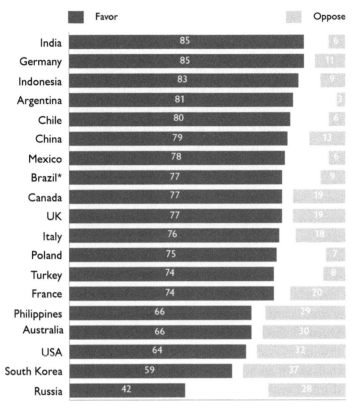

*Asked of 69% of the Brazilian sample

The white space in this chart represents "Depends," "Neither," and "DK/NA."

Obviously, this is not something that will happen soon, and it will take a major crisis or series of crises to bring to pass – just as it took two world wars to bring first the League of Nations and then the UN into existence. However, another finding from GlobeScan's December 2004 poll on UN reform shows majority support in all but one of the countries polled for a central component of world government in the model of the EU – direct representation (Fig. 53). The results are still compelling a decade later (and are probably much the same).

More immediately, the continuing global financial crisis and our mounting climate challenges will likely drive progress by putting in place some additional formal elements of global governance. The aggressive tendencies of Russia in the Ukraine, or indeed China in the South China Sea, may help this along as well.

In 2008, Jacques Attali, an advisor to then French President Nicholas Sarkozy, said, "The core of the international financial crisis is that we have global financial markets but no global rule of law."[2]

As I said to a US congressman at Davos 2002 in New York City, the world today is like the USA a century-and-a-half ago, when interstate commerce forced the creation of federal controls and standards. This is because – as George Soros says and the global banking industry has proven – markets are not self-regulating.

What other crises will arise to cause vested interests to accept new elements of global governance, no one can predict. However, predicting that there *will* be such a crisis over the next 50–100 years is unfortunately one of the surest predictions one can make in today's world made volatile by so many unstable systems and trends.

A next financial crisis is likely to happen within ten years, given we haven't made any significant changes in the inadequate system of checks and balances that led to the 2008 financial crisis. No doubt it will give rise to the actual adoption of some global rules and standards around banking and financial transactions. It may even get the long-proposed and increasingly promoted Tobin Tax on currency speculation implemented in order to pay for international oversight and policing. While this would be a relatively modest step toward world government, it would be hugely symbolic and will make subsequent steps that much easier.

A major global crisis might well stimulate a creative period of global institution-building similar to the period after the Second World War, when all the Bretton Woods global institutions were created, including the World Bank and IMF. In this context, some people worry that, with so many cultures and religions in the world, there is no basis for agreeing on a common set of principles and values on which to base global governance. Here, in addition to our polling, it is useful to look at the work of Professor Hans Kung, President of the Global Ethic Foundation. Kung's study of global religions shows that, once you remove divisive issues such as abortion, gay

2   "And Now for a World Government," *Financial Times*, December 8, 2008.

rights, and the role of women, all major religions in the world have the same basic tenets on which global rules and standards can be based.

In summary, I agree with Gideon Rachman of the *Financial Times*, who concluded his 2008 column on this subject, "For the first time since *homo sapiens* began to doodle on cave walls, there is an argument, an opportunity and a means to make serious steps towards world government."

If the UN succeeds in rallying the actions required to meet the ambitious SDGs (Sustainable Development Goals) by the target year 2030, this would make a good start along this path.

Summary

- Trust in the UN has declined slightly over the last decade, but not as significantly as other institutions. It remains one of the most trusted institutions, and far more trusted than national governments overall.

- Despite the best efforts of Kofi Annan and Mark Malloch Brown, their 2005 UN reform plan lies in the trash bin of history. In most people's judgment this was a much-needed modernization of a 60-year-old institution.

- The December 2004 BBC World Service Poll across 23 countries showed majority public support for even more significant reforms than those defeated by UN member states.

- Colonial-style "ownership" by the USA and Europe of multilateral institutions such as the World Bank and the IMF respectively has undermined the trust that different regions of the world have in these institutions.

- The current relative vacuum of global governance won't last long. One way or another, the demands of the post-superpower world for ever more effective global standards and coordinated action will be met. This is because, increasingly, the world's greatest challenges are global in scope.

- The urgent requirement for international action on a range of pressing issues is giving rise to inspired diplomacy, partnerships and mass collaboration based in part on the legitimacy of global public opinion.

- All of these initiatives, plus polling findings, show that people around the world believe global governance is too important to leave to the inherently conflicted nation-states and ineffective UN system to sort out.

- Whither the United Nations? Our research with both the global public and with global opinion leaders suggests that humanity will have some form of world government within 100 years.

- GlobeScan's December 2004 poll on UN reform showed majority support in all but one of the 19 countries polled for a central requirement of world government – direct representation through electing country representatives to the UN General Assembly.

- Obviously, this is not something that will happen soon, and it will take a major crisis or series of crises to bring to pass; but unfortunately, such a crisis is likely to occur this century.

13
If current trends continue

If we don't change direction soon, we'll end up where we're heading.

Anon.[1]

Show me the direction in which the people are heading, that I might get out in front and lead them.

Mahatma Gandhi

What if the current trends in global opinion covered in this book continue and are instrumental in shaping the world in which we live? What kind of world will result?

And, is it one future or many futures? How consistent are people's views of the future, across the world?

While large differences exist on many topics (and always will), global research finds an amazing degree of consistency in what people around the world want for their children and their children's children.

One of the more interesting projects that I've worked on in my career was a series of focus groups in eight countries for Ford Motor Company in the late 1990s, the first time Bill Ford Jr. tried to make Ford the greenest and most socially responsible car company in the world. (He's having more success today.)

It was one of the times when I literally circumnavigated the globe to sit behind one-way mirrors in focus group facilities in cities as diverse as London, Bangkok, Warsaw, Hong Kong, Los Angeles, Sydney, and Toronto. It was a personal record for me; I did my part of it all in eight days with three nights spent at 35,000 feet.

---

1   This quotation was used to lead off the International Energy Agency's 2011 "World Energy Outlook" report.

The goal was to understand people's expectations for the future of mobility. My colleague Angus McAllister came up with a brilliant research design that began by exploring people's overall expectations of the future, then narrowed in on personal transport.

After welcoming participants to the focus group, we dimmed the lights and asked people to close their eyes and think of waking up 20 years from now in a future where things hadn't worked out as well as they would have liked. We asked them to imagine getting out of bed and going to the shuttered windows and opening the shutters on the world outside, then describing what they imagined they would see.

It was very striking the extent to which the imagined dystopia was similar across the groups, regardless of geography, culture, age, or economic status – the world was dark, it was smelly and there were no birds; it was heavily polluted, and there were sirens wailing. In short, it was no place a human wanted to go out into.

Then we asked participants to sit back and close their eyes again and think of getting out of bed 20 years into the future to a world that had turned out just the way they hoped it would. Again, the close similarity in what most participants across the world saw was incredible – the utopia world was green and lush; there were birds singing; there was bright sunshine and clear air; and people were outside and there was children's laughter.

From this project and a number of more quantitative research projects (including GlobeScan's 30-nation Millennium Poll in 1999, and our annual 20-nation polls since) we can conclude that people want pretty much the same thing for the future. They want peace; they want a clean environment; they want animals and birds in abundance; and they want people to be happy and getting along. While this has probably always been so, what makes today different is that people believe it is possible to get what they most want.

Put another way, if you want to put a label on it, we could say a "sustainable and just world" is what most people want. They don't want as much drama as today, in terms of fighting between nations, cultures, and narrow self-interests. They want nature respected and a future where people are encouraged to bring their best to the world rather than their worst.

However, this is not the world many people see us heading toward. In fact, significant numbers are quite pessimistic about our future, especially in industrialized countries. One example of this pessimism relates to whether our children and grandchildren will have a better life or not. As Figure 54

FIGURE 54   Our children and grandchildren will have a higher quality of life than we do today
"Agree," BRIC vs. G7,* December 2000–January 2012

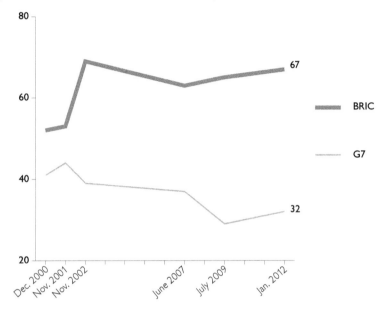

*BRIC includes Brazil, China, India, and Russia. G7 includes Canada, France, Germany, Italy, Japan, UK, and USA.

Brazil not asked 2002 and 2009. China not asked in 2000 and 2001. Italy not asked in 2012. Japan not asked in 2007 and 2012.

shows, belief in a better future has fallen in the G7 industrialized countries even as it has risen in emerging BRIC economies.

This widespread pessimism is what I personally most worry about as we work toward a future most of us want. When we ask people whether the world is heading in the right direction, less than a third of citizens say it is, down from a half in 1999.

Given the danger of this pessimism becoming a self-fulfilling prophesy that keeps humanity from achieving its aspirations, the GlobeScan Foundation's Hope Index is noteworthy in that it sets out to regularly track the degree of hope and hopelessness about the state of the world.

In the inaugural Hope Index poll across 12 countries in 2014, most people (59%) saw "the socioeconomic and environmental challenges the world faces today are *more* difficult than the past." When asked, "How likely, if at all, do you think it is that humanity will find a way to overcome our current challenges?" over six in ten (63%) express optimism. However, significant

FIGURE 55   Will humanity overcome our challenges?
January 2014

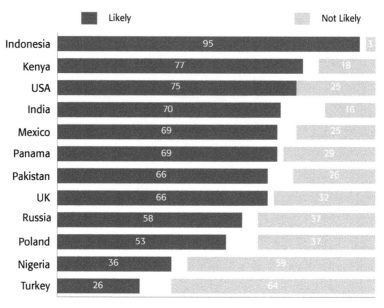

The white space in this chart represents "DK/NA."

minorities in most countries are pessimistic (31% overall). Respondents in Indonesia are especially optimistic, while respondents in Turkey and Nigeria are quite pessimistic (Fig. 55).

Optimistic or pessimistic?

Clearly, hope has always been important at critical points in human history, and the next few decades will, I'm sure, benefit from it.

Actually, the public opinion trends covered in this book suggest a positive – even hopeful – future for humanity. If these trends continue and leaders emerge to convert them into societal change, we can expect a number of themes to play out to varying degrees. I outline the major ones in this chapter.

Obviously, most of the predictions, trends, and ideas in this book will take decades to fully manifest as change. Most in this chapter, however, are what might be called "by-the-numbers predictions," in that a significant and growing weight of public opinion already supports them.

The collaborative economy

One of the most far-reaching trends we see is the emergence of the collaborative economy, including collaborative production and consumption.

The Great Depression in the 1930s gave rise to fundamentally different attitudes and values that lasted for a generation, such as thrift, reuse, and sharing. It is still a bit early to tell what the modern equivalent will look like coming out of the massive uncontrolled experiment called the Great Recession, but our research and observations suggest the growing focus on balance and quality of life over stress and standard of living is leading, at the consumer end of the economy, to more sharing and search for community.

Time magazine has named collaborative consumption one of the "ten ideas that will change the world."[2] Advocates see it as including traditional sharing, bartering, lending, trading, renting, gifting, and swapping, reinvented through network technology. It's sharing access to things rather than individually owning them that is the departure point.

In industrialized countries, young urban consumers are flocking to car-sharing services such as Zipcar, seeing it as both "cool" and providing practical mobility on a budget. The widespread sharing of music and movies over the internet has perhaps most established this open source sharing phenomenon among a new generation of consumers, and other internet tools such as social media help create the communities and other means for collaboration and sharing on a massive scale.

Similarly, at the production end of the economy we're seeing increased collaboration not only among individuals (as with Wikipedia), but between companies with common goals or complementary offerings. A good example is car companies collaborating to develop batteries and drivetrains for plug-in electric cars. Another is content providers (such as publishers or recording studios) partnering with distribution channels (such as iTunes) to extend their markets.

A friend of mine spends his working hours assembling virtual supercomputers to work out complex problems for his global bank employer using the idle capacity of his colleagues' laptop computers. Cloud computing is but another example of the collaborative economy working throughout the value chain, with users sharing massive file storage facilities rather than owning their own.

Whether it is manufacturers using precompetitive collaboration to make breakthroughs in pharmaceuticals or electric vehicles, governments and

2   "Today's Smart Choice: Don't Own. Share," *Time*, March 17, 2011.

companies partnering to build needed energy infrastructure, or young urban consumers flocking to car-sharing services, collaboration is becoming a key competitive advantage.

We believe these trends will accelerate and lead to what can be called a collaborative economy, leading to both greater resource efficiency and better quality of life. Not only will people gain greater utility per dollar from sharing cars, homes, major appliances, and equipment, but they can gain a greater sense of community with those they choose to share with, a major driver of quality of life.

Two other recent developments are helping to bring along the collaborative or "sharing" economy. One is the rapid rise of websites that enable people to monetize the sharing of their vehicles (such as Uber and Lyft) or spare rooms (such as AirBnB). Another development is the rapid rise of crowd-sourced fundraising (such as Kickstarter and Idiegogo) and peer-to-peer lending (such as Lending Club, Prosper, and Payoff).

In the collaborative economy, co-housing may well replace the condominium as the dominant real estate trend, especially for the recently married and retired segments of the market. Developed in Denmark 25 years ago, co-housing communities combine the autonomy of private dwellings with the advantages of shared amenities and a greater sense of community.

As the collaborative economy gains market share, it will become a key context and driver for real progress on sustainability, in that it enables people to do more with less by sharing resources. Having urban Chinese sharing cars makes a lot more sense for the planet and people than each of these 500 million individuals having their own car.

The collaborative economy will also increasingly manifest at the global policy and political level with the kinds of cooperative initiative between a wide range of state and non-state actors that I call *tahaloufs* in Chapter 10. Certainly in global business circles, collaborative initiatives are already seen as the only way individual companies can realistically address global challenges such as climate, water, or youth training.

The challenge in all this is that many organizations are "hard-edged" and don't know how to successfully operate in a more open, engaging, and collaborative context. We have global NGOs running campaigns that are competitive with other NGOs; we have natural resource companies unable to gain a social license for new developments because they try to impose them onto the local population; we have engineer-led renewable energy companies unable to overcome local opposition to wind farms.

The transition to the collaborative economy will tend to be disruptive to existing market leaders as it represents significant opportunities for new entrants and others – not least for social scientists who are needed to help organizations learn the new social process skills required for success in an increasingly collaborative, partnership world.

The rise of local and the new city-state

A significant component of the collaborative economy will be the "100 mile economy," the major driver of which is the steady growth (even through the recession) of the local and natural food movement across both industrialized and emerging economies, and a widespread search for identity and community. In economically fragile times, with people pulling back from globalization, the multiplier effect of buying local is not lost on struggling city and town officials. Add volatile energy markets to the equation, and local is the new frontier.

The growth of the local food phenomenon across a wide range of countries can be seen in Figure 18, based on self-reported findings from Greendex, a major longitudinal study GlobeScan is doing with the National Geographic Society to track a wide range of sustainable behaviors across 18 countries.

But this will not be the "old local." It's the "global local," where excellence will be encouraged and enabled through connectivity to global opportunities, while kept real by being well grounded in community values and relationships. This is the ground on which the future will be reinvented and implemented brick by brick and click by click.

"Cities that work" will be some of the major beneficiaries of this new global local. As occurred during the artisanal trading of the Middle Ages, city-states are again emerging not only as political entities such as Singapore and the Vatican, but as place-brands such as London, Hong Kong, Dubai, and Tianjin Eco-City. Watch this space, as cities the world over rise to the opportunities inherent in dynamic place-branding.

A new realism

After a financial meltdown at the scale of the Great Recession, we can see just how caught up we humans can get in a rose-colored paradigm, which some argue was an unreal and unsustainable fantasy world of ever-increasing wealth and material throughput within a strictly finite planetary biosphere.

Yet, our leaders are trying to keep us focused on simply getting the growth bandwagon going again in the same old way rather than learning our lessons, reforming our institutions, and redefining progress more in line with human aspirations.

Many people are wiser than that, and are weaning themselves off personal debt and addiction to the things money can buy. Even if they have been forced into this by hard times, many are finding real meaning in the things money can't buy and that have been progressively undervalued over the last 20 years – close family life, good friends, a real sense of community, personal projects and hobbies, grow-your-own or local food, spending time cooking real food, etc. While still a subculture, this is already assuming the proportions of a mega-trend in industrialized countries, toward what can be called the "New Realism."

In this search for real, we can seeing consumer preferences changing from artificial to natural products, from material "bling" to real experiences, from wants to needs, from unrealistic expectations to making real choices between practical alternatives.

As for the larger economy, GlobeScan's research shows that most people want stability and fairness more than growth. The New Realists want a real economy where real environmental and social costs are internalized rather than ignored in decision-making. They also want us to face up to our fundamental challenges rather than only addressing the symptoms and papering over the deeper issues. They understand that this will mean departing from the status quo and applying innovative approaches to get to the future they really want.

So, the New Realism that we see emerging from the Great Recession focuses on a real economy, real experiences, real food, and real community.

Near-term predictions

Here are some more tangible predictions that I expect to come to pass over the next 5–10 years.

1. **Carbon divestment.** Events suggest that a tipping point has arrived in the climate change debate. The June 2015 G7 Leaders Summit's declaration that "deep cuts in global greenhouse gas emissions are required with a decarbonization of the global economy over the course

of this century" is unprecedented and a powerful signal to the market. It will speed the pace of investors divesting from carbon industry stocks, especially petroleum and coal company shares. With the support of Archbishop Desmond Tutu as well as early movers such as the Rockefeller Brothers Fund and a growing number of universities, we would predict that divestment will reach proportions that will materially restrict oil exploration and coal production by the year 2020. With the governor of the Bank of England[3] saying that most of the oil reserves that underpin existing share valuations of petroleum companies "are unburnable," even rational shareholders have good reason to sell their shares in Big Oil.

2. **Legalized soft drugs.** Public majority support, coupled with the widely acknowledged ineffectiveness of the war on drugs, combined with the need for new sources of government tax revenues to reduce deficits, will result in the legalization and taxation of soft drugs such as cannabis within 5–10 years in many G7 countries. Compared with the well-documented societal harm of legalized alcohol, most people won't notice any negative social impacts, as long as under-age access is restricted. While I first made this prediction in early 2012, subsequent legalization initiatives in five US states (beginning with Colorado and Washington), as well as in Portugal and Uruguay, make this a safe prediction today.

3. **Water wars.** GlobeScan's polling shows public concern about diminishing fresh water supplies is rising quickly across the world. Add to this the World Bank's list of 28 countries already experiencing sufficient water shortages to negatively affect their economy, and the fact that a number of authors have already drawn links between specific wars and related water disputes. If we thought oil was bad for starting wars, water will be the mega-issue of the next 50 years. We expect there will be a mounting number of water wars of words, trade, and even gunfire by the end of this decade. Rivers passing through a number of countries (such as the Nile, Niger, and Mekong) will be particular flash-points, but large aquifers under multiple jurisdictions in the Middle East and elsewhere will also cause conflict.

4. **New issue: electromagnetic radiation.** Electromagnetic radiation will likely join the ranks of other widely perceived health risks such as smoking and exposure to chemicals (such as dioxins). This will have huge impacts on the electronics and mobile telephony industries, and create major opportunities for early movers offering lower-radiation devices.

3   The Bank of England governor, Mark Carney, was reported by *The Guardian* newspaper to say in an October 2014 World Bank seminar, "The vast majority of [oil] reserves are unburnable."

Summary

- What if the trends in global opinion documented in this book continue and are instrumental in shaping the world in which we live? What kind of world will result? And, is it one future or many futures? How consistent are people's views of the future, across the world?

- While large differences exist on many topics (and always will), global research finds an amazing degree of consistency in what people around the world want for their children and their children's children. They want peace; they want a clean environment; they want animals and birds in abundance; and they want people to be happy and getting along. While this has probably always been so, what makes today different is that people believe it is possible to get what they most want.

- Are most people optimistic or pessimistic about humanity's prospects? The GlobeScan Foundation's inaugural 2014 Hope Index across 12 countries found that over six in ten citizens (63%) express optimism "that humanity will find a way to overcome our current challenges." However, significant minorities in most countries are pessimistic (31% overall).

- Most of the public opinion trends covered in this book suggest a positive – even hopeful – future for humanity. If these trends continue and leaders emerge to convert them into societal change, we can expect a number of themes to play out to varying degrees.

- Obviously, most of the trends, ideas, and predictions in this book will take decades to fully manifest as change. Most in this chapter, however, are what might be called "by-the-numbers predictions," in that a significant and growing weight of public opinion already supports them.

- One of the most far-reaching trends we see is the emergence of the collaborative economy, including collaborative production and consumption. The challenge in this is that many organizations are "hard-edged" and don't know how to successfully operate in a more open, engaging, and collaborative context.

- A significant component of the new sharing economy will be the "100 mile economy," driven by the local food movement. "Cities that work" will be some of the major beneficiaries of this rise of local, and place-branding of cities will bring back the days of the city-state.

- A New Realism is emerging from the Great Recession, focusing on a real economy, real experiences, real food, and real community. In this search for real, we see consumer preferences changing from artificial to natural products, from material "bling" to real experiences, from wants to needs, from unrealistic expectations to making real choices between practical alternatives.

- We also see a number of early trends accelerating, including carbon divestment, the legalization of cannabis, water wars, and the rise of new issues such as electromagnetic radiation.

14
Ideas for the 21st century

> Be the change you wish to see in the world.
>
> Mahatma Gandhi

> It's not enough that we do our best; sometimes we have to do what's required.
>
> Winston Churchill

What makes the 21st century so exciting is that we humans now believe that collectively we can do anything we set out to do. Everything's possible.

This final chapter goes well beyond public opinion findings to suggest some ideas that I believe are as likely as any others to come to reality over the course of the next 80 years of the 21st century.

You could call these ideas the musing of a global pollster who believes we're heading into a period of step change rather than more of the incremental change that most people are focused on and used to. With so many elements of the status quo being unsustainable, "business as usual" is simply not going to work for us much longer. Hence, not only will change be the only constant, it will be accelerated change constantly challenging us humans and our institutions to change quickly enough.

Here are some ideas to unlock our collective thinking. I wish us all well.

Social capitalism

At the November 2014 Business for Social Responsibility conference in New York, Indra Nooyi, CEO of PepsiCo, said, "We need to write the next chapter of capitalism together." What will this chapter look like?

The ever-increasing pressure on business to act better in society's interest will eventually lead, I believe, to a structural fix – such as a legal requirement for incorporated companies to act in the interest of the broader society – in return for being granted their limited financial and legal liability. In the meantime, there will be a progression of business concepts and leaders who will continue to advance the cutting edge of change.

One such concept is social enterprise, or more broadly social capitalism, which we see as a next big thing – bigger than CSR was over the last few decades. Social capitalism is about putting societal purpose at the core of the business enterprise, then applying business discipline and capital to execute on this purpose.

One of the business leaders currently leading this charge is Paul Polman, CEO of Unilever, the third-largest global consumer goods company. In an April 2012 interview with *The Guardian*, he put this new view of capitalism this way:

> I don't think our fiduciary duty is to put shareholders first. I say the opposite. What we firmly believe is that if we focus our company on improving the lives of the world's citizens and come up with genuine sustainable solutions, we are more in synch with consumers and society and ultimately this will result in good shareholder returns.
>
> Why would you invest in a company which is out of synch with the needs of society, that does not take its social compliance in its supply chain seriously, that does not think about the costs of externalities, or of its negative impacts on society?

In a way, this kind of thinking is the inevitable result of business's evolution amid mounting public pressure over the last 30 years, which I detailed in Chapter 7.

My friend John Elkington[1] has been prescient about the importance and promise of social enterprise, and he has been helping major corporations learn from this phenomenon (and vice versa) ever since. While social enterprise has been around as a concept since the 1980s, over the last decade it has become significantly more established and recognized, not least by social entrepreneur Muhammad Yunus being awarded the Nobel Peace Prize in 2006 for his pioneering microcredit work with Grameen Bank in Bangladesh. It is certainly capturing the imagination of a growing number of young entrepreneurs with a social conscience.

---

[1]   Founder of UK consultancies SustainAbility and Volans and author of 19 books, including his exposition on the promise of social enterprises, *The Power of Unreasonable People* (Harvard Business School Press, 2008).

California-based branding consultant Ron Vandenberg uses the term "social capitalism" to describe projecting the concept of social purpose from the enterprise level to a branding and economic systems level.[2]

We are seeing an increasing number of leadership organizations (e.g., Unilever, IKEA, and Natura) awakening to the power and promise of putting societal purpose at the center of their organization. And this will only grow as business attempts to regain its social contract eroded through the Great Recession.

International research shows almost one in four people around the world are ready to abandon the free enterprise system.[3] Yet a majority of people respect the ability of companies to marshal human endeavor – seeing them as the modern-day equivalent of the Roman system of legions in this respect. It is corporate *motives* people don't trust, focused only on maximizing profit for a few. Tying corporate strengths to societal purpose gives the best of both worlds and takes us in a direction that people want and support.

Social capitalism, if fully developed and institutionalized, could create a fundamentally new legal entity combining the societal goals that we used to expect from governments or NGOs with the discipline and leverage of the private sector. This may be essential both for retaining business's social license to operate and grow, and for meeting humanity's challenges in the time-frame required.

Collaborative democracy

Clearly, a democracy is made up of many elements, including free and fair elections, the enshrining of the rule of law, the existence of democratic institutions, how dissent is treated, etc. But most would agree that having citizens believing that their government is run by the will of the people should form part of an adequate definition.

2   Although the term was used earlier by others, including Australian Prime Minister Kevin Rudd in 2009.
3   A BBC World Service Poll, released in November 2009, found 23% of respondents across 27 countries said capitalism "is fatally flawed and a new system is needed," compared with only 11% who said capitalism "works well as it is." Most (51%) took the middle position that capitalism "has problems that can be addressed with more regulation and reform."

FIGURE 56   My country is governed by the will of the people
"Yes," trends: November 2001–February 2015

Increasing or stable at high level

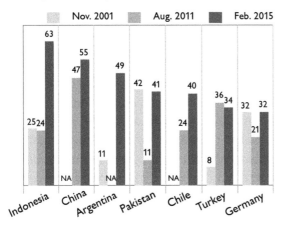

Decreasing or stable at low level

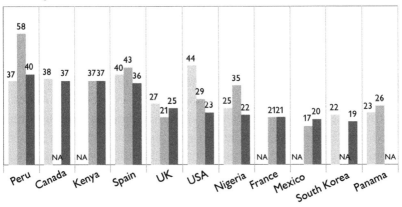

Over the years, GlobeScan (including in partnership with Gallup International) has asked scientific samples of citizens in a total of 65 countries whether they agree that their country is governed by the will of the people, or not. We have only ever found six countries where a majority said yes – and none of these are the so-called established democracies. And as Figure 56 shows, over the first decade-and-a-half of the new millennium, this picture has gotten even worse in some key democracies.[4]

4   See "The Magna Carta: alive but not well", paper by Doug Miller presented at 2015 WAPOR Conference, Buenos Aires, available at http://www.globescan.com/images/ GlobeScan_Foundation/Doug-Miller-WAPOR-Paper-on-Magna-Carta-2015.pdf.

These low and declining levels of engagement in our democracies, as further evidenced by ever-lower levels of voter turnout in elections, are creating what an environmental scientist would call a "stressed ecosystem" in which instability and invasive species flourish; the political equivalent of which is extreme parties and policies, and increasing street protests and radical occupations.

Unfortunately, in the face of this, too many governments are clamping down on the symptoms (dissent) rather than addressing the root causes of alienation, which of course only fuels the degrading political climate even more. Current levels of trust in democratic institutions and political engagement are so low that we don't have very far to go before the wheels begin to fall off. So, the time for truly significant reform in our democracies is fast upon us. Fortunately, the internet (including mass collaboration software and social networking) and new policy development processes (including deliberative polling and citizen cabinets) provide some useful starting points for renewing our democracies.[5]

One attempt to define collaborative democracy calls it a political system in which governmental stakeholders (politicians, parties, ministers, parliamentarians, and public servants) and non-governmental stakeholders (NGOs, political lobbies, scientists, academics, local communities, and individual citizens) collaborate on the development of public policy and laws. But this just begins to describe the breadth of the concept in my opinion.

For me it starts with a fundamental shift in paradigm. Rather than the current political culture of polarized viewpoints warring with each other, collaborative democracy is focused on what Buddhists and Muslims would call the "middle way" and what pollsters would call the average or median point of view. Most powerfully, it is about developing policies that can be supported by the middle two-thirds of citizens.

Collaborative democracy is about reinventing for a digital age and truly enshrining principles of equality, transparency, open deliberation, and participatory democracy back into our system of governance.

Transparency of information and processes, because these are essential to regaining citizen trust in our democracy. *Equal* and participatory, because it hasn't been lately; it is widely perceived to have been captured by self-interest and monetary interests. *Deliberative*, because the complexity of the

---

5   I want to acknowledge the pioneering thinking and work of my long-time colleague Steven Kull, director of the University of Maryland's Program for Public Consultation, in helping shape my ideas on this.

issues requires both extensive research and an iterative process of policy development to get it right for the most people. *Collaborative,* because no single government or organization or profession can solve our complex, interrelated, and transboundary problems by themselves.

Putting all of these elements together unlocks the whole-system views and outside-the-box creativity we need to truly solve our challenges rather than "kicking the can down the road" for someone else to clean up.

All of this is possible. It's the realm of social scientists, and they have perfected a number of innovative tools and processes that can be tailored to local situations and can deliver all the elements of collaborative democracy. It's also the realm of a new breed of politician, and a growing number of local jurisdictions are well along in putting different elements of collaborative democracy into place.

The most ambitious current example of this new approach is Voice of the People, a bipartisan organization launched by my colleague Steven Kull in the USA.[6] Voice of the People is urging the US Congress to take these new methods to scale so that each member of Congress has a large, scientifically selected, representative sample of their constituents – called a Citizen Cabinet – to be consulted on current issues and provide a voice that accurately reflects the values and priorities of their district or state. Voice of the People ultimately seeks to create a large standing national Citizen Cabinet of over 100,000 Americans, all connected by the internet, with a representative sample in every state and district, that will be operated by a congressionally chartered National Academy for Public Consultation. In the meantime, with funds from foundations and individual donors, Voice of the People is establishing interim Citizen Cabinets in several states and districts.

Some elements of collaborative democracy will no doubt be coming to a government near you (and me) in the not-so-distant future.

From duality to diversity (from two to three)

The simplistic duality of most current debates is increasingly debilitating. The left and the right. The progressives and the status quo conservatives. Islam vs. the West. Renewables vs. nuclear. Us vs. Them. This is not how we're

6   See http://www.vop.org.

going to get to a future we really want. Competition of ideas is healthy but, as in nature, we need more diversity of ideas in play than just two opposites.

In an increasingly collaborative world, this Cold War artifact of duality – this arbitrary and limited way of thinking – will naturally give way to more inclusive ways of framing conversations and exploring possibilities.

The truth is, we can no longer afford the luxury of lurching from one extreme to another because, in an "Us vs. Them" policy world, both positions are forced into extreme corners that few actually want and that don't actually work in practice.

While humanity isn't nearly ready to embrace unity or oneness yet, and our governance and other systems can't accommodate too many alternatives, I would argue for an increase in the use of three-way choices and indeed three-party systems that over time will improve decision-making and societal outcomes.

This idea is particularly important when it comes to the essential requirements for human life: food, potable water, breathable air, and energy for temperature control. In all these essentials, we should have "backup to our backup" – three stand-alone systems capable of delivering these essential services. We do this on spacecraft carrying humans; we must with Spaceship Earth.

In this context, the argument for establishing a complete system of organic local food production and distribution, in parallel with the conventional or corporate food system, is logical. The only question is what is the third complete food system we should develop to ensure humanity can produce the nutrients we need under any conceivable future scenarios?

Moving from two to three will help turn adversity into diversity, and log jam into collaborative progress.

Off-worlding risk

A number of long-term trends are on a collision course when it comes to the risks we impose on future generations. The ever-deepening concern for the environment (most striking today among citizens of middle-income countries), and the growing demand for transparency and accountability in all things due to low trust levels, are colliding with rapid increases in what most lay people would consider high-risk experimentation and technology developments with potential planetary-scale impacts.

This is happening at a time when the current scientific governance system has been widely criticized as being inadequate due to revelations about flawed peer-review processes of scientific journals, the overbearing nature of corporate funding for research, the lack of full disclosure, and too little government oversight.

This will lead to a much more public debate on the ecosystem risks associated with certain kinds of scientific research and technological development. The more transparency on this, the less average people will feel comfortable with the scale of risks being taken with scientific developments such as nanotechnology and artificial intelligence (let alone biological warfare).

All of this will culminate in increasingly persuasive calls for companies and governments to move higher risk technology outside the biosphere.

While projects such as NASA's Kepler Mission[7] actively search for other habitable worlds, Earth is the only world humanity knows of that can so wonderfully support our needs, the only one on which we can rely for the next few centuries at least, and will always be our only home planet. It is inevitable that we will take this reality much more seriously as it becomes clear (through challenges such as the ozone hole and now climate change) that humanity can have a huge impact on the planetary systems on which life depends.

Of course, the best way for this off-worlding of risk to happen would be proactively, by scientific institutions, scientists, and technologists leading the way, bringing governments, business, and others with them. The current privatization of space transport (e.g., Virgin Galactic, SpaceX, and Scaled Composites) certainly opens the way for this to occur.

Requiring high-risk scientific experiments and potentially hazardous technologies and manufacturing processes to be pursued in Earth orbit or eventually in Moon or Mars colonies is the ultimate way of having them pay their full cost to humanity, including all "externalities." Well-balanced scientific panels under the auspices of the UN could be given the responsibility for assessing activities based on their planetary risk profile.

And, of course, this policy will have the side benefit of getting humanity to the stars faster, while protecting the home world.

---

7   In December 2011, NASA announced the first confirmed Earth-like planet orbiting in the habitable region of a Sun-like star. The only challenge for colonization: it is 600 light-years from Earth.

Summary

- This final chapter goes well beyond public opinion findings to suggest some ideas that I believe are as likely as any others to come to reality over the course of the next 80 years of the 21st century. You could call these ideas the musing of a global pollster who believes we're heading into a period of step change rather than simply more incremental change.

- **Social capitalism**. The ever-increasing pressure on business to act better in society's interest will eventually lead, I believe, to a structural fix – such as a legal requirement for incorporated companies to act in the interest of the broader society, in return for being granted their limited financial and legal liability. Social capitalism is about putting societal purpose at the core of the business enterprise, then applying business discipline and capital to execute on this purpose. Leading companies are already voluntarily pursuing this, but it will increasingly be required through legislation or other means.

- **Collaborative democracy**. The huge democratic deficit that exists in many countries will lead to the reinvention of democracy for the digital age to truly enshrine principles of equality, transparency, open deliberation, and participatory democracy back into our system of governance. It starts with a fundamental shift in paradigm. Rather than the current political culture of polarized viewpoints warring with each other, collaborative democracy is focused on what pollsters call the average or median point of view. It is about applying proven "social technologies" to involve all parties in developing policies that can be supported by the middle two-thirds of citizens. It will put citizens collectively back in charge of the future.

- **From duality to diversity**. In an increasingly collaborative world, the Cold War artifact of Us and Them – this arbitrary and limited way of thinking – will naturally give way to more inclusive ways of framing conversations and exploring possibilities. Moving from a focus on two points of view to at least three will help turn adversity into diversity, and log jam into collaborative progress.

- **Off-worlding risk.** There will be ever more public debate on the ecosystem risks associated with certain kinds of scientific research and technological development. This will lead to increasingly persuasive calls for companies and governments to move higher-risk activities outside the biosphere. Such a policy will have the side benefit of getting humanity to the stars faster, while protecting our home world.

Appendix 1: Question wording and methodology

Figure 1

Q2t.   How serious a problem do you consider each of the following issues to be? Is each of the following a very serious problem, somewhat serious problem, not very serious problem or not a serious problem at all?

ct)   Climate change or global warming, due to the Greenhouse Effect

Very serious problem
Somewhat serious problem
Not very serious problem
Not a serious problem at all
VOLUNTEERED (DO NOT READ)
Don't know/Not Applicable

Figure 3

G13 a)   Military force should be used to help defeat government leaders who protect international terrorists operating from their country.

Strongly agree
Somewhat agree
Somewhat disagree
Strongly disagree
VOLUNTEERED (DO NOT READ)
Depends/Neither agree nor disagree
Not asked
Don't know/Not Applicable

Figure 4

G9A.   For each of the following statements, please tell me if you strongly agree, somewhat agree, somewhat disagree, or strongly disagree:

gt)   American companies are having a mainly positive influence in the world

Figure 5

M1t.   Please tell me if you think each of the following are having a mainly positive or mainly negative influence in the world:

ct)   The United States

Figure 6

G7.   Who or what would you say is most to blame for the current global financial crisis? Anything else?

"WHO"
Our national government
United States
Western governments/countries
Investment banks/investment bankers
Stock brokers/bond traders
Investors/financial speculators
Consumers/those borrowing money to buy a house – our country
American/Western consumers
Press/media
Business/companies
Banks/financial institutions
International financial institutions like the IMF

"WHAT"
Capitalism/globalization
Greed
Normal economic cycle
Nothing/no one
Other (Specify _____)
Don't know/Not Applicable

Figure 7

1)   For each of the following possible future trends, please tell me if you would see it as mainly positive or mainly negative:

a)   Europe becomes more influential than the United States in world affairs.

Figure 8

M1t.   Please tell me if you think each of the following are having a mainly positive or mainly negative influence in the world:

dt)   The European Union

Figure 9

M1t.   Please tell me if you think each of the following countries are having a mainly positive or mainly negative influence in the world:

at)   China

Figure 10

Q4t.   Please tell me how much you trust each of the following institutions to operate in the best interest of our society. Would you say you have a lot of trust, some trust, not much trust, or no trust at all in …?

at)   Our national government
bt)   Large [COUNTRY] companies
ct)   Global companies operating in [COUNTRY]
dt)   Non-governmental organizations such as environmental and social advocacy groups
et)   Press and media
gt)   The United Nations
ht)   Religious groups and churches

Figure 11

Q28t.   Please tell me if you strongly agree, somewhat agree, somewhat disagree or strongly disagree with each of the following statements:

at)   The world is going in the right direction

Figure 12

G8B.   Which one of the following most causes you to distrust leaders? Is it their …

Not doing what they say
Secrecy
Character flaws
Arrogance
Self-interest
VOLUNTEERED (DO NOT READ)
Other (Do not specify)
Not asked
Don't know/Not Applicable

Figure 13

G2t.   As you may know, there are both positive and negative impacts from the increasing globalization occurring in the world. By globalization, I mean the *increased trade between countries in goods, services and investment*. Thinking of you and your family's interests, do you think the overall effect of globalization is very positive, somewhat positive, somewhat negative or very negative?

Very positive
Somewhat positive
Somewhat negative
Very negative
VOLUNTEERED (DO NOT READ)
Neutral/Neither positive nor negative
Both positive and negative
Never heard of term globalization
Don't know/Not Applicable

Figure 14

9t.   How serious a problem do you consider each of the following issues to be?

Very serious problem
Somewhat serious problem
Not very serious problem
Not a serious problem at all
VOLUNTEERED (DO NOT READ)
Don't know/Not Applicable

at)   Air pollution in general
bt)   Water pollution in rivers, lakes, and oceans
dt)   Climate change due to Greenhouse Effect
et)   Depletion of natural resources
ft)   Automobile emissions
ht)   Loss of animal and plant species
it)   Production, transportation, and use of chemicals
jx)   Loss of rain forests, jungles, and wilderness areas
k)   The genetic modification of food crops

Figure 15

Q4At.   As you may know, there are both positive and negative impacts from the increasing globalization occurring in the world. By globalization, I mean the increased trade between countries in goods, services, and investment. Thinking of you and your family's interests, do you think the overall effect of globalization is very positive, somewhat positive, somewhat negative, or very negative?

Q5At.   For each of the following statements, please tell me if you strongly agree, somewhat agree, somewhat disagree, or strongly disagree:

at)   It is important to protect [COUNTRY'S] industries and jobs by using tariffs and other barriers against competing products from other countries.

Figure 16

G4t. Please tell me if each of the following will get better or worse because of globalization. What about [READ]? Will it get …?

Much better
A bit better
A bit worse
Much worse
VOLUNTEERED (DO NOT READ)
No effect either way
Depends
Don't know/Not Applicable

at) You and your family's income and buying power
bt) The economy of [COUNTRY]
ct) Workers' rights, working conditions, and wages in [COUNTRY]
b) You and your family's quality of life or wellbeing
d) [COUNTRY'S] cultural life
e) The availability of inexpensive products in your community
h) The quality of jobs available in [COUNTRY]
i) Economic equality among people in the world
jt) Environmental quality in the world
j) Access for [COUNTRY'S] exports to foreign markets
ft) Peace and stability in the world
ht) Economic development in poor countries
it) Poverty and homelessness in the world
d) The number of jobs in [COUNTRY]
et) Human rights, individual freedom, and democracy in the world

Figure 17

G3 a) Please tell me which of the following two statements is closer to your own opinion. Is it …?

Globalization concentrates wealth and makes the rich richer and the poor poorer,
    or,
Globalization brings economic opportunities to all people equally, both the rich and the poor.

Not asked
Don't know/Not Applicable

Figure 18

3tm. How often, if at all, do you consume each of the following types of food and beverages?

d) Locally grown foods (e.g., from your province/state or region)

Never
Less than once a month
Once or twice per month

Once per week
Several times per week
Daily

Figure 19

M6a.   Do you think that the current economic crisis points to the need for major changes, minor changes, or no significant changes in [COUNTRY's] economy …?

M6b.   What about the international economic system? Do you think that the current economic crisis points to the need for major changes, minor changes, or no significant changes in the international economic system?

Figure 20

C3t.   For each of the following statements, please tell me if you strongly agree, somewhat agree, somewhat disagree, or strongly disagree:

g)   The free enterprise system and free market economy work best in society's interest when accompanied by strong government regulations.

Figure 21

Q7At.   Thinking about the economic developments of the last few years, how fairly do you think the benefits and burdens have been shared in [COUNTRY]: very fairly, somewhat fairly, not very fairly, or not at all fairly?

Figure 22

7At.   Please tell me if you agree or disagree with each of the following statements:

gt)   Most rich people in [COUNTRY] deserve their wealth.

Strongly agree
Somewhat agree
Somewhat disagree
Strongly disagree
VOLUNTEERED (DO NOT READ)
Depends/Neither agree nor disagree
Don't know/Not Applicable

Figure 23

GDP1t.   As you may know, all countries measure their progress and development through economic statistics such as gross domestic product or GDP, which counts all of a country's money-based income and production of goods and services. Which of the following points of view on the best way for the government to measure our country's progress and development is closest to your own?

The government should measure national progress using the money-based, economic statistics because economic growth is the most important thing for a country to focus on.

Health, social and environmental statistics are as important as economic ones and the government should also use these for measuring national progress.

VOLUNTEERED (DO NOT READ)
Don't know/Not Applicable

Figure 24

Q19At.   Please tell me if you strongly agree, somewhat agree, somewhat disagree, or strongly disagree with each of the following statements:

at.   [COUNTRY'S] economy will be significantly damaged if we try to cut our emissions of climate-changing gases

Figure 25

Q   The profits of large companies help make things better for everyone who uses their products and services

Strongly agree
Somewhat agree
Somewhat disagree
Strongly disagree
VOLUNTEERED (DO NOT READ)
Depends/Neither agree nor disagree
Don't know/Not Applicable

Figure 26

Q1t.   The term "sustainable development" has been used since it first appeared in the Brundtland World Commission Report. In your estimation, is the potency of this term increasing, decreasing, or remaining the same in positively influencing key government and industry decision-makers in your country?

Figure 27

Q7t.   I would like you to think about how you form impressions of particular companies. What are the things that matter most in forming either a favorable or unfavorable impression of a company?

Labor practices and business ethics
Environmental impacts
Economic/financial factors/size
Business strategy and management

Figure 28

Q5At.   For each of the following statements, please tell me if you strongly agree, somewhat agree, somewhat disagree, or strongly disagree:

dt)   The free enterprise system and free market economy is the best system on which to base the future of the world

Figure 29

Q3.   What specific companies do you think are leaders in integrating sustainability into their business strategy?

Figure 30

Q8t.   Please tell me if you strongly agree, somewhat agree, somewhat disagree, or strongly disagree with each of the following statements:

gt)   The more socially responsible my company becomes, the more motivated and loyal I become as an employee

Figure 31

Q10Bt.   I am going to read a list of things some people say should be part of the responsibilities of large companies. For each one, please tell me to what extent you think companies should be held responsible.

01   Not held responsible
02
03   Held partially responsible
04
05   Held completely responsible
     VOLUNTEERED (DO NOT READ)
     Depends
     Don't know/Not Applicable

at)   Treating all employees and job applicants fairly, regardless of gender, race, religion, or sexual orientation
bt)   Applying the same high standards everywhere it operates in the world
ct)   Helping solve social problems like crime, poverty, and lack of education
dt)   Ensuring its products and operations do not harm the environment
et)   Increasing economic stability in the world
ft)   Reducing human rights abuses in the world
gt)   Providing good quality products and services at the lowest possible price
ht)   Supporting progressive government policies and legislation
it)   Helping reduce the gap between rich and poor
jt)   Ensuring that all materials it uses to make its products have been produced in a socially and environmentally responsible manner

Q15Bt.   Please rate each of the following types of companies on how well they fulfill their responsibilities to society. Compared to other types of companies, would you say [INSERT COMPANY TYPE] are …?

Among the very best
Above average
Average
Below average
Among the very worst
VOLUNTEERED (DO NOT READ)
Depends on the company/Some good, some bad
No opinion/Not familiar with this industry
Don't know/Not Applicable

at)   Banks and finance companies
bt)   Oil/petroleum companies
ct)   Auto companies
dt)   Clothing and apparel companies
et)   Chemical companies
ft)   High-tech/computer companies
it)   Food companies
jt)   Pharmaceutical companies
kt)   Mining companies
lt)   Telecommunications companies (telephone)

Figure 32

Q8t.   Please tell me if you strongly agree, somewhat agree, somewhat disagree, or strongly disagree with each of the following statements:

dt)   Our government should create laws that require large companies to go beyond their traditional economic role and work to make a better society, even though this could lead to higher prices and fewer jobs

Figure 33

Q7At.   Please tell me if you strongly agree, somewhat agree, somewhat disagree, or strongly disagree with each of the following statements:

dt)   I am very interested in learning more about the ways that some companies are trying to be socially responsible

Q11Bt.   Please tell me if you agree or disagree with each of the following statements:

at)   Companies communicate honestly and truthfully about their social and environmental performance

Figure 34

Q12Bt. Over the past year, have you considered rewarding a socially responsible company by either buying their products or speaking positively about the company to others? Would you say you have …?

Not considered doing this
Considered this, but didn't actually do it, or
You have actually done this in the past year
VOLUNTEERED (DO NOT READ)
Don't know/Not Applicable

Q16t. In the past year, have you considered punishing a company you see as not socially responsible by either refusing to buy their products or speaking critically about the company to others? Would you say you have …?

Not considered doing this
Considered this, but didn't actually do it, or
You have actually done this in the past year
VOLUNTEERED (DO NOT READ)
Don't know/Not Applicable

Figure 35

Q13Bt. Please tell me if you strongly agree, somewhat agree, somewhat disagree, or strongly disagree with each of the following statements:

at) As a consumer, I can make a difference in how responsibly a company behaves

b) As a citizen, I can make a difference in how responsibly our national government behaves

Figure 36

16P. To what extent have environmentally friendly products, that is products less harmful to the environment, become part of your regular purchases?

Regularly purchase a number of these
Regularly purchase one
Only sample these products
Never purchase them

Figure 37

Q12Bt. Over the past year, have you considered rewarding a socially responsible company by either buying their products or speaking positively about the company to others? Would you say you have …?

Not considered doing this
Considered this, but didn't actually do it, or
You have actually done this in the past year
VOLUNTEERED (DO NOT READ)
Don't know/Not Applicable

Figure 39

Q4t.   Please tell me how much you trust each of the following institutions to operate in the best interest of our society. Would you say you have a lot of trust, some trust, not much trust, or no trust at all in …?

at)   Our national government
bt)   Large [COUNTRY] companies
ct)   Global companies operating in [COUNTRY]
dt)   Non-governmental organizations such as environmental and social advocacy groups
et)   Press and media
ft)   Scientific and academic research institutions
gt)   The United Nations

Figure 40

G4B)   How much trust do you have in each of the following leaders to manage the challenges of the coming year in the best interests of you and your family? Would you say you have a lot, some, not much, or no trust at all in …?

a)   Individuals responsible for managing the global economy
b)   Individuals responsible for managing [COUNTRY'S] economy
c)   Executives responsible for multinational companies
d)   Spiritual and religious leaders
e)   Leaders of the United States of America
f)   Leaders of western European countries
g)   Leaders at the United Nations
h)   Leaders of charitable or non-governmental organizations

Figure 41

Q5At.   For each of the following statements, please tell me if you strongly agree, somewhat agree, somewhat disagree, or strongly disagree:

et)   I see myself more as a global citizen than a citizen of [COUNTRY]

Figure 42

G5t.   Please tell me if you strongly agree, somewhat agree, somewhat disagree, or strongly disagree with each of the following statements:

g)   Leaders of major environmental and social non-government organizations should be excluded when government leaders negotiate globalization agreements, because they are not widely elected

Figure 43

Q1At.   For each of the following possible global problems, please tell me if you see it as a very serious, somewhat serious, not very serious, or not at all serious problem:

    at)   Human rights abuses in the world
    bt)   Pollution and environmental problems in the world
    ct)   The spread of human diseases
    dt)   Extreme poverty in the world
    et)   Terrorism
    ft)   The migration of people between countries
    gt)   War and armed conflicts
    ht)   The state of the global economy
    it)   Religious fundamentalism
    jt)   Corruption
    k)   The gap between rich and poor

Figure 44

Q3At.   What about [READ STATEMENT] … do you strongly support, somewhat support, somewhat oppose, or strongly oppose environmental and social groups being involved in this activity?

    a)   Publicly criticizing the behavior of government and companies
    b)   Using public protests to raise awareness of an issue
    c)   Influencing government policies in [COUNTRY]
    d)   Working with companies to help solve environmental and social issues
    e)   Delivering social services like education or health care
    f)   Communicating about their activities and commitments
    g)   Raising money to support their activities

Figure 45

M5.   Do you think what US leaders refer to as the "war on terror" has made al Qaeda stronger, weaker, or has had no effect either way?

Figure 46

Q5At.   For each of the following statements, please tell me if you strongly agree, somewhat agree, somewhat disagree, or strongly disagree:

    ft)   The use of military force is the most effective way of reducing international terrorism

Figure 47

Q1.   What do you think is the most important problem facing the world today?

Figure 48

Q1At.   For each of the following possible global problems, please tell me if you see it as a very serious, somewhat serious, not very serious, or not at all serious problem:

   at)   Human rights abuses in the world
   bt)   Pollution and environmental problems in the world
   ct)   The spread of human diseases
   dt)   Extreme poverty in the world
   et)   Terrorism
   ft)   The migration of people between countries
   gt)   War and armed conflicts
   ht)   The state of the global economy
   it)   Religious fundamentalism
   jt)   Corruption
   kt)   The gap between rich and poor

Figure 49

Q7At.   Thinking about the economic developments of the last few years, how fairly do you think the benefits and burdens have been shared in [COUNTRY]: very fairly, somewhat fairly, not very fairly, or not at all fairly?

Figure 50

GB6.   Please tell me if you think each of the following are having a mainly positive or mainly negative influence in the world:

   h)   The United Nations

Figure 51

GB4.   The five permanent members of the Security Council are China, France, Russia, Britain, and the United States. Some people have proposed that the permanent membership should be expanded. Would you favor or oppose additional countries becoming permanent members?

GB3.   As you may know, there are currently five permanent members of the United Nations Security Council, and any one of them can veto (block) any resolution. Some people have proposed that this should be changed so that if a decision was supported by all the other members, no one member could veto the decision. Would you favor or oppose this change?

Figure 52

Q3Bt.   Please tell me how much you trust each of the following institutions to operate in the best interest of our society. Would you say you have a lot of trust, some trust, not much trust, or no trust at all in …?

   gt)   The United Nations

Figure 53

GW8A   The United Nations is currently exploring possible reforms. Please tell me if you favor or oppose each of the following proposals:

a)   Having [COUNTRY'S] official representative to the United Nations General Assembly be elected by the people of [COUNTRY]

Favor
Oppose
VOLUNTEERED (DO NOT READ)
Depends
Neither
Don't know/Not Applicable

Figure 54

Q7At.   Please tell me if you agree or disagree with each of the following statements:

ft)   Our children and grandchildren will have a higher quality of life than we do today

Strongly agree
Somewhat agree
Somewhat disagree
Strongly disagree
VOLUNTEERED (DO NOT READ)
Depends/Neither agree nor disagree
Don't know/Not Applicable

Figure 55

Q5.   How likely, if at all, do you think it is that humanity will find a way to overcome our current social, environmental, and economic challenges?

Very likely
Somewhat likely
Not very likely
Not at all likely
VOLUNTEERED (DO NOT READ)
Don't know/Not Applicable

Figure 56

Q8At.   Would you say that [THIS COUNTRY] is governed by the will of the people?

Yes
No
Don't know/no answer

Appendix 2: Detailed tables of poll results (by year and country)

Note: This appendix provides tables of country-by-country results for figures in this book where averages are presented. For figures that already contain actual numerical values, no tables are therefore provided here.

Figure 1

Q2t. How serious a problem do you consider each of the following issues to be? Is each of the following a very serious problem, somewhat serious problem, not very serious problem or not a serious problem at all?

ct. Climate change or global warming, due to the Greenhouse Effect

	Very serious											
	2014	2013	2012	2011	2010	2009	2008	2007	2003	2000	1998	1992
Brazil	88	NA	77	88	92	86	89	84	74	48	47	71
Canada	43	51	47	NA	48	58	70	66	40	44	46	58
China	35	44	40	55	58	57	56	59	37	40	30	NA
France	53	61	54	49	54	65	69	66	46	64	51	NA
Germany	31	52	47	50	47	61	50	48	54	63	68	73
India	36	51	46	47	53	45	42	68	67	69	44	36
Russia	46	53	NA	66	43	46	42	34	43	46	39	40
UK	41	46	46	49	43	59	61	59	50	61	50	62
USA	34	44	39	39	41	45	45	50	31	40	33	47

Figure 4.

G9A. For each of the following statements, please tell me if you strongly agree, somewhat agree, somewhat disagree, or strongly disagree.

gt) American companies are having a mainly positive influence in the world

	Total agree		Strongly agree		Somewhat agree		Somewhat disagree		Strongly disagree		Total disagree	
	2007	2005	2007	2005	2007	2005	2007	2005	2007	2005	2007	2005
Brazil	41	58	15	27	26	31	29	17	21	17	51	35
Canada	41	45	16	14	25	31	23	27	31	23	54	51
Chile	37	43	10	13	27	30	31	21	17	24	49	45
China	62	59	12	22	50	37	24	20	5	9	29	28
France	33	39	11	16	22	24	32	27	28	28	59	55
Germany	20	27	4	6	16	21	38	45	36	21	74	66
India	63	68	31	32	32	36	16	13	6	9	22	22
Indonesia	46	48	10	10	36	38	32	27	14	13	45	41
Italy	36	42	10	12	26	30	35	26	22	23	57	49
Mexico	34	36	11	11	23	25	32	32	31	30	63	62
Nigeria	61	68	21	33	40	34	21	15	12	10	33	26
Philippines	80	84	40	50	40	34	14	8	4	5	18	13
Russia	10	23	1	4	9	18	37	35	33	22	70	57
S. Korea	40	37	7	3	32	34	45	49	11	13	57	62
Turkey	23	23	6	4	17	19	38	38	24	25	62	63
UK	41	47	13	19	28	28	26	24	25	19	51	43
USA	55	60	17	22	38	38	22	20	17	14	39	35

Figure 5.

M1t. Please tell me if you think each of the following are having a mainly positive or mainly negative influence in the world:

ct) The United States

	Mainly positive										Mainly negative									
	2004	2005	2006	2007	2008	2009	2010	2012	2013	2014	2004	2005	2006	2007	2008	2009	2010	2012	2013	2014
Australia	39	29	29	32	32	37	45	50	46	44	52	60	60	58	56	38	40	38	42	46
Canada	34	30	34	27	38	44	40	48	45	43	60	60	56	62	55	38	47	42	45	52
Chile	29	38	32	41	42	55	62	47	62	NA	50	46	51	43	42	26	22	26	27	NA
China	40	22	28	38	34	29	33	29	20	18	42	62	52	46	58	44	53	48	57	59
France	38	25	24	32	36	45	46	62	52	51	54	65	69	51	53	39	40	27	39	41
Germany	27	21	16	20	18	39	37	44	35	21	64	65	74	72	65	47	44	45	39	57
India	54	44	30	18	43	39	42	37	40	42	30	17	28	24	20	28	28	23	24	29
Indonesia	38	40	21	32	33	36	58	43	38	36	51	47	71	55	43	39	25	37	44	47
Mexico	11	10	12	10	12	13	23	38	41	35	57	55	53	56	54	49	38	38	43	41
Russia	16	22	19	19	7	25	38	24	17	21	63	52	59	53	65	50	31	47	53	55
UK	44	36	33	35	41	48	46	60	46	52	50	57	57	53	45	35	43	32	46	42

Figure 6.
G7. Who or what would you say is most to blame for the current global financial crisis?

	Our national government	United States	Banks/financial institutions	Capitalism/ globalization	Western governments/ countries/world superpowers	Greed/corruption/ dishonesty	Investment banks/investment bankers
Australia	13	20	20	28	3	6	6
Canada	27	19	15	22	6	8	5
Chile	7	18	3	5	15	1	2
China	10	30	1	1	7	1	1
Costa Rica	34	36	8	6	17	7	7
France	20	10	18	12	19	4	15
Germany	14	11	38	3	7	9	18
India	30	32	4	12	14	9	17
Indonesia	52	14	1	11	7	14	1
Italy	16	13	4	31	26	34	21
Japan	7	36	15	2	-	4	2
Kenya	56	-	8	3	10	23	1
Mexico	74	24	17	3	2	1	1
Nigeria	47	23	5	19	22	25	4
Pakistan	9	13	1	1	7	1	1
Panama	42	17	5	12	14	9	7
Philippines	83	6	1	1	4	20	1
Russia	34	19	6	1	5	2	1
Spain	14	13	13	11	18	3	15
Turkey	24	35	4	5	5	5	7
UK	27	4	32	20	4	4	13
USA	31	10	13	21	3	6	5

Figure 6.

G7. Who or what would you say is most to blame for the current global financial crisis?

	Business/ companies/ managers	Investors/ financial speculators	Normal economic cycle	International financial institutions like the IMF	People in general / ourselves / selfish/lazy/ irresponsible people	Consumers/those borrowing money to buy a house - our country	Politicians/people in power/politics
Australia	5	3	4	4	6	4	2
Canada	7	3	6	3	5	6	1
Chile	14	2	1	1	3	1	4
China	2	1	1	2	4	1	1
Costa Rica	5	3	5	5	1	7	1
France	7	9	2	2	-	4	-
Germany	14	5	1	1	1	1	2
India	3	7	4	2	-	3	-
Indonesia	7	4	1	3	1	1	1
Italy	2	4	7	1	3	1	1
Japan	5	9	-	1	1	1	9
Kenya	7	3	8	6	1	4	3
Mexico	7	9	-	9	-	1	-
Nigeria	-	7	10	6	-	4	1
Pakistan	1	-	3	1	1	1	2
Panama	4	5	6	5	1	5	1
Philippines	5	3	1	-	24	1	10
Russia	3	4	1	2	-	1	-
Spain	5	5	2	4	2	2	3
Turkey	5	4	2	4	-	10	-
UK	3	1	5	3	6	1	4
USA	7	3	5	1	7	4	12

Figure 7.

1) For each of the following possible future trends, please tell me if you would see it as mainly positive or mainly negative.

a) Europe becomes more influential than the United States in world affairs.

	Positive	Negative
Argentina	57	16
Australia	62	23
Brazil	53	28
Canada	63	26
Chile	48	17
China	66	16
France	70	22
Germany	79	10
India	35	38
Indonesia	56	22
Italy	76	14
Japan	35	13
Lebanon	59	14
Mexico	66	8
Philippines	35	54
Poland	58	12
Russia	60	13
S. Africa	63	25
S. Korea	53	40
Spain	81	9
Turkey	49	19
UK	66	26
USA	34	55

Figure 8.

M1t. Please tell me if you think each of the following are having a mainly positive or mainly negative influence in the world:

dt) The European Union

	Mainly positive								Mainly negative							
	2013	2012	2010	2009	2008	2007	2006	2005	2013	2012	2010	2009	2008	2007	2006	2005
Australia	41	41	58	55	65	67	59	46	42	41	18	16	16	12	21	23
Canada	51	61	70	57	73	71	70	51	26	28	12	12	9	10	17	15
Chile	60	51	69	64	64	64	66	61	18	11	9	10	13	14	14	8
China	40	46	51	41	57	62	58	57	28	26	33	22	28	16	12	15
Egypt	29	51	40	43	39	40	10	30	27	25	22	20	35	42	33	25
France	68	67	70	74	71	71	68	72	23	23	18	12	17	13	21	15
Germany	59	73	69	76	81	72	73	72	21	19	16	12	5	17	15	12
India	33	22	34	23	36	22	29	36	21	24	14	20	11	16	20	13
Indonesia	50	34	54	44	37	46	52	55	22	24	20	23	25	30	27	19
Kenya	60	62	61	69	72	74	62	58	12	21	15	15	17	12	21	9
Mexico	42	42	51	42	37	36	43	37	34	27	17	15	15	12	15	27
Nigeria	58	63	63	58	58	58	64	61	26	26	14	27	26	23	19	16
Russia	41	42	55	50	31	51	46	42	19	16	10	17	23	11	18	9
UK	42	46	50	54	55	61	59	54	47	46	37	22	28	25	25	32
USA	46	56	61	50	62	60	53	42	33	31	21	19	19	19	20	27

Figure 9.

M1t. Please tell me if you think each of the following countries are having a mainly positive or mainly negative influence in the world: at) China

	Mainly positive									Mainly negative								
	2013	2012	2010	2009	2008	2007	2006	2005	2004	2013	2012	2010	2009	2008	2007	2006	2005	2004
Australia	36	61	43	36	47	60	43	43	56	55	29	43	43	37	28	39	38	28
Canada	29	53	35	35	31	45	46	36	48	59	36	49	41	58	40	42	44	39
Chile	57	53	61	55	60	60	62	63	56	25	18	20	22	17	19	16	15	15
France	25	38	26	24	22	35	32	31	49	68	49	64	64	70	46	59	53	33
Germany	13	42	24	20	11	28	30	31	34	67	47	62	71	69	59	53	44	47
India	36	30	25	30	30	22	35	44	66	27	31	52	38	24	18	22	15	20
Indonesia	55	51	63	43	43	58	62	60	68	27	26	18	29	37	25	27	23	20
Mexico	31	37	23	32	34	29	31	28	33	47	37	42	26	26	28	28	26	28
Russia	42	46	52	42	45	46	38	32	42	24	21	18	31	18	21	31	33	27
UK	37	57	38	40	39	48	49	40	46	50	32	48	38	42	38	34	44	35
USA	23	42	36	29	32	33	34	35	39	67	46	51	51	52	54	44	53	46

Figure 10.

Q4. Please tell me how much you trust each of the following institutions to operate in the best interest of our society. Would you say you have a lot of trust, some trust, not much trust, or no trust at all in ...?

at) Our national government

	Total trust (1+2)										Total no trust (3+4)									
	2014	2013	2012	2010	2009	2007	2005	2003	2002	2000	2014	2013	2012	2010	2009	2007	2005	2003	2002	2000
Brazil	26	NA	40	56	38	31	22	54	38	25	74	NA	59	42	61	69	78	46	61	74
Canada	54	67	63	55	67	55	41	63	59	54	46	33	36	44	31	44	58	35	40	44
France	23	37	26	25	38	51	30	33	NA	37	76	61	72	73	60	40	67	65	NA	60
Germany	63	60	38	30	48	55	24	29	51	39	36	38	62	69	52	44	75	70	49	58
India	61	76	65	73	73	71	70	77	62	63	35	23	33	21	18	28	28	22	37	36
Indonesia	55	65	59	52	83	50	66	68	67	69	44	35	41	48	15	48	33	31	33	28
Mexico	32	40	48	23	32	31	31	55	35	54	66	59	52	77	68	69	69	43	64	45
Nigeria	37	43	43	43	32	31	31	38	41	46	60	56	57	57	69	69	68	62	57	54
Russia	55	59	67	54	64	57	56	52	43	43	40	36	31	43	33	40	40	45	51	54
Spain	13	8	27	23	29	NA	49	71	55	49	86	89	71	76	70	NA	50	27	43	50
Turkey	50	69	61	37	30	39	52	54	13	61	47	30	37	61	68	56	46	40	86	39
UK	45	42	55	52	44	49	50	54	50	52	55	58	44	46	54	49	49	45	48	47
USA	43	47	47	56	62	51	59	72	76	58	56	53	51	43	37	48	39	26	23	42

Figure 10.

Q4t. Please tell me how much you trust each of the following institutions to operate in the best interest of our society. Would you say you have a lot of trust, some trust, not much trust, or no trust at all in ...?

bt) Large [COUNTRY] companies

	TOTAL TRUST (1+2)										TOTAL NO TRUST (3+4)									
	2014	2013	2012	2010	2009	2007	2005	2003	2002	2000	2014	2013	2012	2010	2009	2007	2005	2003	2002	2000
Brazil	53	NA	61	74	60	46	35	59	53	44	47	NA	39	21	36	54	63	41	44	55
Canada	48	73	60	53	63	57	59	66	61	60	51	23	36	43	33	40	39	32	35	36
France	40	52	41	49	34	46	40	41	NA	42	59	46	57	49	63	50	55	57	NA	54
Germany	58	64	48	51	37	51	35	41	45	47	41	32	48	46	61	47	64	57	54	47
India	57	75	66	62	65	76	64	75	63	67	32	23	26	31	24	21	33	24	35	30
Indonesia	73	82	66	62	66	55	69	78	64	67	24	18	31	36	29	42	29	21	33	28
Mexico	29	43	57	52	57	56	58	60	49	67	68	55	42	47	42	44	41	38	50	32
Nigeria	63	69	62	59	60	50	58	NA	56	60	34	30	37	39	39	49	41	NA	42	37
Russia	33	44	44	32	31	34	36	28	23	25	56	47	52	64	57	59	57	67	56	68
Spain	13	44	27	43	28	NA	38	62	34	44	86	53	71	54	69	NA	56	36	55	52
Turkey	59	73	64	59	32	50	54	45	40	54	36	25	31	34	63	43	41	41	50	46
UK	51	59	57	65	51	49	50	53	46	54	47	38	40	33	45	46	47	43	48	40
USA	48	54	40	51	49	48	49	53	43	56	51	44	59	47	50	49	49	44	55	44

Figure 10.

Q4t. Please tell me how much you trust each of the following institutions to operate in the best interest of our society. Would you say you have a lot of trust, some trust, not much trust, or no trust at all in ...?

c1) Global companies operating in [COUNTRY]

	Total trust (1+2)										Total no trust (3+4)									
	2014	2013	2012	2010	2009	2007	2005	2003	2002	2000	2014	2013	2012	2010	2009	2007	2005	2003	2002	2000
Brazil	50	NA	57	68	51	43	34	39	47	38	48	NA	43	25	44	56	64	60	48	60
Canada	38	55	49	48	56	46	45	53	48	46	60	40	46	46	39	47	50	40	42	48
France	35	41	32	34	25	32	30	21	NA	29	62	54	66	60	70	59	61	73	NA	65
Germany	49	57	41	45	33	51	36	41	51	41	49	39	55	51	64	47	62	56	42	49
India	48	67	49	57	48	61	54	59	52	54	41	25	39	33	35	35	41	39	44	38
Indonesia	65	77	51	58	46	46	59	62	50	63	30	21	43	39	45	50	38	35	35	29
Mexico	25	38	49	43	42	46	49	51	44	52	69	59	48	56	57	52	50	47	54	47
Nigeria	67	72	73	57	68	60	67	52	59	62	29	27	27	41	27	38	30	40	38	29
Russia	20	31	28	21	22	19	20	19	16	13	68	58	66	74	60	70	70	72	49	76
Spain	17	34	22	31	18	NA	30	52	29	38	77	61	74	63	75	NA	60	46	55	58
Turkey	49	55	50	30	25	32	30	32	26	50	43	41	44	58	70	54	61	50	55	50
UK	38	42	50	52	47	42	41	45	41	45	59	52	44	42	46	50	53	50	50	48
USA	40	49	45	47	50	43	43	51	45	47	57	47	52	49	45	51	52	41	45	50

Figure 10.

Q4t. Please tell me how much you trust each of the following institutions to operate in the best interest of our society. Would you say you have a lot of trust, some trust, not much trust, or no trust at all in ...?

dt) Non-governmental organizations such as environmental and social advocacy groups

	Total trust (1+2)											Total no trust (3+4)									
	2014	2013	2012	2010	2009	2007	2005	2003	2002	2000		2014	2013	2012	2010	2009	2007	2005	2003	2002	2000
Brazil	58	NA	65	71	60	47	51	64	61	59		42	NA	35	24	37	50	47	34	35	39
Canada	75	73	73	72	75	73	73	77	74	74		24	26	25	26	22	23	24	20	22	22
France	74	69	69	71	71	73	68	67	NA	53		25	29	29	26	26	23	27	27	NA	40
Germany	69	79	61	65	55	56	57	63	68	60		29	16	38	33	44	42	41	36	30	33
India	48	56	52	64	57	63	58	79	60	80		34	30	34	23	26	32	33	17	37	18
Indonesia	58	71	66	78	62	64	72	73	62	81		38	24	30	20	25	30	25	23	25	14
Mexico	35	40	59	78	74	71	76	70	44	73		53	50	38	21	25	27	24	28	52	27
Nigeria	65	72	73	59	63	69	68	59	61	64		32	26	26	39	31	30	30	33	36	31
Russia	43	49	57	44	44	42	48	54	46	48		43	39	37	46	38	42	37	35	29	36
Spain	50	52	49	57	46	NA	66	73	68	65		47	43	50	42	52	NA	30	26	24	31
Turkey	71	66	63	52	41	51	52	46	45	58		24	31	31	39	55	36	43	41	42	42
UK	68	71	68	65	69	62	66	72	68	69		31	26	26	29	26	31	27	22	27	25
USA	66	65	63	59	69	68	67	66	67	67		32	33	35	39	29	28	29	30	27	31

Figure 10.

Q4t. Please tell me how much you trust each of the following institutions to operate in the best interest of our society. Would you say you have a lot of trust, some trust, not much trust, or no trust at all in ...?

et) Press and media

	Total trust (1+2)									Total no trust (3+4)								
	2014	2013	2012	2010	2009	2007	2003	2002	2000	2014	2013	2012	2010	2009	2007	2003	2002	2000
Brazil	NA	NA	62	66	52	50	52	58	52	NA	NA	38	31	46	50	47	40	47
Canada	61	55	55	48	51	53	57	56	55	38	44	44	50	47	46	42	43	44
France	25	35	26	24	31	31	27	NA	37	75	64	73	73	68	66	70	NA	61
Germany	45	40	42	40	42	44	40	49	38	54	59	58	57	58	55	59	50	59
India	65	67	74	79	64	80	83	76	80	27	25	19	13	23	18	14	24	18
Indonesia	66	81	81	77	70	74	80	88	77	30	17	17	22	22	23	19	10	22
Mexico	27	42	50	55	49	51	55	44	51	68	57	49	44	51	48	43	55	48
Nigeria	67	71	70	54	78	69	72	61	79	30	28	29	45	20	30	27	37	20
Russia	52	49	54	42	51	47	46	48	47	42	47	44	54	45	48	48	45	50
Spain	31	38	33	26	28	NA	58	55	59	67	59	66	72	71	NA	40	43	39
Turkey	43	42	45	21	21	26	31	25	49	53	57	50	73	75	70	60	69	51
UK	28	30	30	34	31	36	33	29	29	72	69	69	65	66	61	65	70	70
USA	34	43	38	40	36	41	48	52	41	66	55	60	58	63	57	51	45	59

Figure 10.

Q4t. Please tell me how much you trust each of the following institutions to operate in the best interest of our society. Would you say you have a lot of trust, some trust, not much trust, or no trust at all in ...?

g1) The United Nations

	Total trust (1+2)							Total no trust (3+4)						
	2014	2013	2012	2010	2009	2003	2000	2014	2013	2012	2010	2009	2003	2000
Brazil	NA	NA	57	NA	53	52	49	NA	NA	41	NA	39	44	44
Canada	72	69	70	NA	72	77	73	24	26	25	NA	24	19	21
France	52	61	53	53	61	57	NA	45	36	44	43	36	37	NA
Germany	67	77	52	55	57	65	70	30	17	46	43	41	34	28
India	56	53	52	60	56	71	55	24	19	28	23	22	20	36
Indonesia	74	74	64	63	57	65	59	19	18	29	33	29	31	29
Mexico	36	44	55	91	87	88	45	52	46	39	9	11	9	51
Nigeria	47	64	64	58	64	61	63	46	32	34	41	33	33	34
Russia	38	40	41	NA	36	NA	NA	40	43	47	NA	39	NA	NA
Spain	43	51	36	40	41	78	59	53	41	62	56	54	19	33
Turkey	50	50	28	16	26	33	23	42	46	63	75	70	52	64
UK	68	67	71	67	72	73	75	30	29	25	31	24	24	23
USA	53	57	62	58	61	64	68	45	40	34	38	37	32	27

Figure 10.

Q4t. Please tell me how much you trust each of the following institutions to operate in the best interest of our society. Would you say you have a lot of trust, some trust, not much trust, or no trust at all in ...?

ht) Religious groups and churches

	Total trust (1+2)								Total no trust (3+4)							
	2012	2010	2009	2007	2006	2003	2002	2000	2012	2010	2009	2007	2006	2003	2002	2000
Brazil	NA	NA	60	62	NA	NA	65	77	NA	NA	38	38	NA	NA	33	23
Canada	48	NA	50	59	NA	NA	60	65	48	NA	47	38	NA	NA	38	31
France	19	23	22	24	NA	NA	NA	31	80	73	72	68	NA	NA	NA	63
Germany	39	27	30	49	NA	NA	39	47	58	71	68	50	NA	NA	59	48
India	68	58	54	73	NA	NA	69	71	21	29	31	25	NA	NA	30	26
Indonesia	84	85	74	74	NA	NA	92	98	14	13	20	20	NA	NA	5	2
Mexico	48	43	44	43	NA	NA	55	51	50	56	55	55	NA	NA	44	47
Nigeria	87	65	84	87	86	85	76	87	12	34	16	13	12	14	23	12
Russia	55	NA	66	62	NA	NA	47	43	36	NA	27	28	NA	NA	38	41
Spain	NA	25	20	NA	NA	NA	41	48	NA	72	79	NA	NA	NA	55	49
Turkey	52	29	27	26	NA	NA	49	43	40	67	70	67	NA	NA	46	57
UK	55	54	52	51	NA	NA	62	59	41	43	44	45	NA	NA	35	36
USA	66	71	69	68	NA	NA	72	81	31	27	29	30	NA	NA	25	18

Figure 11

Q28t. Please tell me if you strongly agree, somewhat agree, somewhat disagree, or strongly disagree with each of the following statements
jt) The world is going in the right direction

TOTAL AGREE

	2014	2011	2010	2009	2007	2005	2004	2003	2002	2001	2000
France	17	10	10	15	17	17	14	15	15	24	44
Germany	37	23	22	32	36	22	24	19	13	23	47
India	46	62	64	48	50	39	51	51	49	38	58
Indonesia	58	43	52	64	57	65	58	44	35	56	73
Mexico	24	28	24	29	29	31	43	47	39	39	65
Nigeria	32	41	38	34	45	28	19	26	33	39	53
Russia	35	46	42	41	36	35	32	31	37	34	31
Turkey	34	29	17	19	17	19	12	19	31	17	44
UK	29	24	27	29	33	36	20	33	25	31	52
USA	25	19	20	29	31	35	34	45	37	53	53

Figure 12.
G8B. Which one of the following most causes you to distrust leaders? Is it their...

	Not doing what they say	Secrecy	Character flaws	Arrogance	Self interest	Other	DK/NA
Argentina	50	6	1	3	34	3	4
Australia	34	18	4	18	20	4	1
Canada	39	13	3	14	27	2	1
Chile	56	7	4	4	25	1	2
France	39	24	1	4	30	1	2
Germany	44	8	7	10	28	1	2
India	34	1	9	5	51	0	1
Indonesia	57	4	2	2	35	1	1
Italy	23	36	1	17	19	3	2
Japan	40	5	14	11	28	2	1
Mexico	43	7	11	14	22	0	3
Netherlands	47	17	4	5	26	0	1
Nigeria	46	5	5	6	34	0	4
Qatar	29	15	11	13	31	2	0
Russia	70	3	4	5	13	2	2
S. Africa	43	6	6	8	30	2	4
S. Korea	60	6	2	3	28	0	1
Spain	39	13	8	7	25	0	8
Turkey	58	6	9	3	24	0	0
UK	41	18	2	14	22	1	1
USA	35	18	9	11	23	2	2

Figure 14.
9t. How serious a problem do you consider each of the following issues to be?

at) Air pollution in general

	2000	1998
Argentina	84	82
Australia	54	55
Canada	54	53
China	72	37
France	74	66
Germany	59	56
India	83	85
Indonesia	66	56
Italy	76	72
Mexico	81	75
Russia	76	67
S. Africa	60	54
Turkey	63	71
UK	57	53
USA	54	49

bt) Water pollution in rivers, lakes and oceans

	2000	1998
Argentina	92	87
Australia	69	72
Canada	71	68
China	69	60
France	81	73
Germany	69	72
India	80	73
Indonesia	56	53
Italy	83	79
Mexico	83	72
Russia	76	71
S. Africa	59	59
Turkey	49	55
UK	67	61
USA	72	64

dt) Climate change due to Greenhouse Effect

	2000	1998
Argentina	73	72
Australia	49	54
Canada	44	46
China	40	30
France	64	51
Germany	63	68
India	69	44
Indonesia	33	22
Italy	64	60
Mexico	74	73
Russia	46	39
S. Africa	28	29
Turkey	36	41
UK	61	50
USA	40	33

et) Depletion of natural resources

	2000	1998
Argentina	89	87
Australia	68	69
Canada	68	63
China	62	55
France	74	67
Germany	72	74
India	85	68
Indonesia	48	50
Italy	75	74
Mexico	84	78
Russia	69	64
S. Africa	42	40
Turkey	58	59
UK	71	64
USA	64	61

Figure 14.

9t. How serious a problem do you consider each of the following issues to be?

ft) Automobile emissions

	2000	1998
Argentina	79	80
Australia	59	57
Canada	50	52
China	68	58
France	67	60
Germany	49	49
India	84	84
Indonesia	54	45
Italy	73	72
Mexico	79	71
Russia	57	52
S. Africa	38	39
Turkey	47	50
UK	57	53
USA	46	41

ht) Loss of animal and plant species

	2000	1998
Argentina	89	86
Australia	67	70
Canada	59	57
China	52	77
France	68	63
Germany	66	71
India	84	71
Indonesia	42	40
Italy	71	63
Mexico	87	77
Russia	61	55
S. Africa	44	41
Turkey	59	61
UK	66	59
USA	56	53

ft) Production, transportation and use of chemicals

	2000	1998
Argentina	77	75
Australia	47	50
Canada	50	46
China	40	22
France	66	57
Germany	56	56
India	66	52
Indonesia	41	37
Italy	61	59
Mexico	75	71
Russia	56	51
S. Africa	39	39
Turkey	45	48
UK	58	47
USA	46	41

Figure 14.

9t. How serious a problem do you consider each of the following issues to be?

jx) Loss of rainforests, jungles and wilderness areas

	2000	1998
Argentina	92	NA
Australia	76	NA
Canada	70	NA
China	52	NA
France	71	NA
Germany	85	NA
India	80	NA
Indonesia	51	NA
Italy	80	NA
Mexico	89	NA
Russia	42	NA
S. Africa	44	NA
Turkey	48	NA
UK	77	NA
USA	70	NA

k) The genetic modification of food crops

	2000	1998
Argentina	60	NA
Australia	39	NA
Canada	37	NA
China	25	NA
France	62	NA
Germany	48	NA
India	52	NA
Indonesia	20	NA
Italy	51	NA
Mexico	56	NA
Russia	32	NA
S. Africa	28	NA
Turkey	43	NA
UK	51	NA
USA	34	NA

Figure 15.

Q4At. As you may know, there are both positive and negative impacts from the increasing globalization occurring in the world. By globalization, I mean the increased trade between countries in goods, services and investment. Thinking of you and your family's interests, do you think the overall effect of globalization is very positive, somewhat positive, somewhat negative, or very negative?

	Positive (1+2)								Negative (3+4)							
	2015	2011	2009	2005	2003	2002	2001	2000	2015	2011	2009	2005	2003	2002	2001	2000
Brazil	-	62	62	52	72	NA	62	64	-	22	26	36	22	NA	26	29
Chile	50	50	52	63	54	51	60	61	19	23	18	15	22	21	20	16
China	48	47	58	46	60	76	75	NA	29	27	12	37	13	12	10	NA
France	45	36	32	38	35	30	37	29	50	56	56	50	45	50	34	36
Germany	53	53	52	43	55	61	77	51	21	33	34	30	38	35	20	26
India	51	47	43	64	73	70	79	70	22	25	19	19	18	22	15	23
Indonesia	60	52	42	60	61	54	74	63	21	20	31	21	22	35	16	23
Italy	-	NA	55	55	53	59	61	57	-	NA	34	30	31	28	22	29
Mexico	61	42	65	69	67	69	69	71	15	22	24	23	19	23	23	25
Nigeria	64	78	70	68	70	68	70	71	29	17	24	19	15	21	10	16
Russia	-	27	34	23	28	26	33	37	-	19	12	14	16	16	13	13
Spain	52	38	41	NA	55	30	36	41	34	17	34	NA	19	30	33	28
Turkey	33	50	22	33	30	37	27	51	27	35	56	24	31	41	61	29
UK	73	61	60	63	67	69	73	60	23	32	30	32	28	27	22	33
USA	57	52	60	65	65	70	76	68	39	44	36	31	31	27	21	29

Figure 15.

Q5At. For each of the following statements, please tell me if you strongly agree, somewhat agree, somewhat disagree, or strongly disagree.

at) It is important to protect [Country's] industries and jobs by using tariffs and other barriers against competing products from other countries.

	Total agree					Strongly agree					Somewhat agree				
	2015	2013	2008	2005	2001	2015	2013	2008	2005	2001	2015	2013	2008	2005	2001
Australia	71	76	61	NA	77	42	43	28	NA	45	28	33	33	NA	31
Brazil	-	75	69	85	77	-	35	44	62	51	-	40	26	22	26
Canada	68	71	71	75	64	25	32	32	36	28	43	39	39	39	36
Chile	77	NA	79	84	82	41	NA	61	51	52	37	NA	19	33	30
China	62	NA	73	51	69	15	NA	33	27	32	47	NA	40	24	37
France	75	80	73	69	71	33	42	33	36	30	42	38	39	33	41
Germany	52	NA	65	71	54	12	NA	23	37	26	40	NA	42	34	28
Kenya	89	NA	85	90	NA	52	NA	60	68	NA	37	NA	25	23	NA
Nigeria	89	77	83	80	73	51	26	52	40	45	38	51	31	40	28
Pakistan	81	67	63	NA	NA	47	36	35	NA	NA	33	31	28	NA	NA
Russia	78	68	77	78	73	46	41	36	41	39	32	26	41	37	34
S. Korea	87	87	74	88	68	38	40	17	40	21	49	47	57	48	47
Spain	68	NA	67	NA	49	35	NA	24	NA	23	34	NA	43	NA	26
Turkey	61	67	78	80	43	21	23	28	23	7	40	44	50	57	37
UK	65	71	64	62	61	26	35	22	29	31	39	35	42	33	30
USA	63	72	66	67	61	28	35	35	31	28	35	37	30	35	32

Figure 16.

G4t. Please tell me if each of the following will get better or worse because of globalization. What about [read]? Will it get...?

d) The number of jobs in [COUNTRY]

	Better	Worse
Argentina	22	73
Australia	33	58
Brazil	39	54
Canada	47	45
Chile	40	42
China	49	41
France	17	72
Germany	28	70
India	43	50
Indonesia	33	65
Italy	48	29
Japan	10	76
Kazakhstan	59	19
Mexico	45	41
Netherlands	59	41
Nigeria	59	28
Qatar	75	21
Russia	33	26
S. Africa	29	61
S. Korea	45	52
Spain	24	48
Turkey	70	13
UK	44	43
USA	46	45
Venezuela	55	39

et) Human rights, individual freedom and democracy in the world.

	Better	Worse
Argentina	31	56
Australia	54	38
Brazil	53	38
Canada	61	33
Chile	53	23
China	70	16
France	34	53
Germany	71	27
India	64	28
Indonesia	65	32
Italy	59	27
Japan	45	22
Kazakhstan	55	10
Mexico	46	35
Netherlands	80	20
Nigeria	60	25
Qatar	69	24
Russia	36	12
S. Africa	54	30
S. Korea	77	20
Spain	23	49
Turkey	66	11
UK	63	27
USA	71	22
Venezuela	67	24

Figure 16.

G4t. Please tell me if each of the following will get better or worse because of globalization. What about [read]? Will it get...?

ft) Peace and stability in the world

	Better	Worse
Argentina	18	69
Australia	44	47
Brazil	43	48
Canada	48	44
Chile	40	38
China	73	15
France	20	67
Germany	56	40
India	51	40
Indonesia	36	62
Italy	46	36
Japan	39	26
Kazakhstan	60	13
Mexico	40	40
Netherlands	65	35
Nigeria	55	32
Qatar	50	41
Russia	33	20
S. Africa	39	45
S. Korea	65	31
Spain	22	49
Turkey	69	9
UK	47	42
USA	63	29
Venezuela	57	33

ht) Economic development in poor countries.

	Better	Worse
Argentina	19	74
Australia	52	40
Brazil	45	48
Canada	57	36
Chile	46	36
China	79	11
France	29	57
Germany	51	46
India	59	35
Indonesia	49	48
Italy	48	37
Japan	50	26
Kazakhstan	62	10
Mexico	41	41
Netherlands	70	30
Nigeria	58	28
Qatar	47	50
Russia	31	17
S. Africa	38	48
S. Korea	55	43
Spain	19	54
Turkey	69	11
UK	59	29
USA	75	18
Venezuela	58	35

it) Poverty and homelessness in the world.

	Better	Worse
Argentina	18	75
Australia	32	59
Brazil	38	55
Canada	40	52
Chile	42	38
China	61	23
France	21	66
Germany	40	57
India	48	45
Indonesia	27	69
Italy	38	43
Japan	24	44
Kazakhstan	53	15
Mexico	46	43
Netherlands	58	42
Nigeria	55	31
Qatar	41	56
Russia	21	24
S. Africa	34	54
S. Korea	49	45
Spain	18	56
Turkey	69	13
UK	48	41
USA	53	38
Venezuela	52	40

Figure 16.

G4t. Please tell me if each of the following will get better or worse because of globalization. What about [read]? Will it get...?

jt) Environmental quality in the world

	Better	Worse
Argentina	20	73
Australia	39	56
Brazil	40	53
Canada	42	52
Chile	32	50
China	69	21
France	22	69
Germany	45	53
India	52	40
Indonesia	39	57
Italy	37	50
Japan	31	48
Kazakhstan	47	23
Mexico	37	48
Netherlands	43	56
Nigeria	61	24
Qatar	40	56
Russia	20	40
S. Africa	40	43
S. Korea	33	66
Spain	18	53
Turkey	70	12
UK	44	47
USA	48	43
Venezuela	54	41

j) Access for [COUNTRY'S] exports to foreign markets

	Better	Worse
Argentina	42	47
Australia	70	20
Brazil	64	27
Canada	73	19
Chile	74	13
China	81	11
France	52	33
Germany	76	21
India	75	19
Indonesia	70	27
Italy	71	15
Japan	43	43
Kazakhstan	56	15
Mexico	54	31
Netherlands	87	13
Nigeria	62	21
Qatar	90	9
Russia	50	13
S. Africa	58	24
S. Korea	73	26
Spain	40	35
Turkey	64	13
UK	71	17
USA	70	21
Venezuela	81	14

Figure 16.

G4t. Please tell me if each of the following will get better or worse because of globalization. What about [read]? Will it get...?

e) The availability of inexpensive products in your community

	Better	Worse
Argentina	67	27
Australia	64	25
Brazil	55	36
Canada	66	26
Chile	68	17
China	67	17
France	51	37
Germany	64	30
India	65	28
Indonesia	53	44
Italy	70	17
Japan	67	9
Kazakhstan	63	11
Mexico	56	30
Netherlands	81	19
Nigeria	60	29
Qatar	81	19
Russia	36	21
S. Africa	42	41
S. Korea	76	19
Spain	35	34
Turkey	72	10
UK	67	21
USA	70	20
Venezuela	66	27

h) The quality of jobs available in [COUNTRY]

	Better	Worse
Argentina	20	74
Australia	46	42
Brazil	41	52
Canada	52	39
Chile	39	42
China	63	28
France	22	65
Germany	50	44
India	54	41
Indonesia	51	46
Italy	53	30
Japan	30	49
Kazakhstan	54	22
Mexico	47	39
Netherlands	65	34
Nigeria	59	27
Qatar	82	14
Russia	30	19
S. Africa	31	56
S. Korea	58	39
Spain	23	48
Turkey	70	12
UK	48	38
USA	55	37
Venezuela	58	36

i) Economic equality among people in the world

	Better	Worse
Argentina	19	71
Australia	33	58
Brazil	39	50
Canada	50	42
Chile	44	37
China	57	30
France	24	63
Germany	45	52
India	57	35
Indonesia	36	59
Italy	38	44
Japan	38	37
Kazakhstan	45	14
Mexico	46	39
Netherlands	64	36
Nigeria	56	27
Qatar	72	25
Russia	23	21
S. Africa	44	41
S. Korea	45	52
Spain	20	57
Turkey	66	11
UK	48	41
USA	63	27
Venezuela	65	27

Figure 16.

G4t. Please tell me if each of the following will get better or worse because of globalization. What about [read]? Will it get...?

b) You and your family's quality of life or wellbeing

	Better	Worse
Argentina	34	56
Australia	60	24
Brazil	64	25
Canada	66	22
Chile	60	19
China	70	15
France	37	41
Germany	64	28
India	80	14
Indonesia	77	17
Italy	55	16
Japan	35	21
Kazakhstan	59	10
Mexico	59	28
Netherlands	81	19
Nigeria	71	19
Qatar	90	7
Russia	28	17
S. Africa	54	32
S. Korea	76	20
Spain	37	30
Turkey	40	46
UK	69	15
USA	69	16
Venezuela	76	16

d) [COUNTRY'S] cultural life

	Better	Worse
Argentina	47	44
Australia	60	29
Brazil	62	29
Canada	63	25
Chile	63	20
China	80	12
France	44	39
Germany	70	26
India	58	33
Indonesia	49	49
Italy	69	17
Japan	38	36
Kazakhstan	68	11
Mexico	52	33
Netherlands	75	25
Nigeria	60	29
Qatar	75	24
Russia	43	21
S. Africa	47	38
S. Korea	71	26
Spain	38	32
Turkey	66	17
UK	60	30
USA	67	22
Venezuela	69	25

Figure 16.

G4t. Please tell me if each of the following will get better or worse because of globalization. What about [read]? Will it get...?

a1) You and your family's income and buying power

	Better	Worse
Argentina	31	59
Australia	49	34
Brazil	58	30
Canada	55	31
Chile	56	22
China	71	13
France	31	45
Germany	46	47
India	78	16
Indonesia	70	23
Italy	46	22
Japan	27	25
Kazakhstan	58	10
Mexico	59	28
Netherlands	71	29
Nigeria	71	17
Qatar	92	6
Russia	27	17
S. Africa	48	35
S. Korea	67	25
Spain	33	32
Turkey	34	52
UK	62	19
USA	61	24
Venezuela	74	17

b1) The economy of [COUNTRY]

	Better	Worse
Argentina	24	69
Australia	63	29
Brazil	50	41
Canada	59	34
Chile	55	30
China	83	10
France	31	57
Germany	59	37
India	69	26
Indonesia	40	57
Italy	62	21
Japan	40	43
Kazakhstan	69	11
Mexico	54	34
Netherlands	74	26
Nigeria	61	31
Qatar	88	11
Russia	46	16
S. Africa	42	46
S. Korea	62	36
Spain	39	34
Turkey	45	43
UK	64	25
USA	65	27
Venezuela	64	30

c1) Workers' rights, working conditions and wages in [COUNTRY]

	Better	Worse
Argentina	18	77
Australia	40	49
Brazil	40	51
Canada	50	39
Chile	41	40
China	58	29
France	27	62
Germany	30	66
India	58	35
Indonesia	52	45
Italy	48	32
Japan	16	67
Kazakhstan	59	15
Mexico	47	39
Netherlands	58	42
Nigeria	60	27
Qatar	76	21
Russia	25	22
S. Africa	40	44
S. Korea	55	43
Spain	25	44
Turkey	70	12
UK	61	29
USA	54	36
Venezuela	60	33

Figure 19.
M6a. Do you think that the current economic crisis points to the need for major changes, minor changes, or no significant changes in [COUNTRY's] economy...?

	Major changes	Minor changes	No significant changes	DK/NA
Australia	48	40	9	4
Brazil	71	22	5	2
Canada	56	34	8	2
Central America	75	7	2	15
Chile	75	20	2	3
China	59	35	4	2
Egypt	68	20	7	5
France	79	12	5	3
Germany	67	26	4	2
Ghana	71	19	3	7
India	39	36	12	14
Indonesia	73	16	4	7
Italy	79	14	4	3
Japan	39	51	5	5
Kenya	87	10	2	1
Mexico	52	30	3	15
Nigeria	66	22	8	4
Philippines	92	6	1	1
Portugal	90	7	1	2
Russia	47	41	3	9
Spain	82	12	2	4
Turkey	69	22	5	5
UK	73	18	6	3
USA	75	18	6	2

Figure 19.

M6b. What about the international economic system? Do you think that the current economic crisis points to the need for major changes, minor changes or no significant changes in the international economic system?

	Major changes	Minor changes	No significant changes	DK/NA
Australia	76	17	3	5
Brazil	77	17	4	2
Canada	69	22	5	4
Central America	80	5	2	13
Chile	80	14	1	4
China	75	19	3	4
Egypt	73	16	5	6
France	83	9	4	4
Germany	75	19	4	2
Ghana	72	15	2	11
India	40	33	12	15
Indonesia	62	19	4	15
Italy	81	11	2	6
Japan	45	45	3	7
Kenya	84	10	3	3
Mexico	42	27	3	29
Nigeria	55	28	9	8
Philippines	88	10	1	1
Portugal	92	6	1	2
Russia	47	36	3	15
Spain	84	10	1	5
Turkey	67	22	4	8
UK	76	17	4	3
USA	64	26	5	6

Figure 20.

C3t. For each of the following statements, please tell me if you strongly agree, somewhat agree, somewhat disagree, or strongly disagree.

g) The free enterprise system and free market economy work best in society's interest when accompanied by strong government regulations.

	Total agree (1+2)					Strongly agree					Somewhat agree				
	2008	2007	2005	2002	2001	2008	2007	2005	2002	2001	2008	2007	2005	2002	2001
Canada	79	66	68	64	65	30	24	22	20	21	49	43	46	44	44
China	92	87	76	78	68	47	39	31	30	24	45	48	45	48	44
France	54	50	57	49	47	16	13	17	12	10	39	38	40	36	37
Germany	70	62	68	71	74	31	21	35	28	39	39	42	33	43	35
Indonesia	70	71	86	79	89	32	26	42	31	40	39	44	44	48	49
Italy	84	71	71	68	74	48	33	32	24	35	36	38	39	44	39
Mexico	64	64	68	63	64	19	21	24	23	23	45	43	44	41	41
Nigeria	71	65	71	64	66	33	26	39	28	39	39	39	32	36	27
Russia	68	61	67	74	71	28	17	26	35	36	40	45	42	39	35
Turkey	56	35	55	54	50	17	3	9	10	9	39	31	46	44	41
UK	75	62	69	59	65	31	20	25	19	24	44	41	44	39	41
USA	70	57	59	50	50	31	20	20	18	15	39	37	39	32	34

Figure 21.

Q7At. Thinking about the economic developments of the last few years, how fairly do you think the benefits and burdens have been shared in [Country]: very fairly, somewhat fairly, not very fairly, or not at all fairly?

	Very fairly			Somewhat fairly			Not very fairly			Not at all fairly			Depends (Volunteered)			DK/NA		
	2015	2009	2007	2015	2009	2007	2015	2009	2007	2015	2009	2007	2015	2009	2007	2015	2009	2007
Australia	5	9	10	45	55	47	30	24	27	19	8	12	1	1	0	1	3	3
Brazil	3	6	2	22	37	16	37	25	32	35	31	37	2	1	4	1	1	9
Canada	6	8	8	51	50	50	24	28	29	15	11	10	1	1	0	4	3	3
Chile	1	5	1	19	32	13	37	36	38	36	21	44	2	1	1	3	5	3
China	9	4	4	44	40	54	32	34	30	7	15	7	7	3	1	2	4	4
France	1	0	2	13	14	11	54	50	44	32	32	34	0	1	2	1	2	7
Germany	2	2	3	38	20	20	35	46	45	15	29	26	8	2	4	3	1	2
India	23	15	12	29	29	31	18	16	18	15	11	6	4	6	16	11	22	18
Indonesia	4	4	1	33	35	16	47	41	51	8	7	28	2	4	0	6	10	4
Kenya	15	8	8	47	28	35	24	32	30	12	25	26	2	4	0	1	4	2
Mexico	9	6	7	31	11	13	33	30	30	17	39	37	8	4	4	2	8	9
Nigeria	22	9	10	28	31	43	21	32	26	26	25	16	1	1	1	2	2	3
Spain	1	4	5	7	23	19	31	21	44	58	45	23	1	2	3	2	5	6
Turkey	5	2	1	10	11	8	22	42	40	59	34	42	0	2	2	5	9	7
UK	4	4	5	33	35	37	37	37	41	24	20	15	0	1	1	2	4	2
USA	4	6	6	37	35	40	29	33	31	29	22	21	0	1	0	2	4	1

Figure 22

Q7At. Please tell me if you strongly agree, somewhat agree, somewhat disagree, or strongly disagree with each of the following statements.

g1) Most rich people in [COUNTRY] deserve their wealth

Country	TOTAL AGREE (1+2)		Strongly agree		Somewhat agree		Somewhat disagree		Strongly disagree		TOTAL DISAGREE (3+4)		Depends / Neither agree nor disagree		DK/NA	
	2012	2008	2012	2008	2012	2008	2012	2008	2012	2008	2012	2008	2012	2008	2012	2008
Argentina	39		9		23		26		23		50		7		12	
Australia	61	53	18	16	43	37	22	22	12	13	34	35	4	9	2	3
Brazil	43	43	8	12	35	31	32	17	21	36	53	54	4	3	0	3
Canada	58	61	16	17	42	44	20	21	16	11	37	32	4	2	2	2
Chile	30		11		19		23		28		51		6		14	
China	52	50	14	15	38	35	26	28	16	14	42	41	5	6	1	2
Costa Rica		41		22		19		23		27		50		6		3
France	31		6		25		31		31		63		6		1	
Germany	35	29	12	4	23	24	35	32	23	15	58	47	5	22	2	2
Ghana	43		16		27		26		15		41		9		7	
Greece	9		4		5		15		64		79		8		4	
India	51	51	28	23	24	27	11	16	18	16	29	33	4	9	15	7
Indonesia	54	43	14	10	40	33	22	31	8	13	29	43	12	6	4	8
Italy		24		3		20		34		35		69		7		1
Kenya	44	31	25	16	19	15	19	30	32	32	51	62	4	6	1	0
Mexico	40	29	16	13	24	16	24	23	22	43	46	65	12	6	3	
Nigeria	39	38	20	18	18	20	18	24	36	36	54	60	4	2	3	0
Pakistan	41	40	20	12	20	28	15	15	23	23	38	37	8	7	14	16
Panama	29	39	8	15	21	24	21	24	33	29	54	53	8	5	9	3
Philippines	16	22	3	8	13	14	31	27	33	41	54	68	8	10	9	0
Russia	16	17	3	5	13	12	31	29	44	43	75	72	5	6	4	5
South Korea	42	39	7	3	35	37	38	39	18	12	55	51	2	7	1	2
Spain	20	18	5	5	15	14	29	42	39	22	67	65	11	17	2	1
Turkey	20	14	4	4	15	10	34	35	30	35	63	70	7	8	10	8
UK	45	47	15	11	31	36	25	26	21	18	46	44	7	5	2	5
USA	58	57	22	24	37	33	20	20	16	14	36	34	4	7	1	2

Figure 24.

Q19At. Please tell me if you strongly agree, somewhat agree, somewhat disagree, or strongly disagree with each of the following statements: at. [Country's] economy will be significantly damaged if we try to cut our emissions of climate changing gases

	Total agree (1+2)							Total disagree (3+4)						
	2015	2012	2010	2009	2008	2007	2000	2015	2012	2010	2009	2008	2007	2000
Australia	48	49	41	49	49	NA	NA	48	46	52	46	45	NA	NA
Brazil	-	41	45	48	57	49	36	-	50	48	45	34	44	61
Canada	43	45	38	42	47	50	NA	51	52	54	53	47	45	NA
Chile	43	NA	34	43	38	51	46	37	NA	40	36	38	35	44
China	54	46	42	42	53	48	40	43	45	50	52	40	48	56
France	44	46	46	44	50	NA	40	54	49	50	50	44	NA	51
Germany	32	35	43	47	45	45	35	22	26	24	26	26	22	63
India	59	61	62	54	38	73	60	13	17	37	26	28	33	33
Indonesia	76	70	55	50	48	57	50	29	33	36	45	45	42	46
Kenya	70	45	54	50	44	53	NA	27	32	29	51	46	32	NA
Mexico	63	52	24	16	47	25	18	33	34	43	38	36	35	30
Nigeria	62	57	55	59	53	60	NA	35	29	33	18	7	35	NA
Pakistan	55	53	45	65	15	NA	NA	56	67	50	52	15	NA	NA
Spain	32	11	38	34	74	45	33	32	29	41	28	35	44	59
Turkey	46	40	43	56	46	43	NA	55	49	53	55	51	35	NA
UK	43	44	34	38	44	44	37	54	49	46	47	56	47	59
USA	41	44	42	48	34	41	45	54	49	46	47	56	52	51

Figure 26.

Q1t. The term "sustainable development" has been used since it first appeared in the Brundtland World Commission Report. In your estimation, is the potency of this term increasing, decreasing, or remaining the same in positively influencing key government and industry decision-makers in your country?

Number of responses

	2008 TOTAL	SECTOR					REGION			
		Corporate	Government	Voluntary	Institutional	Service	West Europe	North America	Asia/Pacific	Other
TOTAL	353	87	33	56	98	79	113	157	43	40
Decreasing potency	21	11	27	27	24	20	17	24	16	28
Remaining the same	22	22	24	25	19	23	24	22	21	20
Increasing potency	57	67	48	48	56	57	59	55	63	53

	2006 TOTAL	SECTOR					REGION			
		Corporate	Government	Voluntary	Institutional	Service	West Europe	North America	Asia/Pacific	Other
TOTAL	360	90	41	47	111	71	135	153	44	28
Decreasing potency	26	21	37	30	24	24	21	32	11	36
Remaining the same	20	17	17	19	19	27	22	16	20	25
Increasing potency	54	62	46	51	56	49	56	52	68	39
Not stated					1		1			

	2002 TOTAL	SECTOR					REGION			
		Corporate	Government	Voluntary	Institutional	Service	West Europe	North America	Asia/Pacific	Other
TOTAL	246	79	29	33	58	47	87	99	28	32
Decreasing potency	16	13	17	21	14	19	11	18	11	25
Remaining the same	28	29	21	33	29	26	37	27	14	19
Increasing potency	55	58	62	45	57	51	51	54	75	56

Figure 28.

Q5At. For each of the following statements, please tell me if you strongly agree, somewhat agree, somewhat disagree, or strongly disagree.
dt) The free market system and free market economy is the best system on which to base the future of the world

	Total agree (1+2)									Total disagree (3+4)								
	2015	2012	2011	2010	2009	2007	2005	2002	2001	2015	2012	2011	2010	2009	2007	2005	2002	2001
Chile	49	NA	42	45	45	47	NA	61	61	21	NA	38	31	33	28	NA	16	20
China	65	72	64	68	65	66	74	77	66	28	12	23	19	25	23	20	14	22
France	45	39	35	30	34	41	36	39	42	50	51	55	58	55	45	50	40	41
Germany	63	62	69	69	65	62	65	68	75	27	28	27	28	30	30	32	30	23
India	55	61	61	58	46	68	70	66	73	21	30	23	27	26	20	17	30	20
Indonesia	65	65	52	55	48	63	68	57	69	24	21	37	37	29	23	29	35	24
Mexico	53	46	39	57	51	56	61	63	63	33	39	38	41	38	38	38	30	31
Nigeria	65	60	54	58	60	61	66	55	62	30	33	44	39	36	34	29	40	20
Turkey	36	35	46	27	43	34	47	57	42	39	33	31	55	37	41	36	30	24
UK	62	57	51	56	61	59	66	61	62	30	29	33	26	26	30	27	25	24
USA	64	71	62	59	74	70	71	77	80	30	24	27	29	21	23	24	14	12

Figure 30.

Q8t. Please tell me if you strongly agree, somewhat agree, somewhat disagree or strongly disagree with each of the following statements?

gt) The more socially responsible my company becomes, the more motivated and loyal I become as an employee.

	Total agree (1+2)						Strongly agree						Somewhat agree					
	2013	2010	2008	2005	2003	2001	2013	2010	2008	2005	2003	2001	2013	2010	2008	2005	2003	2001
Australia	90	NA	87	87	79	82	44	NA	53	57	39	48	45	NA	34	30	40	34
Brazil	86	NA	31	NA	99	95	58	NA	26	NA	91	88	28	NA	5	NA	8	7
Canada	78	NA	88	90	88	79	48	NA	52	62	58	44	30	NA	36	28	30	35
Chile	72	83	76	NA	85	91	19	40	48	NA	61	64	53	42	28	NA	24	27
China	89	95	98	NA	83	95	42	51	76	NA	48	63	47	44	22	NA	35	32
France	82	NA	84	76	75	71	45	NA	51	45	37	30	38	NA	33	31	38	41
Germany	88	NA	95	95	86	89	35	NA	39	70	62	45	54	NA	56	25	24	44
Mexico	75	83	78	NA	63	89	44	48	51	NA	41	72	30	35	27	NA	22	17
Nigeria	82	92	84	NA	NA	83	45	59	38	NA	NA	60	37	33	46	NA	NA	23
Russia	71	71	53	NA	79	60	45	27	25	NA	48	30	26	45	28	NA	31	30
S. Korea	77	98	83	NA	NA	90	37	65	56	NA	NA	37	40	33	27	NA	NA	53
Turkey	77	66	66	NA	66	97	37	11	15	NA	42	6	40	55	51	NA	24	91
UK	80	74	83	79	71	72	31	37	36	48	37	32	49	37	47	31	34	40
USA	75	76	87	79	75	80	44	53	55	48	46	37	31	23	32	31	29	43

Figure 31.

Q10Bt. I am going to read a list of things some people say should be part of the responsibilities of large companies. For each one, please tell me to what extent you think companies should be held responsible.

Q10 AGGREGATE NET EXPECTATIONS. EXPECTATIONS INCLUDED ARE LISTED TO THE RIGHT OF THE TABLE BELOW.

	2015	2011	2009	2007	2005	2003	2001
Argentina	65	68	69	66	69	-	64
Australia	55	61	55	59	57	68	59
Brazil	74	73	75	82	71	-	61
Canada	53	53	54	60	62	62	55
Chile	63	56	59	61	66	77	52
China	30	30	45	46	31	37	26
France	40	48	38	42	53	43	59
Germany	33	50	66	56	55	58	48
Greece	68	65	61	67	69	-	-
India	9	22	17	53	59	76	75
Indonesia	52	61	48	60	63	53	62
Italy	-	76	65	63	61	65	54
Mexico	35	45	39	37	41	44	38
Nigeria	29	60	45	57	56	55	26
Russia	-	69	72	69	71	81	72
S. Korea	38	50	48	46	46	25	50
Spain	46	58	51	-	-	54	55
Turkey	62	54	63	55	62	55	41
UK	55	61	54	59	62	64	59
USA	46	47	50	57	53	58	53

at) Treating all employees and job applicants fairly, regardless of gender, race, religion or sexual orientation

bt) Applying the same high standards everywhere it operates in the world

ct) Helping solve social problems like crime, poverty, and lack of education

dt) Ensuring its products and operations do not harm the environment

et) Increasing economic stability in the world

ft) Reducing human rights abuses in the world

gt) Providing good quality products and services at the lowest possible price

ht) Supporting progressive government policies and legislation

it) Helping reduce the gap between rich and poor

jt) Ensuring that all materials it uses to make its products have been produced in a socially and environmentally responsible manner

Figure 31.
Q15Bt. Please rate each of the following types of companies on how well they fulfill their responsibilities to society.
Compared to other types of companies, would you say [INSERT COMPANY TYPE] are...?
Q15 AGGREGATE NET PERFORMANCE. INDUSTRIES INCLUDED ARE LISTED TO THE RIGHT OF THE TABLE BELOW.

at) Banks and finance companies
bt) Oil/Petroleum companies
ct) Auto companies
dt) Clothing and apparel companies
et) Chemical companies
ft) High-tech/computer companies
it) Food companies
jt) Pharmaceutical companies
kt) Mining companies
lt) Telecommunications companies (telephone)

	2015	2013	2011	2009	2007	2005	2003	2001
Argentina	-11	-23	-15	-17	-13	-13	-	0
Australia	-12	-24	-20	-17	-26	-24	-18	-21
Brazil	-19	-8	4	-8	21	-3	-	24
Canada	-13	-26	-16	-17	-21	-10	-10	-7
Chile	3	6	4	13	17	17	11	21
China	3	-2	11	8	4	19	23	24
France	-16	-27	-19	-23	-18	-6	-14	1
Germany	-15	-12	-14	-21	-11	-8	-5	4
Greece	-8	-17	-4	-10	-9	-12	-	-
India	51	41	33	20	45	35	45	43
Indonesia	36	33	28	16	35	30	19	29
Italy	-	-	-11	-24	-27	-25	-12	-9
Mexico	14	20	17	20	30	30	28	27
Nigeria	55	37	44	27	44	21	13	47
Russia	-	-3	-7	-7	-6	-6	-1	1
S. Korea	-4	-18	-1	-14	-27	-1	-4	-4
Spain	-6	-11	-10	-12	-	-	-5	3
Turkey	-4	-4	-24	-2	5	21	20	32
UK	-13	-23	-13	-15	-14	-10	-7	-6
USA	-8	-15	-19	-18	-15	-6	-9	-8

Figure 32.
Q8t. Please tell me if you strongly agree, somewhat agree, somewhat disagree, or strongly disagree with each of the following statements.
dt) Our government should create laws that require large companies to go beyond their traditional economic role and work to make a better society, even though this could lead to higher prices and fewer jobs

	Strongly agree								Somewhat agree							
	2013	2009	2007	2005	2004	2003	2002	2001	2013	2009	2007	2005	2004	2003	2002	2001
Australia	26	19	19	17	17	17	14	19	38	37	36	36	36	31	38	35
Canada	20	22	20	16	15	15	12	11	37	33	34	34	38	35	38	33
Chile	40	36	31	30	26	35	28	34	23	23	30	23	28	30	19	23
China	23	29	28	25	36	12	22	24	48	38	34	37	34	46	39	43
France	20	16	17	11	12	12	9	16	28	27	18	23	22	27	21	32
Germany	8	11	7	9	12	14	7	14	31	28	28	21	22	24	21	24
India	32	39	31	17	23	28	45	29	26	24	19	24	27	31	30	42
Indonesia	34	24	17	26	26	13	10	20	35	28	25	35	32	38	26	42
Italy	NA	12	10	8	9	13	11	15	NA	26	24	27	18	29	22	26
Mexico	31	1	1	1	1	26	14	21	32	11	10	9	11	28	10	30
Nigeria	40	22	32	18	33	36	23	37	35	22	28	32	23	24	23	23
Russia	18	15	18	16	16	11	11	19	29	26	23	28	23	24	18	26
UK	18	17	22	19	18	14	12	20	36	33	35	31	37	32	39	37
USA	18	14	21	14	13	10	8	9	27	25	23	28	28	24	33	27

Figure 33.

Q7At. Please tell me if you strongly agree, somewhat agree, somewhat disagree, or strongly disagree with each of the following statements. PROMPT: Is that somewhat or strongly?

dt) I am very interested in learning more about the ways that some companies are trying to be socially responsible.

	Total agree (1+2)						Total disagree (3+4)						DK/NA					
	2012	2009	2007	2004	2003	2001	2012	2009	2007	2004	2003	2001	2012	2009	2007	2004	2003	2001
Australia	75	66	72	72	74	79	22	29	25	22	22	19	0	1	2	2	1	1
Canada	79	73	73	83	77	85	20	21	24	15	21	14	1	5	1	1	2	1
Chile	64	62	50	58	59	67	24	25	41	31	29	23	8	10	4	7	7	8
China	83	63	78	82	67	73	14	25	18	12	22	16	1	4	3	3	6	6
Germany	75	69	70	70	66	79	23	27	27	26	31	20	1	2	1	1	1	1
Indonesia	69	59	59	74	69	75	16	31	35	16	23	20	9	7	3	4	3	4
Russia	64	54	46	56	44	58	22	24	34	27	32	23	8	15	10	8	17	10
Turkey	72	51	66	65	68	63	12	28	25	22	20	29	9	14	3	8	4	5
UK	65	62	62	70	61	73	32	31	35	26	36	23	0	5	1	1	1	1
USA	78	67	73	78	67	77	20	27	25	20	30	20	2	4	1	1	2	1

Figure 33.

Q1Bt. Please tell me if you agree or disagree with each of the following statements. PROMPT: Is that somewhat or strongly? at) Companies communicate honestly and truthfully about their social and environmental performance.

	Total agree (1+2)					Total disagree (3+4)					DK/NA				
	2012	2009	2007	2004	2002	2012	2009	2007	2004	2002	2012	2009	2007	2004	2002
Australia	19	45	39	18	21	78	48	58	78	74	2	4	2	1	1
Canada	22	50	51	44	37	77	44	46	54	61	1	4	2	1	1
Chile	30	29	21	20	28	59	52	71	68	56	7	16	6	7	13
China	76	40	72	82	51	19	47	25	14	43	1	3	1	2	3
Germany	28	16	24	29	19	59	80	74	66	80	2	2	-	1	1
Indonesia	75	61	57	76	64	16	31	39	19	32	3	5	2	2	2
Russia	49	21	23	30	11	35	56	51	53	65	9	21	21	13	21
Turkey	28	30	38	42	42	36	47	53	46	53	26	14	2	8	-
UK	26	44	32	44	27	72	47	63	53	70	1	7	3	1	1
USA	22	44	29	50	36	75	51	70	48	61	2	4	-	1	2

Figure 34.

Q12Bt. Over the past year, have you considered rewarding a socially responsible company by either buy-ing their products or speaking positively about the company to others? Would you say you have...?

	Have actually done this								
	2015	2013	2010	2008	2006	2004	2001		
Australia	57	52	52	54	49	53	60		
Canada	58	48	54	52	45	44	50		
Chile	14	5	4	9	15	12	13		
China	33	14	10	25	21	14	24		
France	40	36	32	24	29	19	13		
Germany	12	13	32	16	33	40	42		
Indonesia	10	8	18	9	15	9	9		
Italy	-	NA	38	36	34	29	25		
Mexico	9	8	16	20	18	20	17		
Nigeria	54	51	59	42	48	29	33		
Russia	18	14	6	11	10	14	12		
Turkey	8	8	10	34	21	13	15		
UK	49	44	41	41	36	30	40		
USA	63	49	57	59	48	44	53		

Figure 34.

Q16t. In the past year, have you considered punishing a company you see as not socially responsible by either refusing to buy their products or speaking critically about the company to others? Would you say you have...?

	Have actually done								
	2013	2010	2008	2006	2004	2003	2002	2001	2000
Australia	46	44	61	56	51	60	54	68	57
Canada	37	45	57	54	40	51	37	54	40
Chile	6	8	12	21	14	16	14	14	14
China	13	9	34	30	18	13	14	25	13
France	33	31	33	35	31	25	24	20	17
Germany	15	29	19	38	42	44	39	48	21
Indonesia	6	3	7	9	3	6	4	7	1
Italy	NA	44	47	47	34	40	30	33	27
Mexico	9	21	17	21	20	22	29	28	29
Nigeria	18	23	22	26	14	17	12	25	18
Russia	13	7	11	13	7	8	5	12	6
Turkey	8	16	37	29	23	18	12	13	14
UK	40	36	46	41	38	37	34	52	31
USA	38	47	62	56	42	49	39	58	43

Figure 35.

Q13Bt. Please tell me if you strongly agree, somewhat agree, somewhat disagree, or strongly disagree with each of the following statements. at) As a consumer, I can make a difference in how responsibly a company behaves.

	Total agree (1+2)							Total disagree (3+4)						
	2015	2013	2010	2008	2006	2003	2001	2015	2013	2010	2008	2006	2003	2001
Argentina	73	51	56	49	58	44	NA	23	36	31	34	26	27	NA
Australia	76	71	75	75	76	58	77	23	27	23	22	21	40	22
Brazil	79	77	69	74	76	76	77	20	20	29	21	21	21	18
Canada	75	70	78	84	81	72	76	24	28	22	15	18	26	21
Chile	57	52	50	63	71	60	62	33	23	35	30	25	27	25
China	61	76	73	81	78	67	76	34	20	25	15	16	23	15
France	55	50	58	51	64	38	39	43	48	39	44	32	46	47
Germany	44	62	55	38	52	49	59	51	33	43	51	45	49	40
Greece	81	67	77	69	73	NA	NA	17	28	18	27	22	NA	NA
India	72	70	45	45	82	76	81	20	13	37	34	10	17	11
Indonesia	78	77	69	65	75	77	76	12	13	22	23	17	15	15
Italy	NA	NA	83	79	67	52	56	NA	NA	15	18	30	40	34
Kenya	75	77	70	63	72	NA	NA	24	19	25	35	25	NA	NA
Mexico	62	64	61	60	61	62	60	29	33	24	21	23	20	23
Nigeria	75	78	70	70	78	56	71	23	19	29	28	19	39	13
Peru	68	70	60	67	71	NA	NA	23	23	26	22	15	NA	NA
Russia	-	50	22	36	45	40	36	-	35	62	48	34	39	36
S. Korea	64	72	69	67	72	NA	58	31	26	29	33	28	NA	36
Turkey	55	58	33	67	68	57	62	27	34	46	25	16	29	31
UK	67	60	70	74	75	60	73	32	38	26	24	22	37	23
USA	70	66	78	76	76	65	79	29	34	20	23	21	32	20

Figure 35.

Q13Bt. Please tell me if you strongly agree, somewhat agree, somewhat disagree, or strongly disagree with each of the following statements.

b) As a citizen, I can make a difference in how responsibly our national government behaves.

	Total agree	Strongly agree	Somewhat agree	Somewhat disagree	Strongly disagree	Total disagree	Depends	DK/NA
Argentina	67	30	37	16	12	28	2	3
Australia	72	29	42	16	12	27	0	0
Brazil	76	31	45	12	10	22	0	1
Canada	66	29	37	17	15	33	0	1
Chile	48	10	38	28	14	42	4	6
China	68	22	46	25	4	29	3	0
France	64	21	43	22	12	34	1	1
Germany	40	7	33	37	18	54	4	1
Greece	71	49	21	16	11	26	3	0
India	66	29	37	15	7	22	6	6
Indonesia	81	28	54	13	1	14	2	4
Italy	NA	NA	NA	NA	NA	NA	NA	NA
Kenya	76	43	33	14	8	23	1	0
Mexico	63	26	37	19	9	28	5	4
Nigeria	74	46	28	17	6	23	2	1
Peru	69	29	40	14	10	23	3	5
S. Korea	54	16	38	28	14	41	2	3
Turkey	55	13	42	22	6	28	6	11
UK	56	18	38	22	22	44	0	0
USA	59	23	36	18	22	40	0	0

Figure 37.

Q12Bt. Over the past year, have you considered rewarding a socially responsible company by either buying their products or speaking positively about the company to others? Would you say you have...?

	Have actually done this								
	2015	2013	2010	2008	2006	2003	2001	1999
Argentina	9	7	11	7	18	12	24	22
Australia	57	52	52	54	49	53	60	NA
Brazil	12	12	20	18	11	17	16	NA
Canada	58	48	54	52	45	44	50	50
Chile	14	5	4	9	15	12	13	NA
China	33	14	10	25	21	14	24	23
France	40	36	32	24	29	19	13	NA
Germany	12	13	32	16	33	40	42	37
Greece	39	35	38	31	35	4	NA	NA
India	9	21	10	18	17	19	14	16
Indonesia	10	8	18	9	15	9	9	12
Mexico	9	8	16	20	18	20	17	17
Nigeria	54	51	59	42	48	29	33	45
S. Korea	48	34	41	44	33	NA	13	NA
Spain	40	13	24	24	NA	10	11	22
Turkey	8	8	10	34	21	13	15	8
UK	49	44	41	41	36	30	40	31
USA	63	49	57	59	48	44	53	46

Figure 39.
Q4t. Please tell me how much you trust each of the following institutions to operate in the best interest of our society. Would you say you have a lot of trust, some trust, not much trust, or no trust at all in ...?
at) Our national government

	Total trust (1+2)	A lot of trust	Some trust	Not much trust	No trust at all	Total no trust (3+4)	Other	DK/NA
Argentina	32	8	24	33	32	65	0	3
Australia	55	11	44	28	17	45	0	0
Brazil	26	2	24	31	43	74	0	0
Canada	54	14	40	24	22	46	0	0
Chile	49	10	38	37	12	49	0	2
China	87	26	61	11	1	12	0	0
France	23	2	21	41	35	76	0	1
Germany	63	8	55	29	7	36	0	0
Ghana	45	20	25	32	21	54	0	2
Greece	28	9	19	29	43	72	0	0
India	61	22	39	19	16	35	0	5
Indonesia	55	17	38	36	7	44	0	1
Israel	33	4	29	40	27	67	0	0
Kenya	61	24	37	22	17	39	0	0
Mexico	32	4	28	46	21	66	0	1
Nigeria	37	10	27	30	30	60	0	3
Pakistan	53	23	30	29	18	47	0	0
Peru	44	7	38	33	21	55	0	1
Russia	55	12	43	26	14	40	0	4
S. Korea	40	6	33	42	17	58	0	2
Spain	13	4	9	32	54	86	0	0
Turkey	50	23	27	20	27	47	1	0
UK	45	5	40	34	21	55	0	3
USA	43	4	39	27	28	56	0	1

Figure 39.

Q4t. Please tell me how much you trust each of the following institutions to operate in the best interest of our society. Would you say you have a lot of trust, some trust, not much trust, or no trust at all in ...?

bt) Large [COUNTRY] companies

	Total trust (1+2)	A lot of trust	Some trust	Not much trust	No trust at all	Total no trust (3+4)	Other	DK/NA
Argentina	28	2	25	41	25	67	0	6
Australia	51	6	45	35	12	47	0	2
Brazil	53	9	44	33	14	47	0	0
Canada	48	10	38	32	19	51	0	1
Chile	44	6	38	39	14	53	0	3
China	69	20	49	30	0	30	1	0
France	40	3	37	41	18	59	0	1
Germany	58	8	50	33	8	41	0	0
Ghana	62	18	43	26	9	35	0	4
Greece	49	10	39	28	20	48	0	3
India	57	15	42	21	12	32	0	11
Indonesia	73	11	62	22	2	24	1	2
Israel	25	3	23	43	32	75	0	0
Kenya	63	21	43	27	9	36	0	1
Mexico	29	3	26	52	15	68	1	2
Nigeria	63	13	50	26	8	34	0	3
Pakistan	57	12	45	31	10	41	0	2
Peru	59	9	50	28	11	39	0	2
Russia	33	3	30	34	22	56	0	11
S. Korea	33	3	30	46	18	64	0	3
Spain	13	4	8	56	31	86	1	0
Turkey	59	15	44	23	14	36	1	4
UK	51	5	46	33	14	47	0	2
USA	48	4	44	28	22	51	0	1

Figure 39.

Q4t. Please tell me how much you trust each of the following institutions to operate in the best interest of our society. Would you say you have a lot of trust, some trust, not much trust, or no trust at all in …?

ct) Global companies operating in [COUNTRY]

	Total trust (1+2)	A lot of trust	Some trust	Not much trust	No trust at all	Total no trust (3+4)	Other	DK/NA
Argentina	NA	NA	NA	NA	NA	NA	NA	NA
Australia	37	5	33	35	26	61	0	2
Brazil	50	8	42	35	14	48	0	2
Canada	38	9	29	33	27	60	0	2
Chile	30	3	28	44	18	61	0	8
China	62	8	54	28	3	31	2	5
France	35	2	33	38	24	62	0	3
Germany	49	4	45	38	11	49	0	2
Ghana	63	16	47	28	6	34	0	3
Greece	26	6	20	31	40	72	0	3
India	48	16	32	26	15	41	1	10
Indonesia	65	11	54	28	2	30	0	5
Israel	31	3	28	43	26	69	0	0
Kenya	62	26	36	25	11	36	0	2
Mexico	25	1	23	43	25	69	1	5
Nigeria	67	20	48	23	6	29	0	4
Pakistan	58	17	42	30	10	40	0	2
Peru	51	9	42	30	13	43	0	6
Russia	20	3	17	36	33	68	0	12
S. Korea	41	2	39	38	10	49	1	9
Spain	17	2	16	47	30	77	1	5
Turkey	49	16	33	26	17	43	1	7
UK	38	3	36	39	20	59	0	3
USA	40	3	36	33	25	57	0	3

Figure 39.

Q4t. Please tell me how much you trust each of the following institutions to operate in the best interest of our society. Would you say you have a lot of trust, some trust, not much trust, or no trust at all in ...?

dt) Non-governmental organizations such as environmental and social advocacy groups

	Total trust (1+2)	A lot of trust	Some trust	Not much trust	No trust at all	Total no trust (3+4)	Other	DK/NA
Argentina	45	7	38	27	13	41	0	14
Australia	74	14	60	15	9	24	0	2
Brazil	58	14	44	30	12	42	0	1
Canada	75	28	47	15	9	24	0	1
Chile	61	21	40	22	8	30	0	9
China	56	8	47	34	3	37	1	6
France	74	15	59	19	7	25	0	1
Germany	69	12	56	24	5	29	0	2
Ghana	68	32	36	22	4	26	0	6
Greece	28	5	23	25	44	69	1	2
India	48	18	30	21	13	34	2	16
Indonesia	58	12	46	32	6	38	1	4
Israel	75	24	51	20	5	25	0	0
Kenya	65	33	32	26	6	32	0	2
Mexico	35	6	28	33	19	53	0	12
Nigeria	65	17	48	26	6	32	0	3
Pakistan	59	18	41	23	12	35	0	5
Peru	61	11	50	21	11	32	0	7
Russia	43	9	33	23	19	43	0	15
S. Korea	58	6	52	32	5	37	0	5
Spain	50	9	41	33	14	47	1	3
Turkey	71	26	46	17	6	24	1	4
UK	68	10	57	22	8	31	0	2
USA	66	9	57	18	15	32	0	2

Figure 39.

Q4t. Please tell me how much you trust each of the following institutions to operate in the best interest of our society. Would you say you have a lot of trust, some trust, not much trust, or no trust at all in ...?

et) Press and media

	Total trust (1+2)	A lot of trust	Some trust	Not much trust	No trust at all	Total no trust (3+4)	Other	DK/NA
Argentina	33	3	29	41	23	64	0	3
Australia	36	5	31	35	30	64	0	0
Brazil	NA	NA	NA	NA	NA	NA	NA	NA
Canada	61	15	46	20	18	38	0	0
Chile	56	7	49	32	11	43	0	2
China	64	10	55	30	2	33	1	2
France	25	2	23	45	30	75	0	0
Germany	45	4	40	43	10	54	0	2
Ghana	61	22	39	28	9	37	0	2
Greece	16	3	13	30	54	84	0	0
India	65	29	36	15	13	27	1	7
Indonesia	66	14	52	28	2	30	1	3
Israel	47	9	38	32	21	53	0	0
Kenya	70	38	32	18	11	29	0	1
Mexico	27	3	24	51	17	68	0	5
Nigeria	67	20	47	22	7	30	0	3
Pakistan	69	26	43	22	6	28	1	2
Peru	66	14	52	22	10	32	0	2
Russia	52	5	46	26	16	42	0	6
S. Korea	30	3	27	48	17	66	1	3
Spain	31	4	27	51	16	67	2	0
Turkey	43	17	26	28	25	53	1	3
UK	28	2	26	40	32	72	0	0
USA	34	4	30	30	36	66	0	1

Figure 39.

Q4t. Please tell me how much you trust each of the following institutions to operate in the best interest of our society. Would you say you have a lot of trust, some trust, not much trust, or no trust at all in ...?

ft) Scientific and academic research institutions

	Total trust (1+2)	A lot of trust	Some trust	Not much trust	No trust at all	Total no trust (3+4)	Other	DK/NA
Argentina	NA	NA	NA	NA	NA	NA	NA	NA
Australia	91	43	49	4	3	7	0	1
Brazil	NA	NA	NA	NA	NA	NA	NA	NA
Canada	88	39	49	8	3	11	0	1
Chile	68	26	42	18	5	23	0	9
China	67	12	55	28	2	31	1	1
France	85	20	65	10	4	14	0	1
Germany	77	22	55	16	4	20	0	3
Ghana	68	30	38	20	7	28	0	5
Greece	73	24	49	16	6	22	0	5
India	63	27	36	15	8	22	1	14
Indonesia	82	28	54	12	3	14	1	3
Israel	75	27	47	19	6	25	0	0
Kenya	58	21	36	26	11	37	2	4
Mexico	47	14	33	33	14	47	0	6
Nigeria	65	15	50	26	4	30	0	5
Pakistan	71	32	39	16	7	23	0	6
Peru	63	16	47	19	7	26	0	11
Russia	72	26	46	12	7	19	0	9
S. Korea	61	9	51	28	2	30	0	9
Spain	74	28	46	20	5	24	0	1
Turkey	78	33	45	10	7	17	1	4
UK	89	35	53	7	2	10	0	2
USA	83	27	57	8	7	15	0	1

Figure 39.

Q4t. Please tell me how much you trust each of the following institutions to operate in the best interest of our society. Would you say you have a lot of trust, some trust, not much trust, or no trust at all in ...?

gt) The United Nations

	Total trust (1+2)	A lot of trust	Some trust	Not much trust	No trust at all	Total no trust (3+4)	Other	DK/NA
Argentina	NA	NA	NA	NA	NA	NA	NA	NA
Australia	73	17	55	13	12	25	0	2
Brazil	NA	NA	NA	NA	NA	NA	NA	NA
Canada	72	20	52	14	10	24	1	3
Chile	51	13	38	26	9	35	1	12
China	59	12	48	28	3	31	2	9
France	52	7	45	30	15	45	0	3
Germany	67	12	55	24	6	30	0	3
Ghana	75	31	44	17	5	21	1	4
Greece	36	5	30	32	29	61	0	3
India	56	22	34	16	8	24	1	19
Indonesia	74	22	52	17	3	19	1	6
Israel	24	3	21	33	43	76	0	0
Kenya	74	35	40	15	7	22	0	3
Mexico	36	6	30	38	15	52	1	11
Nigeria	47	15	33	31	15	46	1	5
Pakistan	50	21	28	28	18	45	0	5
Peru	58	15	42	19	11	30	0	12
Russia	38	8	30	22	18	40	0	22
S. Korea	78	20	58	14	1	15	0	6
Spain	43	11	33	40	13	53	1	2
Turkey	50	18	32	17	24	42	1	7
UK	68	16	53	21	9	30	0	1
USA	53	11	42	18	28	45	0	1

Figure 40.

G4B) How much trust do you have in each of the following leaders to manage the challenges of the coming year in the best interests of you and your family? Would you say you have a lot, some, not much, or no trust at all in . . .?

	a) Individuals responsible for managing the global economy	b) Individuals responsible for managing (COUNTRY)'s economy	c) Executives responsible for multinational companies	d) Spiritual and religious leaders	e) Leaders of the United States of America	f) Leaders of Western European countries	g) Leaders at the United Nations	h) Leaders of charitable or non-governmental organizations
Argentina	13	14	11	34	10	19	17	48
Canada	50	56	35	51	43	60	69	74
Germany	33	23	39	18	26	49	58	52
India	59	55	49	35	30	31	40	56
Italy	30	30	18	44	28	39	45	52
Japan	30	23	29	14	29	33	57	41
Mexico	15	18	18	42	23	29	36	56
Netherlands	50	59	33	18	25	64	61	55
Nigeria	36	35	36	62	43	41	46	50
Qatar	47	-	60	58	-	27	36	65
Russia	31	27	16	38	12	18	22	38
S. Korea	29	19	31	34	16	27	38	59
Turkey	33	44	33	32	16	25	27	54
UK	41	47	34	36	33	47	66	64
USA	56	66	40	68	75	55	66	66

Figure 41.

Q5At. For each of the following statements, please tell me if you strongly agree, somewhat agree, somewhat disagree, or strongly disagree.
et) I see myself more as a global citizen than a citizen of [COUNTRY].

	Total agree							Strongly agree							Somewhat agree						
	2015	2011	2009	2007	2005	2002	2001	2015	2011	2009	2007	2005	2002	2001	2015	2011	2009	2007	2005	2002	2001
Brazil	-	55	NA	49	49	24	26	-	34	NA	19	24	13	10	-	21	NA	30	25	12	16
Canada	46	NA	56	60	48	44	43	21	NA	29	36	21	21	20	25	NA	27	24	27	23	23
Chile	27	24	30	36	NA	28	40	5	5	10	14	NA	11	20	22	19	20	22	NA	16	20
China	57	62	70	56	76	NA	NA	11	26	32	29	48	NA	NA	46	35	38	26	28	NA	NA
France	53	52	51	56	52	36	35	18	18	18	25	22	14	13	35	34	33	31	30	21	21
Germany	33	44	43	41	51	62	43	7	20	23	10	28	35	19	27	25	20	31	23	27	24
India	54	54	47	63	48	67	52	26	34	18	34	22	42	31	27	20	29	30	26	24	22
Indonesia	47	28	30	25	38	30	46	11	7	6	5	9	10	14	36	21	24	20	29	20	32
Kenya	64	48	47	31	37	NA	NA	24	15	21	11	19	NA	NA	39	34	26	20	18	NA	NA
Mexico	51	31	42	41	42	47	51	19	6	23	26	27	17	24	32	25	19	15	15	30	27
Nigeria	60	59	56	53	45	52	49	27	31	25	26	22	28	18	33	29	31	27	23	24	31
Russia	-	25	19	15	16	22	40	-	7	5	4	5	10	15	-	18	14	11	11	11	25
Spain	59	46	57	NA	NA	49	48	39	23	37	NA	NA	29	15	20	23	20	NA	NA	20	33
Turkey	41	54	34	39	31	33	49	12	25	9	12	4	9	9	28	29	25	27	26	24	40
UK	46	45	54	59	52	49	48	19	25	27	26	24	26	21	26	20	27	33	28	23	27
USA	32	42	54	50	47	35	39	12	22	23	24	22	14	16	20	19	31	26	25	22	22

Figure 42.

G5t. Please tell me if you strongly agree, somewhat agree, somewhat disagree, or strongly disagree with each of the following statements.

g) Leaders of major environmental and social non-government organizations should be excluded when government leaders negotiate globalization agreements, because they are not widely elected

	Strongly agree	Somewhat agree	Somewhat disagree	Strongly disagree	Depends / Neither agree nor disagree	DK/NA
Argentina	17	11	18	37	5	12
Australia	12	21	27	34	2	4
Brazil	16	20	18	34	3	9
Canada	14	25	28	28	1	4
China	-	-	-	-	-	-
France	7	23	26	20	6	17
Germany	8	13	37	39	-	3
India	23	34	20	12	1	10
Indonesia	6	25	49	13	2	5
Japan	4	17	31	18	6	24
Mexico	22	25	23	19	4	7
Russia	9	16	27	13	4	31
S. Africa	9	19	21	27	8	16
S. Korea	8	27	46	17	1	2
Turkey	6	15	41	18	1	20
UK	13	26	29	26	2	5
USA	11	24	32	27	1	5

Figure 43.

Q1At. For each of the following possible global problems, please tell me if you see it as a very serious, somewhat serious, not very serious or not at all serious problem.

at) Human rights abuses in the world

	Very serious					
	2015	2010	2009	2007	2003	2000
Brazil	-	93	86	78	83	81
Canada	69	54	64	65	53	61
Chile	77	69	67	49	69	70
China	15	31	27	34	NA	NA
France	61	69	59	NA	71	56
Germany	31	54	60	49	47	45
India	61	50	43	57	58	70
Indonesia	61	50	56	51	47	46
Italy	-	79	77	71	77	81
Kenya	53	58	51	47	NA	NA
Mexico	72	61	59	56	54	78
Nigeria	65	34	59	60	60	48
Russia	-	31	29	25	38	28
Spain	67	73	90	NA	82	71
Turkey	73	56	60	51	45	46
UK	61	59	58	54	56	66
USA	60	59	58	57	54	59

bt) Pollution and environmental problems in the world

	Very serious					
	2015	2010	2009	2007	2003	2000
Brazil	-	92	90	83	81	83
Canada	63	65	64	74	65	70
Chile	78	81	78	67	70	76
China	28	70	69	59	43	NA
France	49	59	64	NA	72	64
Germany	30	62	57	51	55	49
India	54	59	56	74	77	87
Indonesia	63	57	51	56	51	40
Italy	-	75	78	66	73	81
Kenya	47	51	43	34	NA	NA
Mexico	63	78	74	75	79	77
Nigeria	56	31	47	45	51	43
Russia	-	63	56	46	57	53
Spain	58	62	78	NA	64	67
Turkey	67	55	71	52	36	51
UK	51	60	63	63	65	73
USA	48	59	54	53	54	58

Figure 43.

Q1At. For each of the following possible global problems, please tell me if you see it as a very serious, some-what serious, not very serious or not at all serious problem.

ct) The spread of human diseases

	Very serious					
	2015	2010	2009	2007	2003	2000
Brazil	-	92	83	89	83	83
Canada	48	39	46	60	60	67
Chile	73	74	83	69	78	77
China	23	40	44	40	37	NA
France	47	47	51	NA	70	69
Germany	20	29	29	40	40	43
India	57	45	40	68	70	85
Indonesia	62	54	68	70	54	35
Italy	-	49	48	55	60	72
Kenya	47	67	73	69	NA	NA
Mexico	69	74	79	79	79	78
Nigeria	61	32	70	65	74	59
Russia	-	50	52	50	57	62
Spain	47	53	65	NA	78	68
Turkey	69	54	65	63	44	54
UK	44	47	49	52	55	69
USA	50	46	48	49	59	68

dt) Extreme poverty in the world

	Very serious				
	2015	2010	2009	2007	2003
Brazil	-	97	94	84	87
Canada	70	72	70	66	57
Chile	82	81	86	63	80
China	16	42	38	34	19
France	75	77	74	NA	70
Germany	32	60	61	50	48
India	53	51	52	56	64
Indonesia	61	78	76	64	54
Italy	-	84	79	74	77
Kenya	48	82	81	75	NA
Mexico	63	77	73	72	70
Nigeria	62	37	73	70	NA
Russia	-	51	54	46	53
Spain	77	81	91	NA	75
Turkey	67	64	76	57	43
UK	64	70	75	67	54
USA	59	64	66	56	54

Figure 43.

Q1At. For each of the following possible global problems, please tell me if you see it as a very serious, some-what serious, not very serious or not at all serious problem.

et) Terrorism

	Very serious				
	2015	2010	2009	2007	2003
Brazil	-	92	79	67	83
Canada	71	51	49	58	61
Chile	73	69	60	51	71
China	12	28	38	29	21
France	85	65	63	NA	69
Germany	62	55	58	58	59
India	51	67	57	73	79
Indonesia	64	49	75	59	44
Italy	-	71	75	65	76
Kenya	55	41	27	46	NA
Mexico	64	66	65	72	70
Nigeria	68	35	37	27	41
Russia	-	66	52	55	75
Spain	69	69	87	NA	83
Turkey	67	73	77	73	50
UK	71	64	64	65	73
USA	80	67	57	64	70

ft) The migration of people between countries

	Very serious			
	2015	2010	2009	2007
Brazil	-	41	31	39
Canada	21	13	18	20
Chile	42	42	36	21
China	11	14	5	5
France	20	16	18	NA
Germany	22	17	12	23
India	34	21	21	31
Indonesia	18	11	18	12
Italy	-	31	31	28
Kenya	25	22	21	20
Mexico	45	57	50	50
Nigeria	48	25	24	24
Russia	-	15	19	11
Spain	35	38	51	NA
Turkey	53	33	53	33
UK	28	32	26	36
USA	38	37	26	30

Figure 43.

Q1At. For each of the following possible global problems, please tell me if you see it as a very serious, somewhat serious, not very serious or not at all serious problem.

gt) War and armed conflicts

	Very serious			
	2015	2010	2009	2004
Brazil	-	90	86	NA
Canada	72	64	62	NA
Chile	73	72	63	NA
China	12	25	30	NA
France	76	72	76	NA
Germany	50	57	65	NA
India	36	38	31	NA
Indonesia	53	34	51	NA
Italy	-	81	76	NA
Kenya	39	42	38	63
Mexico	57	40	32	NA
Nigeria	55	30	52	52
Russia	-	55	54	NA
Spain	65	72	87	NA
Turkey	69	64	75	NA
UK	64	68	72	NA
USA	70	67	65	NA

ht) The state of the global economy

	Very serious		
	2015	2010	2009
Brazil	-	68	60
Canada	45	46	47
Chile	59	60	73
China	10	27	33
France	35	45	52
Germany	16	30	49
India	38	32	28
Indonesia	51	72	64
Italy	-	45	43
Kenya	32	56	51
Mexico	52	64	81
Nigeria	52	31	55
Russia	-	30	47
Spain	49	52	79
Turkey	54	49	76
UK	37	57	56
USA	50	72	65

it) Religious fundamentalism

	Very serious		
	2015	2010	2009
Brazil	-	52	44
Canada	42	30	33
Chile	47	44	35
China	9	8	11
France	51	40	35
Germany	39	38	42
India	42	35	25
Indonesia	46	40	42
Italy	-	44	64
Kenya	34	27	27
Mexico	30	13	11
Nigeria	45	37	31
Russia	-	15	16
Spain	48	41	47
Turkey	53	41	62
UK	47	35	40
USA	39	34	34

Figure 43.

Q1At. For each of the following possible global problems, please tell me if you see it as a very serious, somewhat serious, not very serious or not at all serious problem.

jt) Corruption	Very serious		k) The gap between rich and poor	Very serious	
	2015	2010		2015	2001
Brazil	-	96	Brazil	-	78
Canada	55	54	Canada	57	61
Chile	78	75	Chile	76	72
China	36	73	China	27	-
France	53	52	France	51	52
Germany	18	44	Germany	33	45
India	49	66	India	47	65
Indonesia	77	81	Indonesia	51	37
Italy	-	72	Italy	-	62
Kenya	58	86	Kenya	44	NA
Mexico	63	62	Mexico	57	68
Nigeria	64	43	Nigeria	62	47
Russia	-	67	Russia	-	37
Spain	76	66	Spain	57	60
Turkey	64	67	Turkey	69	52
UK	48	50	UK	49	65
USA	62	68	USA	54	49

Figure 44.

Q3At. What about [read statement] ... do you strongly support, somewhat support, somewhat oppose, or strongly oppose environmental and social groups being involved in this activity?

a) Publicly criticizing the behaviour of government and companies.

	Total Support	Total oppose	Depends	DK/NA
Australia	73	21	4	2
Brazil	75	18	4	3
Canada	74	23	2	2
China	55	30	12	3
Germany	85	12	2	1
India	80	14	2	4
Indonesia	88	8	3	1
Kenya	74	23	3	1
Mexico	63	28	6	3
Nigeria	90	10	0	0
Pakistan	74	14	4	9
Peru	70	20	2	8
Spain	68	15	8	10
Turkey	61	20	12	7
UK	72	24	2	2
USA	66	31	2	1

b) Using public protests to raise awareness of an issue.

	Total Support	Total oppose	Depends	DK/NA
Australia	69	26	3	1
Brazil	75	19	3	4
Canada	66	32	2	1
China	53	33	11	2
Germany	83	14	2	2
India	80	15	2	3
Indonesia	62	30	7	1
Kenya	71	26	3	0
Mexico	64	29	4	3
Nigeria	84	15	1	0
Pakistan	71	16	4	9
Peru	62	31	2	6
Spain	67	17	7	9
Turkey	64	17	14	5
UK	71	25	2	1
USA	69	28	2	1

Figure 44.
Q3At. What about [read statement] ... do you strongly support, somewhat support, somewhat oppose, or strongly oppose environmental and social groups being involved in this activity?

c) Influencing government policies in [COUNTRY]

	Total Support	Total oppose	Depends	DK/NA
Australia	75	20	4	2
Brazil	66	26	4	4
Canada	78	18	1	3
China	45	42	11	3
Germany	69	25	3	3
India	75	19	2	3
Indonesia	63	24	8	5
Kenya	76	22	2	0
Mexico	53	38	4	4
Nigeria	86	13	2	0
Pakistan	61	24	5	11
Peru	55	34	2	9
Spain	52	17	13	18
Turkey	56	22	15	7
UK	76	19	2	2
USA	68	28	2	2

d) Working with companies to help solve environmental and social issues.

	Total Support	Total oppose	Depends	DK/NA
Australia	92	6	1	1
Brazil	89	7	2	2
Canada	92	6	1	1
China	88	6	5	1
Germany	89	9	2	0
India	73	20	3	4
Indonesia	91	5	2	2
Kenya	90	9	1	1
Mexico	71	22	2	4
Nigeria	94	6	0	0
Pakistan	66	19	5	10
Peru	83	11	0	5
Spain	71	14	7	9
Turkey	71	13	10	7
UK	88	10	0	2
USA	86	12	0	1

Figure 44.

Q3At. What about [read statement] ... do you strongly support, somewhat support, somewhat oppose, or strongly oppose environmental and social groups being involved in this activity?

e) Delivering social services like education or health care.

	Total Support	Total oppose	Depends	DK/NA
Australia	86	8	4	2
Brazil	91	6	1	3
Canada	86	13	1	1
China	92	4	3	1
Germany	93	5	1	2
India	73	20	2	4
Indonesia	93	4	2	2
Kenya	93	7	0	0
Mexico	76	19	2	3
Nigeria	93	7	0	0
Pakistan	71	15	5	9
Peru	85	9	0	6
Spain	75	14	3	8
Turkey	76	10	9	6
UK	87	13	0	1
USA	85	13	0	2

f) Communicating about their activities and commitments

	Total Support	Total oppose	Depends	DK/NA
Australia	85	11	2	2
Brazil	85	9	2	4
Canada	87	10	1	2
China	73	14	11	2
Germany	89	9	1	1
India	64	24	4	7
Indonesia	75	8	10	7
Kenya	89	10	1	0
Mexico	67	24	2	7
Nigeria	92	7	0	0
Pakistan	63	19	6	12
Peru	77	13	1	8
Spain	67	15	4	14
Turkey	72	11	9	7
UK	87	9	2	1
USA	77	19	2	2

Figure 44.

Q3At. What about [read statement] ... do you strongly support, somewhat support, somewhat oppose, or strongly oppose environmental and social groups being involved in this activity?

g) Raising money to support their activities.

	Total Support	Total oppose	Depends	DK/NA
Australia	79	17	3	1
Brazil	72	21	4	4
Canada	78	19	2	1
China	69	21	9	1
Germany	75	19	3	3
India	65	24	3	8
Indonesia	75	14	7	4
Kenya	75	23	1	0
Mexico	61	27	7	6
Nigeria	90	9	1	0
Pakistan	63	19	6	12
Peru	63	24	3	9
Spain	51	23	16	10
Turkey	56	20	17	8
UK	83	12	3	1
USA	71	25	2	2

Figure 45.
M5. Do you think what USA leaders refer to as the 'war on terror' has made al Qaeda stronger, weaker, or has had no effect either way?

	Made al Qaeda stronger	Made al Qaeda weaker	Has had no effect	Never heard of al Qaeda	DK/NA
Australia	41	17	31	0	10
Brazil	34	9	28	13	15
Canada	32	15	38	2	13
China	23	25	29	3	21
Costa Rica	27	22	36	6	8
Egypt	21	44	31	1	3
France	48	7	33	1	11
Germany	31	34	24	1	10
India	16	27	19	23	16
Indonesia	24	12	33	4	27
Italy	43	13	36	1	7
Kenya	16	58	15	2	8
Lebanon	39	18	32	1	11
Mexico	48	8	33	4	8
Nigeria	22	37	18	9	15
Pakistan	24	13	30	4	29
Panama	28	21	26	7	19
Philippines	19	21	40	4	16
Russia	12	16	31	10	30
Turkey	31	32	18	0	19
UAE	27	17	23	3	31
UK	40	13	36	0	10
USA	33	34	26	1	7

Figure 46.

Q5At. For each of the following statements, please tell me if you strongly agree, somewhat agree, somewhat disagree, or strongly disagree.

ft) The use of military force is the most effective way of reducing international terrorism

	Total agree						Strongly agree						Somewhat agree					
	2015	2009	2007	2004	2003	2001	2015	2009	2007	2004	2003	2001	2015	2009	2007	2004	2003	2001
Australia	52	45	46	34	NA	54	26	16	18	14	NA	26	25	29	28	20	NA	28
Brazil	NA	NA	52	58	53	64	-	-	22	29	26	40	-	-	30	29	27	24
Canada	60	34	39	37	45	53	28	11	16	16	17	25	32	23	23	21	28	28
Chile	38	43	40	42	42	51	12	18	19	17	17	26	26	25	22	25	25	24
China	54	51	54	41	34	NA	13	22	31	20	9	NA	41	29	24	21	26	NA
France	64	37	38	35	35	59	23	12	14	16	11	29	41	25	24	19	24	30
Germany	48	34	55	38	30	39	17	15	19	17	13	15	31	19	36	21	17	24
India	73	50	78	87	77	83	44	23	53	65	51	63	29	27	26	22	26	21
Indonesia	74	73	59	63	61	54	32	37	21	30	20	20	42	36	38	32	42	34
Mexico	61	31	28	18	51	43	18	11	11	4	26	16	43	20	17	14	25	27
Nigeria	81	67	65	75	50	68	42	33	25	39	26	46	39	34	40	36	24	22
Russia	NA	56	43	55	48	56	-	24	18	28	18	28	-	32	25	27	30	28
Spain	47	32	NA	32	32	44	24	16	NA	16	7	21	22	16	NA	16	25	22
Turkey	47	65	64	54	37	55	18	18	21	24	7	13	29	47	44	30	30	42
UK	48	37	39	36	49	46	19	14	14	17	25	18	28	23	25	19	24	28
USA	61	48	51	58	64	76	38	23	24	35	34	43	23	25	27	23	30	32

Figure 48.

Q1At. For each of the following possible global problems, please tell me if you see it as a very serious, somewhat serious, not very serious or not at all serious problem.

at) Human rights abuses in the world

	Very serious	Somewhat serious	Not very serious	Not at all serious	Depends	Not familiar with the issue	Other	DK/NA
Australia	67	24	6	2	1	0	0	1
Canada	69	24	5	1	0	0	0	-
Chile	77	14	5	1	1	1	0	1
China	15	31	34	11	2	5	0	1
France	61	34	3	1	0	0	0	0
Germany	31	45	16	0	6	2	0	0
Ghana	61	25	6	2	2	1	0	3
India	61	26	5	2	0	3	0	3
Indonesia	61	33	5	0	0	0	0	0
Kenya	53	29	10	4	1	2	0	0
Mexico	72	19	6	1	1	1	0	1
Nigeria	65	23	9	2	1	0	0	0
Pakistan	66	28	4	2	0	0	0	0
Peru	73	19	6	1	0	0	0	1
S. Korea	22	53	19	1	2	0	0	3
Spain	67	31	1	0	0	0	0	1
Turkey	73	17	2	0	5	2	0	0
UK	61	32	7	0	0	1	0	0
USA	60	30	7	1	0	0	0	1

Figure 48.

Q1At. For each of the following possible global problems, please tell me if you see it as a very serious, somewhat serious, not very serious or not at all serious problem.

bt) Pollution and environmental problems in the world.

	Very serious	Somewhat serious	Not very serious	Not at all serious	Depends	Not familiar with the issue	Other	DK/NA
Australia	59	34	5	2	0	0	0	0
Canada	63	32	4	1	0	0	0	0
Chile	78	16	4	0	0	1	0	1
China	28	45	21	3	1	1	0	0
France	49	43	7	0	0	0	0	0
Germany	30	53	15	1	1	0	0	0
Ghana	54	27	9	4	4	0	0	0
India	54	37	5	2	0	1	0	2
Indonesia	63	32	4	0	0	0	0	1
Kenya	47	28	17	5	2	1	0	0
Mexico	63	29	7	1	0	0	0	1
Nigeria	56	29	12	2	0	1	0	0
Pakistan	46	37	12	4	1	0	0	0
Peru	79	16	3	1	0	0	0	1
S. Korea	41	45	11	1	1	0	0	1
Spain	58	36	4	1	0	1	0	0
Turkey	67	27	1	0	4	0	0	0
UK	51	40	8	1	0	0	0	0
USA	48	39	10	3	0	0	0	0

Figure 48.

Q1At. For each of the following possible global problems, please tell me if you see it as a very serious, somewhat serious, not very serious or not at all serious problem.

ct) The spread of human diseases

	Very serious	Somewhat serious	Not very serious	Not at all serious	Depends	Not familiar with the issue	Other	DK/NA
Australia	45	40	12	2	0	0	0	0
Canada	48	43	8	0	0	0	0	1
Chile	73	20	5	0	1	1	0	1
China	23	36	30	6	2	2	0	1
France	47	46	6	0	0	0	0	0
Germany	20	39	34	2	3	2	0	0
Ghana	57	28	10	1	3	0	0	1
India	57	32	7	2	1	1	0	1
Indonesia	62	29	7	1	0	0	0	0
Kenya	47	31	13	6	1	1	0	0
Mexico	69	22	7	1	0	0	0	0
Nigeria	61	23	12	2	0	0	0	0
Pakistan	57	30	9	4	0	0	0	0
Peru	66	25	5	2	0	0	0	1
S. Korea	21	46	30	1	1	0	0	1
Spain	47	44	7	1	0	0	0	0
Turkey	69	25	1	0	4	0	0	0
UK	44	43	12	1	0	0	0	0
USA	50	38	10	1	0	0	0	0

Figure 48.

Q1At. For each of the following possible global problems, please tell me if you see it as a very serious, somewhat serious, not very serious or not at all serious problem.

dt) Extreme poverty in the world

	Very serious	Somewhat serious	Not very serious	Not at all serious	Depends	Not familiar with the issue	Other	DK/NA
Australia	71	24	4	1	0	0	0	0
Canada	70	25	4	1	0	0	0	0
Chile	82	14	2	0	1	0	0	1
China	16	34	36	7	4	2	0	0
France	75	23	1	0	0	0	0	0
Germany	32	50	13	0	4	1	0	0
Ghana	65	24	7	3	2	1	0	0
India	53	30	11	4	1	1	0	1
Indonesia	61	34	3	0	0	0	0	1
Kenya	48	32	13	5	1	0	0	0
Mexico	63	25	8	2	1	1	0	1
Nigeria	62	25	9	4	0	0	0	0
Pakistan	59	25	7	7	1	0	0	0
Peru	70	24	5	1	0	0	0	0
S. Korea	27	51	16	2	2	0	0	2
Spain	77	22	1	0	0	0	0	0
Turkey	67	26	2	0	4	0	0	1
UK	64	31	4	1	0	0	0	0
USA	59	32	7	2	0	0	0	0

Figure 48.

Q1At. For each of the following possible global problems, please tell me if you see it as a very serious, somewhat serious, not very serious or not at all serious problem.

et) Terrorism

	Very serious	Somewhat serious	Not very serious	Not at all serious	Depends	Not familiar with the issue	Other	DK/NA
Australia	72	21	5	1	0	0	0	0
Canada	71	23	4	2	0	0	0	0
Chile	73	20	4	1	1	0	0	1
China	12	37	32	11	4	3	0	0
France	85	14	1	0	0	0	0	0
Germany	62	31	7	0	0	0	0	0
Ghana	48	30	12	5	5	1	0	1
India	51	32	8	5	1	1	0	2
Indonesia	64	30	5	0	0	0	0	1
Kenya	55	24	11	8	2	0	0	0
Mexico	64	23	6	2	2	0	0	2
Nigeria	68	22	9	1	0	1	0	0
Pakistan	57	21	7	11	3	1	0	0
Peru	66	23	7	3	0	0	0	2
S. Korea	38	36	18	4	1	0	0	3
Spain	69	29	1	0	0	0	0	0
Turkey	67	24	3	0	4	0	0	1
UK	71	24	4	1	0	0	0	0
USA	80	14	3	1	0	1	0	0

Figure 48.

Q4At. For each of the following possible global problems, please tell me if you see it as a very serious, somewhat serious, not very serious or not at all serious problem.

ft) The migration of people between countries

	Very serious	Somewhat serious	Not very serious	Not at all serious	Depends	Not familiar with the issue	Other	DK/NA
Australia	28	37	20	12	1	0	0	1
Canada	21	39	25	11	1	1	1	1
Chile	42	24	22	7	1	1	0	5
China	11	22	31	19	8	8	0	1
France	20	35	33	11	1	0	0	0
Germany	22	39	31	4	3	1	0	0
Ghana	29	27	26	9	6	2	0	1
India	34	29	17	9	4	2	1	4
Indonesia	18	40	35	5	0	0	0	3
Kenya	25	26	27	16	4	1	0	1
Mexico	45	29	16	7	1	1	0	0
Nigeria	48	27	20	4	1	0	0	0
Pakistan	40	30	14	11	4	2	0	0
Peru	29	38	20	7	1	1	0	5
S. Korea	14	42	32	4	2	0	0	6
Spain	35	38	18	4	3	0	0	1
Turkey	53	32	6	3	5	0	0	1
UK	28	34	28	10	0	0	0	0
USA	38	29	23	7	1	0	0	1

Figure 48.

Q1At. For each of the following possible global problems, please tell me if you see it as a very serious, somewhat serious, not very serious or not at all serious problem.

gt) War and armed conflicts

	Very serious	Somewhat serious	Not very serious	Not at all serious	Depends	Not familiar with the issue	Other	DK/NA
Australia	65	27	6	1	0	0	0	0
Canada	72	22	3	2	0	0	0	0
Chile	73	18	5	1	0	1	0	1
China	12	26	28	14	13	6	0	1
France	76	22	1	0	0	0	0	0
Germany	50	39	8	0	1	1	0	0
Ghana	52	25	9	7	5	1	0	2
India	36	32	11	7	4	3	2	6
Indonesia	53	34	9	3	0	0	0	1
Kenya	39	36	15	8	2	0	0	0
Mexico	57	30	9	2	1	0	0	1
Nigeria	55	31	10	3	0	0	0	0
Pakistan	44	33	13	7	1	1	0	0
Peru	65	23	7	2	0	1	0	2
S. Korea	26	45	23	2	2	0	0	2
Spain	65	29	4	0	1	0	0	1
Turkey	69	26	1	0	3	0	0	1
UK	64	27	8	0	0	0	0	0
USA	70	23	5	1	0	0	0	1

Figure 48.

Q1At. For each of the following possible global problems, please tell me if you see it as a very serious, somewhat serious, not very serious or not at all serious problem.

ht) The state of the global economy

	Very serious	Somewhat serious	Not very serious	Not at all serious	Depends	Not familiar with the issue	Other	DK/NA
Australia	36	46	9	5	1	1	0	1
Canada	45	44	6	3	0	1	0	1
Chile	59	24	9	2	1	2	0	3
China	10	30	31	11	8	8	0	1
France	35	50	12	1	0	0	0	1
Germany	16	41	29	4	3	7	0	0
Ghana	33	41	11	5	4	1	0	5
India	38	28	12	8	4	4	1	5
Indonesia	51	39	6	1	0	0	0	3
Kenya	32	32	23	9	3	1	0	0
Mexico	52	34	8	1	2	1	0	2
Nigeria	52	28	17	3	0	0	0	0
Pakistan	43	33	11	8	2	1	0	1
Peru	49	34	9	1	1	0	0	5
S. Korea	30	50	13	2	1	0	0	3
Spain	49	40	6	1	1	0	0	2
Turkey	54	36	3	0	5	1	0	1
UK	37	49	11	1	0	1	0	0
USA	50	37	9	2	0	0	0	2

Figure 48.

Q1At. For each of the following possible global problems, please tell me if you see it as a very serious, somewhat serious, not very serious or not at all serious problem.

it) Religious fundamentalism

	Very serious	Somewhat serious	Not very serious	Not at all serious	Depends	Not familiar with the issue	Other	DK/NA
Australia	48	28	14	4	0	2	0	4
Canada	42	37	11	4	1	2	1	3
Chile	47	17	17	8	2	2	0	6
China	9	22	37	14	6	10	0	1
France	51	32	11	3	0	2	0	0
Germany	39	39	18	1	1	2	0	0
Ghana	31	31	23	6	4	2	0	2
India	42	31	13	7	3	1	0	3
Indonesia	46	40	8	3	0	0	0	3
Kenya	34	32	21	9	3	1	0	0
Mexico	30	33	14	10	4	1	0	7
Nigeria	45	36	14	4	1	0	0	0
Pakistan	52	25	14	6	1	1	1	0
Peru	33	33	17	9	2	1	0	6
S. Korea	25	37	24	4	2	0	0	8
Spain	48	30	12	3	2	1	0	4
Turkey	53	25	6	3	5	2	0	5
UK	47	32	12	5	1	3	0	0
USA	39	33	15	6	1	2	0	4

Figure 48.

Q1At. For each of the following possible global problems, please tell me if you see it as a very serious, somewhat serious, not very serious or not at all serious problem.

j1) Corruption

	Very serious	Somewhat serious	Not very serious	Not at all serious	Depends	Not familiar with the issue	Other	DK/NA
Australia	55	36	7	1	0	0	0	1
Canada	55	35	8	1	0	0	0	0
Chile	78	16	3	1	1	1	0	1
China	36	35	18	7	3	1	0	0
France	53	37	9	1	0	1	0	0
Germany	18	43	23	4	6	5	0	0
Ghana	80	13	3	1	2	0	0	0
India	49	33	9	4	2	1	0	2
Indonesia	77	20	2	0	0	0	0	0
Kenya	58	23	12	5	1	0	0	0
Mexico	63	25	7	5	1	0	0	0
Nigeria	64	27	7	2	0	0	0	0
Pakistan	58	25	7	8	1	1	0	0
Peru	77	17	4	1	0	0	0	0
S. Korea	47	43	6	1	1	0	0	1
Spain	76	22	1	1	0	0	0	0
Turkey	64	27	1	1	5	1	0	0
UK	48	38	11	2	0	1	0	0
USA	62	29	8	0	0	0	0	0

Figure 48.

Q1At. For each of the following possible global problems, please tell me if you see it as a very serious, somewhat serious, not very serious or not at all serious problem.

kt) The gap between rich and poor

	Very serious	Somewhat serious	Not very serious	Not at all serious	Depends	Not familiar with the issue	Other	DK/NA
Australia	53	29	14	3	0	0	0	1
Canada	57	32	6	2	1	0	0	1
Chile	76	17	5	0	1	0	0	1
China	27	40	23	8	2	0	0	0
France	51	40	9	0	0	0	0	0
Germany	33	45	17	1	3	1	0	0
Ghana	60	26	10	3	0	0	0	0
India	47	32	10	4	3	1	1	2
Indonesia	51	40	7	2	0	0	0	0
Kenya	44	29	19	5	2	1	0	0
Mexico	57	26	10	6	0	1	0	0
Nigeria	62	23	9	5	1	0	0	0
Pakistan	58	21	8	6	3	1	0	2
Peru	52	31	9	5	1	0	0	2
S. Korea	51	40	6	2	1	0	0	0
Spain	57	36	6	1	0	0	0	1
Turkey	69	24	0	1	5	0	0	0
UK	49	34	14	3	0	0	0	0
USA	54	29	13	4	0	0	0	0

Figure 49.

Q7At. Thinking about the economic developments of the last few years, how fairly do you think the benefits and burdens have been shared in [Country]: very fairly, somewhat fairly, not very fairly, or not at all fairly?

	Total fairly				Very fairly				Somewhat fairly			
	2015	2011	2009	2007	2015	2011	2009	2007	2015	2011	2009	2007
Australia	49	62	64	57	5	7	9	10	45	54	55	47
Brazil	25	25	43	18	3	2	6	2	22	23	37	16
Canada	57	55	58	58	6	9	8	8	51	46	50	50
Chile	21	18	37	14	1	2	5	1	19	16	32	13
China	53	46	44	58	9	6	4	4	44	40	40	54
France	13	12	14	13	1	1	0	2	13	11	14	11
Germany	40	32	22	23	2	2	2	3	38	30	20	20
India	52	51	44	43	23	21	15	12	29	30	29	31
Indonesia	38	27	39	17	4	4	4	1	33	23	35	16
Kenya	62	56	36	43	15	22	8	8	47	34	28	35
Mexico	40	40	17	20	9	8	6	7	31	32	11	13
Nigeria	50	43	40	53	22	12	9	10	28	31	31	43
Spain	8	7	27	24	1	0	4	5	7	6	23	19
Turkey	15	19	13	9	5	7	2	1	10	12	11	8
UK	36	37	39	42	4	3	4	5	33	34	35	37
USA	40	32	41	46	4	7	6	6	37	25	35	40

Figure 50.

GB6. Please tell me if you think each of the following are having a mainly positive or mainly negative influence in the world?

h) The United Nations

	Mainly positive	Mainly negative	Depends	Neither, no difference	DK/NA
Argentina	43	20	6	4	27
Australia	67	19	4	7	3
Brazil	64	18	5	1	12
Canada	77	15	2	3	3
Chile	67	9	5	7	13
China	77	9	6	2	5
France	73	18	2	3	5
Germany	86	8	3	2	2
India	57	20	10	4	9
Indonesia	84	6	6	1	2
Italy	73	15	4	4	4
Japan	44	4	-	29	23
Lebanon	57	23	10	6	4
Mexico	41	18	17	4	20
Philippines	87	9	2	1	1
Poland	74	5	3	4	15
Russia	54	8	11	8	19
S. Korea	73	22	3	-	1
Spain	77	7	3	1	13
Turkey	45	25	14	3	12
UK	76	16	1	4	3
USA	59	31	2	2	6

Figure 51.

GB4. The five permanent members of the Security Council are China, France, Russia, Britain, and the United States. Some people have proposed that the permanent membership should be expanded. Would you favor or oppose additional countries becoming permanent members?

	Favor	Oppose	Depends	Neither	DK/NA
Argentina	63	8	1	1	27
Australia	81	13	3	1	2
Brazil	73	12	2	-	13
Canada	84	12	1	-	3
Chile	55	21	4	2	18
China	54	33	5	1	7
France	67	25	1	2	5
Germany	81	16	1	-	1
India	87	6	1	1	5
Indonesia	69	21	3	1	5
Italy	86	9	2	1	3
Japan	59	5	-	17	19
Lebanon	72	7	16	3	2
Mexico	52	14	11	3	19
Russia	44	28	1	11	16
Philippines	73	25	1	-	1
Poland	67	9	2	6	16
S. Africa	76	16	1	-	6
S. Korea	56	40	1	-	2
Spain	80	7	2	1	11
Turkey	59	21	3	10	7
UK	74	21	2	1	3
USA	70	23	3	-	4

Figure 51.

GB3. As you may know, there are currently five permanent members of the United Nations Security Council, and any one of them can veto (block) any resolution. Some people have proposed that this should be changed so that if a decision was supported by all the other members, no one member could veto the decision. Would you favor or oppose this change?

	Favor	Oppose	Depends	Neither	DK/NA
Argentina	48	17	3	1	31
Australia	75	20	2	-	2
Brazil	62	19	2	-	18
Canada	68	26	1	1	4
Chile	47	22	3	8	21
China	47	36	5	1	11
France	44	43	1	4	8
Germany	70	25	2	1	2
India	77	13	3	1	6
Indonesia	73	13	4	2	8
Italy	67	25	2	1	5
Japan	46	13	-	19	23
Lebanon	84	9	2	2	3
Mexico	39	15	16	8	21
Russia	25	29	10	10	25
Philippines	58	35	4	-	3
Poland	52	23	2	5	19
S. Africa	61	29	2	1	8
S. Korea	52	40	5	-	4
Spain	71	13	2	-	14
Turkey	53	24	5	1	7
UK	56	35	2	1	5
USA	57	34	2	1	6

Figure 52.
Q3Bt. Please tell me how much you trust each of the following institutions to operate in the best interest of our society. Would you say you have a lot of trust, some trust, not much trust, or no trust at all in...?
gt) The United Nations

Total trust

	2015	2014	2013	2012	2010	2009	2003	2002
Canada	74	72	69	70	NA	72	77	73
Chile	48	51	55	45	NA	54	51	NA
China	47	59	67	64	55	57	56	NA
France	59	52	61	53	53	61	57	NA
Germany	56	67	77	52	55	57	65	70
India	61	56	53	52	60	56	71	55
Indonesia	69	74	74	64	63	57	65	59
Kenya	74	74	80	81	79	76	NA	NA
Mexico	44	36	44	55	91	87	88	45
Nigeria	68	47	64	64	58	64	61	63
Pakistan	55	50	43	31	31	31	NA	NA
Spain	42	43	51	36	40	41	78	59
Turkey	33	50	50	28	16	26	33	23
UK	75	68	67	71	67	72	73	75
USA	55	53	57	62	58	61	64	68

Total no trust

	2015	2014	2013	2012	2010	2009	2003	2002
Canada	23	24	26	25	NA	24	19	21
Chile	41	35	35	38	NA	33	42	NA
China	42	31	23	23	31	26	33	NA
France	37	45	36	44	43	36	37	NA
Germany	39	30	17	46	43	41	34	28
India	27	24	19	28	23	22	20	36
Indonesia	21	19	18	29	33	29	31	29
Kenya	24	22	13	18	20	19	NA	NA
Mexico	51	52	46	39	9	11	9	51
Nigeria	30	46	32	34	41	33	33	34
Pakistan	43	45	47	56	55	49	NA	NA
Spain	55	53	41	62	56	54	19	33
Turkey	56	42	46	63	75	70	52	64
UK	24	30	29	25	31	24	24	23
USA	45	45	40	34	38	37	32	27

Figure 54.

Q7At. Please tell me if you agree or disagree with each of the following statements.

ft) Our children and grandchildren will have a higher quality of life than we do today.

	Total agree (1+2)						Total disagree (3+4)					
	2012	2009	2007	2002	2001	2000	2012	2009	2007	2002	2001	2000
Brazil	65	NA	36	NA	42	50	31	NA	53	NA	54	49
Canada	43	44	53	51	48	45	54	52	53	44	44	50
China	83	81	83	92	NA	NA	15	12	12	5	NA	NA
France	16	14	16	16	27	24	81	78	75	76	61	63
Germany	28	24	36	22	29	33	67	72	58	75	67	53
India	64	58	78	67	65	67	19	16	19	26	30	30
Italy	NA	19	23	37	44	39	NA	77	71	54	44	51
Japan	NA	17	NA	26	33	34	NA	83	NA	72	61	50
Russia	56	57	54	47	53	40	25	20	20	32	33	42
UK	43	43	49	60	60	56	53	51	47	32	30	37
USA	32	42	46	60	65	59	65	53	48	35	28	38

Appendix 3: GlobeScan's national research partners

Country	Research institute	Location	Contact	Methodology
Argentina	TNS Argentina	Buenos Aires	Mariana Souto mariana.souto@tns-gallup.com.ar +54 11 48 91 64 17	National/Face to face
Australia	GlobeScan	Toronto	Robin Miller robin.miller@globescan.com +1 416 962 0707	National/Telephone
Brazil	Market Analysis	Florianópolis	Fabián Echegaray fabian@marketanalysis.com.br +55 48 3364 0000	Urban/Telephone
Canada	GlobeScan	Toronto	Robin Miller robin.miller@globescan.com +1 416 962 0707	National/Telephone
Chile	Mori Chile	Santiago	Marta Lagos mlagos@morichile.cl +56 2334 4544	National/Face to face
China	GlobeScan	Toronto	Robin Miller robin.miller@globescan.com +1 416 962 0707	Urban/Telephone
Ecuador	Propraxis/Sigma Dos	Quito	Carlos Moreno cmoreno@propraxismarketing.com +593 7 2888519	Urban/Face to face
Egypt	Attitude Market Research	Cairo	Mohamed Al Gendy mgendy@attitude-eg.com +202 2702438	Urban/Face to face
France	Efficience 3	Paris and Rheims	Christian de Thieulloy christian.t@efficience3.com +33 1 4316 5442	National/Telephone

Country	Research institute	Location	Contact	Methodology
Germany	Ri*QUESTA GmbH	Teningen	Bernhard Rieder riquesta.rieder@t-online.de +49 7641 93 43 36	National/Telephone
Ghana	Business Interactive Consulting Limited	Accra	Razaaque Animashaun info@bigghana.com +233 302 783140/782892	National/Face to face
Greece	Institute of Communication	Athens	Vivian Antonopoulou vantonopoulou@mrb.gr +30 2103318065	National/Telephone
India	Team C Voter	Noida	Yashwant Deshmukh yashwant@teamcvoter.com +91 120 424 7135	National/Face to face
Indonesia	DEKA Marketing Research	Jakarta	Irma Malibari irma.malibari@deka-research.co.id info@deka-research.co.id +62 21 723 6901	Urban/Face to face
Italy	Gfk Eurisko	Milan	Paolo Anselmi Paolo.Anselmi@gfk.com +39 02 438091	National/Telephone
Japan	The Yomiuri Shimbun	Tokyo	Susumu Arai arai8138@yomiuri.com +81 3 3217 1963	National/Face to face
Kenya	Research Path Associates Ltd.	Nairobi	Charles Onsongo charles.onsongo@rpa.co.ke +254 20 2734770	Urban/Face to face
Mexico	Parametria	Mexico City	Francisco Abundis fabundis@parametria.com.mx +52 55 2614 0089	National/Face to face

Country	Research institute	Location	Contact	Methodology
Nigeria	Market Trends	Lagos	Jo Ebhomenye joebhomenye@hotmail.com +234 1734 7384	National/Face to face
Pakistan	Gallup Pakistan	Islamabad	Ijaz Shafi Gilani isb@gallup.com.pk +92 51 2655630	National/Face to face
Panama	Dichter & Neira	Panama City	Gabriel Neira gneira@dichter-neira.com +507 236 4000	Urban/Telephone
Peru	Datum	Lima	Urpi Torrado urpi@datum.com.pe +511 215 0600	National/Face to face
Philippines	M&S-Sigma Dos	Makati City	Teodora "Dory" Marasigan tmmarasigan@ms-sigmados.com +63 2 8172780	Urban/Face to face
Poland	Public Opinion Research Centre	Warsaw	Mirosława Grabowska m.grabowska@cbos.pl +48 22 693 46 93	National/Face to face
Russia	CESSI Institute for Comparative Social Research	Moscow	Vladimir Andreenkov vladimir.andreenkov@cessi.ru +7 495 650 55 18	National/Face to face
South Korea	East Asia Institute	Seoul	Bomi Kim spring@eai.or.kr +82 2 2277 1683	National/Telephone
Spain	Sigma Dos Int.	Madrid	Petrana Valentinova petrana@sigmados.com +34 91 360 0474	National/Telephone

Country	Research institute	Location	Contact	Methodology
Turkey	Yöntem Research Consultancy	Istanbul	Mehmet Aktulga mehmet.aktulga@yontemresearch.com +90 212 278 12 19	Urban/Face to face
UK	Populus Data Solutions	London	Patrick Diamond pdiamond@populusdatasolutions.com +44 207 553 4148	National/Telephone
USA	GlobeScan	Toronto	Robin Miller robin.miller@globescan.com +1 416 962 0707	National/Telephone

About the author

Doug Miller is recognized as one of the pioneers of global public opinion research, having conducted his first 30-country poll in 1996 and annual polls ever since.

His 30-country Millennium Poll on the changing expectations of companies in 1999 was particularly influential in the business community. For the last decade, he and his colleagues have conducted the annual BBC World Service Poll that has received wide  media coverage around the world. (Googling "Doug Miller BBC" yields 9 million results.)

Doug is the founder and chairman of GlobeScan, the evidence and ideas company with offices in London, San Francisco, Toronto, and Cape Town – and licensed research partners in 30 countries. Clients include leading global companies, NGOs, and multilateral agencies.

Doug has presented GobeScan's research at the World Economic Forum in Davos, the World Social Forum in Porto Alegre (Brazil), the International Business Leaders Forum in London, the World Business Council for Sustainable Development, United Nations Headquarters in New York, the White House in Washington, and conferences and boardrooms around the world.

He is also President of the GlobeScan Foundation, established in 2012 to "Let everyone speak." The foundation applies social science tools to give voice to global publics and empower collaboration to advance a sustainable and just world.

After six years in the UK and 20 years of global travel he now lives in the countryside north of Toronto and works from The GlobeScan Foundation's headquarters building there. *Can the World be Wrong?* is his first book.

For updates on the trends covered in this book, you can visit http://www.globescanfoundation.org.

For Product Safety Concerns and Information please contact our EU
representative GPSR@taylorandfrancis.com
Taylor & Francis Verlag GmbH, Kaufingerstraße 24, 80331 München, Germany